C000218863

Winning is Everything

By Sheila Willcox

© 2018

Epona Publishing

Table of Contents

Introduction by Cate Bryant

I had read Sheila Willcox's original autobiography *Three Days Running* when I was at school. There were not many horsy books in the library as the Pullein-Thompson sisters' novels were deemed 'not good literature'. I was a typical pony-mad girl riding my first pony bareback for want of a saddle and devoured anything horsy that I could lay my hands on.

Later in my life, when I was living in Cornwall I read an article about Sheila Willcox in *Horse and Hound* - about how she had broken her back and was divorced, and I was upset. I wrote to her asking if she had considered writing a sequel to her autobiography and I was thrilled when she wrote back saying that this was one of her projects. Sheila loved her public and I personally experienced this.

Many years later I learnt of her death and I contacted her son and asked about the possibility of a sequel to her original autobiography. So, this project fell into my lap. Sheila had left a huge box of manuscripts behind, some of which had been sent to publishers in earlier years but had been rejected. I found it hard to believe that someone should be able to write such detailed accounts of so many years full of action and excitement. Apparently, she also had a roomful of personal diaries, but these mysteriously disappeared when she died.

I found that there was the darker side of her story that had not been included in *Three Days Running*, which included not only her seduction by a much older married man high up in the male hierarchy of eventing, but also the chauvinistic way in which she had been treated in the days when women were prohibited from competing in three-day eventing at the Olympics. So, as to be able to tell the whole story I re-wrote *Three Days Running* in a revised edition and extended the time line to include her marriage to John Waddington. I also typed out her non-fiction book *The Event Horse*, which is also available now as an e-book on Amazon.

This is the sequel of Sheila's life which picks up from her wedding and runs until her death in 2017. She suffered from Alzheimer's and her family have arranged that 20% of the profits of these publications should go to an Alzheimer's charity.

Editing this autobiography was a challenge, deciding what to include and what not. The sheer volume of the manuscripts was daunting. I have not included the surnames of her lovers who were all married, wishing to protect their families. She is very frank and truthful when it came to her sex life and I have followed her wishes and included such details. It would appear that she was as athletic in bed as she was in the sporting arena, up until her accident in 1971. One can see why she was referred to as a 'glamour girl'.

As a young woman Sheila had been a staunch Catholic and it was this that prevented her from marrying her much older married lover when she was still a girl. Later on, when she was divorced from John Waddington she felt rejected by the church and lost her faith. One of her best friends regularly 'used a pendulum' to communicate with the 'spirits' and although Sheila went along with this she didn't really believe.

I have included two momentous occasions when Sheila drugged her horses, once using a sedative and the other time using 'go faster powder'. It is important to remember the social context at this time when it was considered perfectly normal to dose a horse with bute so he could compete and there was no scientific understanding of tranquilisers and amphetamines. It was more part of an old-fashioned country lore that was passed down through generations of horsemen such as Bert Cleminson.

A more contentious practice that Sheila regularly carried out, with no demur or apology, was rapping. This is now a banned practice and, quite rightly, decried by all serious and intelligent horse people. Rather than judge her too harshly for this it is important to remember that it was quite a conventional training method in its time.

Sheila's life connected with some famous contemporary horse people. One example is Mary King, who as a young girl went to Sheila's stables to be rigorously trained for three years. Mary devotes a whole chapter entitled "The Sheila Willcox Years" in her autobiography *Mary King: the autobiography* published in 2009 by Orion. Mary's account of Sheila is well-written and accurate. Sheila was also closely involved with the Bechtolsheimers, going to live at their place in Germany before they moved to England. She helped them train their horses, and also instructed Wilfried when he was younger and hoping to compete in eventing. Their youngest daughter, Laura Tomlinson, was only a baby at that stage.

To many Sheila is an icon in the eventing world and I hope that this autobiography does not take the shine off her public image. She was also known as being hard-hearted – "She could be so very kind but if you got in the way of her winning God help you!" Her ex-husband, John Waddington, summed her up as very extreme – "If she thought you were not with her she assumed you were against her."

After immersing myself in the mind of Sheila for over a year now I believe that she was a complex person. Undoubtedly, she was very intelligent, but without the benefit of tertiary education which might have helped her to discern subtlety and different facets of opinion and belief. When it came to men Sheila was really quite clueless! She seemed to view the whole male-female dynamic as some sort of horse competition where if she was beautiful, entertaining and good in bed she would win the prizes. She seemed to entirely disregard the feelings of her lovers' wives but when her own husband indulged in a little public flirtation that would have gone nowhere, she publicly punched him in the face.

However, one cannot deny that she was a horsewoman of undeniable ability and in that way can be an inspiration to many. She knew her horses and she knew how to train a dressage horse, and then take them on to show jumping and cross-country. She was fearless and brave, and she rode head first into life, which sometimes resulted in complete disaster. She was a wonderful friend but a fearsome enemy.

Chapter One – Back to Badminton

On the first day of our marriage we were on our way to the honeymoon in Torquay. For the following two weeks we lived in the lap of luxury: lazy breakfast in bed; making love in every way we could think of, at any time of day; and emerging in the requisite black tie and long frock for dinner every evening in the imposing dining room, where we would be served with a sumptuous dinner. John's shoulder, which he had injured just before the wedding, began to mend. I was tiring of all this food and nothing much to do. All my life I had been busy riding and working, or doing something constructive, and we both agreed how much we were looking forward to starting our proper married life at Long Acre.

We settled in quickly. My horses, Chips (High and Mighty) and Cresta (Airs and Graces) were moved to a nearby rented field. I had also been given permission to use some of the other fields for my dressage practice and show jumping work when training began.

In fact, looking back it is surprising how happy and exciting were the early days of our marriage. We followed the conventional path to happiness promised in the story books. John's parents, the Waddingtons, had provided our beautiful home and I loved it. Other young married couples in the surrounding villages of the Ribble Valley were happy to accept us into their charmed circle.

Most of the people had an interest in horses one way or another, many of them loved their fox hunting as a way of life, and it undoubtedly provided a valuable means of introducing their horses to jumping all kinds of fences. The youngsters learnt to jump boldly and cleverly in the company of experienced older brethren. It gave them confidence and led to their enjoyment of galloping and jumping out of their stride across country. The horses loved their days out hunting and even the worst rain and wind would not stop them. In the good crisp days of winter weather, with a touch of frost in the air, and the sun showing its face, the hunting field was hard to beat for sheer enjoyment of galloping along with one's friends. There were some falls, some riders lost their horses who galloped gleefully away to catch up with the others, a few broken bones, but hunting provided an unequalled method for training horses for their role in whichever facet of equine sport they were to adopt. Most of the point-to-point horses and some of the best steeplechasers learnt their cleverness over fences from the days they spent in the hunting field.

John worked hard from Monday to Friday at the mills, the Waddington family business. He left home at eight in the morning and was not back until getting on for seven o'clock in the evening, sometimes even later. We had Saturdays and Sundays free and at first behaved like an old married couple, dealing with the mowing of the lawns to the front of the house, and in the private garden at the back, trying to encourage the passion flower to stay alive in the greenhouse and keeping the gravel raked in straight lines.

Before we were married, people had shaken their heads sadly, and said, 'Poor John. He'll have nothing to eat but bran mashes.' So, while the horses were still in the field I put my mind to learning to cook and armed with the Constance Spry Cookery Book I launched myself into this challenge. Accounts had been opened in the butcher and the grocer in Clitheroe. I had an account with the garage for my Mini and the horsebox and John's car. I also had a generous dress allowance. All round I found that this marriage business was very enjoyable.

The 1959 eventing season would begin in mid-March. Thus, on January 1st Cresta began his training and fittening programme which would culminate in his first attempt to win at Badminton in the third week of April. Chips, now retired from eventing, was due not to start a second career in Grand Prix dressage after all, but was to go to Ted Marsh, my first lover and with whom he would enjoy hunting in the Heythrop country. I brought him in as well, so he would arrive at Ted's fit and ready for hunting. I was hoping that my generous gift of the use of Chips would help to heal the rift between myself and Ted. He had to adjust to my marital status. We began to talk again, back to our easy conversation and entertaining repartee.

I was quite well-known now and I received a letter from Mrs Mirabel Topham of Aintree fame, asking me to be her guest at Liverpool on Grand National Day, and to be the one to put the sash of honour around the neck of the winning horse when he or she came into the winner's enclosure at the end of the most famous steeplechase in the world. I felt very honoured and went down to the paddock to look at the horses before the race. The atmosphere was mounting tangibly as three o'clock approached. Thrilled, excited and tense with expectation, the vast crowds were milling around trying to place their last-minute bets and searching for a spot as near as they could to the rails - to ensure the best possible view of the race. I sometimes wished over the years that I could have lived more in the future, when a three-day eventer had access to huge amounts of sponsorship and women were as accepted in the sport as men. But this was something different. The adulation of the crowd, the intense high, the danger and thrill of the sport, I wished I could have been the first real 'National Velvet'. Oxo was the winner, and there was me in the Winner's Enclosure clutching the sash, poised to manoeuvre it around his neck and I was suddenly shoved backwards as all the connections literally erupted. I found it hard to push my way through the melee. If only I had been the winning jockey!

Back at home, Cresta's training programme continued relentlessly, and in just over 12 weeks from the first of January we were at Cottesbrooke for the opening event of the season. Even the weather showed its delight as spring approached. Beautiful sun beamed as we converged on the estate in Northamptonshire. The going underfoot was almost perfect and everything augured well.

Cresta and I were reported in the leading newspaper as having "executed a brilliant test" for only 24.26 penalties, followed by a clear round in the show jumping. Gill Kent, Head Girl for Captain Edy Goldman in Cheshire was in second place, 16.33 marks behind us. Anneli Drummond-Hay riding Pluto was third, with Ted Marsh, on Wild Venture and Blue Jeans and Derek Allhusen waiting in the wings to catch up on the cross-country. Colonel Weldon, my own *bête noir*, was riding Samuel Johnson for Mrs Marshall. I knew that Cresta still needed experience at cross-country and I was intent on riding him steadily around the course to boost his confidence, hoping that by the time we got to Badminton he would be ready to have a real go. I took great care to bring him into each obstacle on the right stride for take-off. Our lack of speed was the forfeit I paid for this tactic. Ted had a nasty fall on Wild Venture but shot round the course on Blue Jeans to finish 90 seconds faster than Cresta and me. But we still managed to win by 24.26 marks.

9

The following week was our last competitive opportunity at Stowell Park before Badminton. I went into the dressage and Cresta did a rather ragged rein back and had been overbent on one of the extended trots across the diagonal. To my dismay I found that I had been marked down severely, with 55 penalties against the leader's 31, with other competitors' scores closely following the leader. I looked at my dressage sheets and Sheila Inderwick, who was one of my worst enemies and detractors had not only marked me down on every movement but with barely a comment to explain her marks. I knew that there was no use in making a formal complaint as the 'old boys brigade' would close ranks behind her. In those days competitors did not have the power that they have these days.

The show jumping phase was running far behind time and when it was due to begin I went to the secretary and asked them to withdraw Cresta's entry from the competition. I gave no explanation, and no one queried the reason. Then Beryl, who was helping me, came over to tell me that the press were saying that my horse must be lame. That did it! I was determined to prove this rumour untrue and went back to the Secretary's tent to ask if I might be allowed to jump the show jump course *hors concours*. Cresta produced a copybook clear round with no time faults. Later I jumped fast and clear around the cross-country. I was then utterly determined to go to Badminton and to try my very hardest to win.

The Eventing Committee met afterwards and felt that my objection to the way one of the judges had marked me was a sin of the highest order. Not to be tolerated. They summoned me to appear before them in the male protectorate of the Cavalry Club in Park Lane. I had to travel to London, heart in my mouth. I was still young enough to be scared of these men, especially when they were hunting in a pack, and I had to run the gauntlet of first the Commissionaire at the door who could not believe that a single woman had permission to enter the holy portals, and then beckoned me to follow him through their smoking room and up the stairs to a private room where I would be judged.

For me the whole business was distinctly daunting, but I stood my ground before the Committee, and carefully stated my reasons for withdrawing Cresta, explaining the obvious request that I should still to be allowed to jump, *hors concours*. I then screwed up more courage and told them that I thought it most unfair that I should be

10

judged on a different level to everyone else just because High and Mighty had been so brilliant in the dressage phase. I felt that it was hardly fair to judge Cresta as if he had High and Mighty's ability. Then there was silence and I was sent from the room while they decided what to do with me. In the end, they dismissed me, and I returned to Clitheroe to tell John what had happened.

I was amazed later to read in the press that Pat Smythe was quoted as saying, "She was always something of a prima donna". I had never met her, nor spoken to her, but then again it might have been a misquote by the press. If she did say it then I considered it uncharitable and unfair.

Badminton 1959 was on. The weather was appalling. The trade stands were soaked through and dripping forlornly, looking out onto a sea of mud and on the day the event was due to start the rain continued to fall with depressing regularity. With the traffic of horses, people, official vehicles and competitors the ground was trodden in and there was not one shoot of grass. There was talk that it should be cancelled. I could not bear it. Then it was all go ahead and the cross-country would remain unaltered.

I had so many issues to juggle in my mind, related to my withdrawal from Stowell Park, the inexperience of Cresta, the way the old guard who ran eventing thought of me, my relationship with the public who had always supported me, not to mention the terrible conditions which we were going to have to jump in. My parents had arrived to support me with Patch, and he gave me his special dog-kiss. Then John arrived, accompanied by his Uncle Stanley and Aunt Mary. These relatives were not horsy and had not brought gumboots so they gallantly strapped polythene bags on top of their shoes and slithered round to view the cross-country course. Mud, mud and more mud!

1959 was the first year that Badminton was split into two events, Little Badminton for those horses who had not won more than £30, and Great Badminton for the experienced horses. I had drawn number 19 which meant I would go towards the end of the day.

Dressage day and the rain was still falling relentlessly. The going was now so wet that there was no 'drag' on the horses' legs, little or no suction. The dressage tests were judged by Henry Wynmalen, Mrs V D S Williams and Mr Reg Hindley from Gisburn. By this time Ted

11

and Vivian Eason and Barbara Cooper, my close friends had arrived to swell the ranks of Cresta's supporters. I got dressed for the dressage in my short black coat and velvet hat. I was envious of the men who wore top hats and a version of a tail coat that made them look much more elegant.

The heavy rain continued to bucket down, and a strong easterly wind made conditions even more unpleasant. The dressage arena was a squelching morass and the Duke of Beaufort's beautiful park was ravaged to the extent that everyone was saying that there would probably never be another Badminton after such terrible damage. Frank Weldon was competing on Fermoy who had won an intermediate division at Cottesbrooke but did not appear at Stowell. He also had a second chance with Mrs Marshall's Samuel Johnson. Ted Marsh was on his two very experienced horses Wild Venture and Blue Jeans, and Derek Allhusen had Laurien. David Somerset, heir to the Duke of Beaufort, was riding the great Countryman, and was going to be a danger on his home ground. All these horses were very experienced compared with Cresta.

I will quote Colonel Hope's assessment of our performance in his *Light Horse* magazine: "Airs and Graces. Trot perfectly straight and even. Good halt in the centre of the ring, slightly bunched; good start off after it. Two track work excellent, smooth and nicely positioned. Good straight quiet walk, not very long strides; canter gait absolutely straight; good controlled extended canter; quite nice smooth transitions; the rein back the best I have seen today – steady and with good diagonal cadence; turns on the haunches well-nigh perfect. Halts remarkably good under these conditions. This should turn out to be the best test of the day. Penalties 38.34." Colonel Hope's opinion on how we should be marked was correct and Cresta, the novice went into the lead at the end of the first day.

The equestrian correspondent of The Times wrote: "We had to wait until after the interval to see the star performance of the day by Mrs Waddington and Airs and Graces. This produced only 38.34 penalties, a really good performance in such conditions and a real rejoinder to Cottesbrooke and Stowell".

Cresta was just under 20 points better than Judy Guinness's extremely promising horse Dapper who lay second, with the Frenchman M. Cochinet in third position. Laurien was fourth on 69. Ted on Venture

– 80, and David Somerset with Countryman on 95.34. The game was set.

Tactics were going to be of primary importance for me in the speed and endurance test the next day. I knew that Ted, Derek and David Somerset would go very fast over the cross-country. Weldon, also, would see his opportunity to catch me on both the experienced Samuel Johnson and the eight-year-old Fermoy he had had for the last two years. I could not afford to take the risk of riding fast with my inexperienced Cresta. I would have to look at the steeplechase and cross-country again to see if and where we could save time.

After the dressage was completed, a rumour started that the event was about to be cancelled. I was appalled. Then it was announced that there was to be further inspection of the cross-country course at six o'clock, after which a decision would be made as to whether or not the event was to continue. The directors waded around phase D and eventually decided to eliminate five fences which were clearly waterlogged and impossible, and to lower four more. The length of the course would remain the same. We would still be covering nearly 17 miles for the speed and endurance. Whilst all this was going on I decided it was imperative to inspect the steeplechase track again, to see how it had been affected by rain, which showed no sign of stopping. Puddles were wherever there was an indentation. I was thinking about the effect on Cresta, with all the mud splashing up onto his belly, even if the weather cleared.

Returning to the stable yard I found my parents and John with a copy of *The Field* magazine displaying a colour photograph of both High and Mighty and Airs and Graces on its front cover. We decided to take this as a good omen, although there was a belief in the equestrian world that if a horse and rider appears on a magazine, intimating that here is a picture of the possible winner, it usually guarantees the end of their chances. There was also a telegram from George Greenfield, my literary agent saying, "All best wishes for Badminton and make it Three Years Running". This referred to my autobiography published the previous year which was called *Three Days Running*.

I woke on Saturday morning, the all-important day, and the rain had stopped, but it was dull and cold. We set off on the course and I set a sensible pace, which I knew was much slower than that of the more experienced horses. I wanted to conserve Cresta's energy for the

13

cross-country, when the fences needed attacking with purpose and determination. The first cross-country fence was a plain fence that led down to the hermit's cave where there was a rail with a drop, placed over an ill-defined ditch. Then a long run towards Allen Grove and jumping into the wood over park palings and out again on the other side over a wall birched up to look like an impressive bullfinch. The palings and the bullfinch and the last fence on the course caused more trouble than all of the rest of them put together. The take-off at the palings was very deep and the bullfinch was thick. Cresta jumped them out of his stride. He was full of running and looking for the fences.

By the time we reached the vicarage ditch, with its huge spread and yawning gulf below, full of stinking water, he was leaping like an experienced horse. He only faltered towards the end after we had jumped down over the rails at the head of the quarry, sailed over the fence at the bottom, and came to a field of heavy plough. This was the only really heavy, sucking going on the course and as soon as we emerged from it to cross the road, Cresta resumed his lightness of foot, jumping a stile, a post-and-rails and fence of fir boughs. We were then back in the park and only the last fence stood between us and the finish. It always causes trouble with its drop into the lake, and I brought Cresta towards it on a very clear line so that he could have no doubt where I intended we should jump. He popped over the rails neatly, threw up a few splashes as we navigated along the shallow edge and was quickly out and away to the finish of the cross-country and the run-in. Others were not as lucky. This fence alone claimed four falls and nine refusals. A colonel, two women and one man went for a swim.

Afterwards, I went over to check the score board and I was rather taken aback that we had earned only four bonus marks, too slow even though I had meant to be careful over the steeplechase phases, and a more respectable 30 over the cross-country. That meant nothing until one took into account that David Somerset had gone round like the wind to gain 35 on the steeplechase and 58 on the cross-country. Ted with Wild Venture had also meant business and had gained 18.4 on the steeplechase and 50.4 on the cross-country. Derek on Laurien had gained 12.8 on the steeplechase and 26 on the cross-country. I had given away too much and although Cresta had been a star for me, I had failed him and everyone else by not asking for just a little more speed on the steeplechase.

Now, these men were in a good position to win. David Somerset deserved to go into the lead with his fast round, but I had handed it to them all on a plate. There was no-one to blame but myself. I was muttering away to myself in disgust. Winning meant so much to me. I turned to Ted Eason, a very retiring gentleman and said, "I should be kicked", I was taken aback when he kissed me, he had thought I said, "I should be kissed". This shook me out of my black mood of self-recrimination as I laughed.

After we had tended to Cresta washing him down and watching intently for any signs of fatigue and pain, Beryl ran him up for me and he was sound. He had come through this first big test with flying colours. The next morning everyone was assembled for the veterinary inspection. The tenth Duke of Beaufort, known as Master, came into the yard with the Queen, who leant casually against the stables wall to watch the proceedings. There was an air of anticipation hanging over everyone, and the yard hummed. I let Beryl present Cresta when the ground jury called him up, he was fine.

At two o'clock that afternoon, with Cresta's mane plaited, we were ready for the parade of all the horses and riders still left in the competition. The weather remained depressingly cold and dull. The show jumping arena was very cut up. As the top layer of the ground was drying it started to acquire the holding power of treacle and would not only cause suction but was also slippery and unpleasant. We screwed the longest studs we could find into his shoes to give him better grip.

David Somerset was in the lead with a plus score of 0.66, Cresta was second on minus 3.54 and Ted on Wild Venture was third on minus 10.4 and Derek Allhusen was on minus 30.2. In the show jumping there was a penalty of 10 points for a fence down so this would be a very close competition. Spectators had braved the cold and arrived in droves wearing every type of warm weather clothing with rugs under their arms. The British are very stoic when facing the vagaries of the weather and the grandstand was soon packed and benches and chairs filled to overflowing all around the arena.

15

In those days horse and riders were not ordered from last to first as it is today, and Countryman ridden by David Somerset was the first to go. If they jumped a clear round then they would win, and they set off at a smart pace, moving fluently. They knocked down one fence, so I still had the chance of winning but only if I jumped clear. Cresta was not in the least bit tired from the day before and the bell rang, and we set off on what was probably to be the most important show jumping round of my life. At stake here was not just the honour of winning but creating a record for being the first person to win the Badminton Horse Trials for three years in succession.

I gave Cresta every chance to jump clear by placing him in the very best place for take-off, so that he would lose neither impetus nor balance. We had a few close shaves when he slightly tapped a fence, but the pole didn't fall, then he jumped big into the double and had to get out cleverly and cleanly. We passed through the finishing posts to a huge burst of applause. We had won. My parents and John rushed to greet us as we went out of the main arena into the collecting ring, and the Easons joined us, quite overcome to have bred a horse which had won the Badminton Three-Day Event. Cresta was petted, stroked and admired and I was patted on the back. Then for the fourth year I was interviewed by Dorian Williams and after that surrounded by the press. Beryl took Cresta back to his stable with a posse of his devoted fans following him.

It is hard to describe how I felt. I think I really did not properly appreciate the enormity of what Cresta and I had done. Three years in a row. I received a telegram from my publishers: "Congratulations from all at St James's Place, particularly on proving that it wasn't just the horse". The Duke of Beaufort was always very kind and supportive of me and my family. On opening day Daddy had disappeared with the Duke into his personal stable yard for a man-to-man chat and after my father wrote congratulating David Somerset, the Duke replied: "Dear Mr Willcox, It was extremely kind of you to write and I will be pleased to convey your congratulations to David Somerset. It was a marvellous performance by your daughter to win on such a young horse. If only she could represent us at the next Olympics, we would be sure to win. Your sincerely, Beaufort."

Everyone in our family was much impressed by this.

Chapter Two – European Championships

After the heady excitement of winning Badminton three years running I went home with John to Long Acre and normal life. Cresta was roughed off and went out into the field for a well-earned rest. I would go down to see him every day, taking his bowl of lightly crushed oats. I would stroke his neck while he stretched it down to the food. He would take a mouthful and then raise his head with eyes half-closed with contentment while he chewed and swallowed, enjoying the company and my voice. It evoked memories of Lytham Hall when I would visit Chips each day with Patch, my dog, and Smudge, the cat.

John and I had talked about getting a dog, but I felt I couldn't do this while Patch was still alive. When he visited he would have been deeply resentful of another dog now claiming my affection. In my deep conversations with Cresta during that summer break I told him that the Harewood Three-Day Event in the following autumn was to be the European Championships.

I would be defending my title of winning gold with Chips at Copenhagen. I had been invited to go into team training at Ascot and was not too happy on two counts. Firstly, John had not been at all pleased at the thought of losing his wife to a five-week training programme, and I saw no real reason to spend all that time doing nothing very constructive, when we could just as well train at home. Thus, it was amicably agreed that I would work at home and inform them honestly and truthfully of our progress and would meet with the selectors at Catterick for a one-day event before going on to Harewood. Apart from me, those chosen to go into training were all men: David Somerset with Countryman, Ted Marsh with both Blue Jeans and Wild Venture, Derek Allhusen with Laurien, and Frank Weldon (Acting Captain) with Samuel Johnson, Jeremy Beale with Fulmer Folly and S. Walford with Absalom.

Cresta's training went exceptionally well and his legs remained sound and clean. We went to several horse shows to compete in the show jumping classes, and also took part in working hunter classes where the horse is not judged simply on his looks and conformation but also on his jumping ability over rustic fences. We were invited to give a demonstration of dressage at the Northern International Horse Show in a big arena in Manchester, which was reminiscent of the White City in London. We also did the same programme for our local Clitheroe Agricultural Show just up the road from Long Acre. Everything went well, and I could hardly wait for Harewood to begin.

Driving along in the horsebox from Long Acre, we climbed up and over the Pennines into Yorkshire and I started scanning the moors on either side for signs of yellow flowers in the gorse bushes. Chips had been prone to go off his food when he was away from home and one of my friends, a horse dealer had told me that a twig or two of gorse hung up in the loosebox might do the trick. Although I was somewhat sceptical I tried it and had been astonished that somehow, this gave him back his appetite. Cresta was a good doer but still I hung the gorse up, it was a superstitious precaution, just in case!

Meeting the men in the team at Harewood was somewhat strained. I had the distinct feeling that they resented the fact that I had been given what was obviously considered to be special treatment. It was alright for them, as soon as the morning session was over they usually jumped in their cars to scoot home or visit friends. Whereas, whenever I had been in Windsor for training I had spent the rest of the day in the stables, hanging about, talking to the grooms. Now I had Cresta, and I suspected that they weren't going to be thrilled if he turned out to be as good as Chips!

I decided to ignore this chill factor and cheerfully pretended that I did not notice it. As ever, I was warmly welcomed by the Stable Manager at Harewood where the totally charming and helpful event organisers in the tent found time to deal with every small problem. Northern hospitality and enthusiasm abounded.

I settled Cresta in his box. There were temporary stables erected that went directly onto the grass of the field but fortunately the good weather meant this didn't matter. The horses were crowded together in close proximity.

Our team had four days by ourselves before the rest of the competitors rolled in and Colonel Weldon dictated our daily work and the team vet kept a close eye on each of the horses for continuing soundness. Although we had meant to all meet up at Catterick the going had been rock hard and Weldon, along with the Eventing Committee decided that it was not worth the risk of hammering precious tendons on what was virtually concrete going.

The Russian team arrived in the dead of night, two days after us, having travelled overland from Russia through Europe, then over the Channel to England and from the port by road. There had been no Russian representatives since 1914 and we were keen to see what sort of horses they might bring with them. The horses all looked very tired when they arrived, and small. I would have liked to speak to the Russians and I walked past their stables several times smiling but without their interpreter it was not possible.

Before I had left Long Acre, I had been visited by Paul Tanfield of the Daily Mail and his photographer. The next day there was an evocative photograph in the newspaper while I was galloping along a ridge, passing beneath a tree. The article quoted me as saying that both the Germans and Russians were fielding a strong team and that the hard going was bound to be difficult for everyone.

Reg Hindley, Director of the European Championships, welcomed the ten competing nations' teams and the individual competitors, a total of 72 entries. After a short briefing we piled into Land Rovers to be driven around the roads and tracks of phases A and C, and got out to walk around B – the steeplechase. We all commented on the hardness of the ground. The grass on the steeplechase course had turned brown.

The fourth fence of the cross-country, the slide, was quickly followed by three other obstacles. It was a high island post-and-rails set almost at the bottom of a steep slope and approached by three alternative lines, the second being off a straight but very steep line from the rim of the bowl above in the centre, and the other two set at equal but opposite angles attached to a central alternative with the outside running away downhill, the first one losing the least time by being on the shortest route. All three ran steeply downhill through unpleasantly coarse rough grass. I would make up my mind later which would be the best option for Cresta when we team members went around alone for a more concentrated look. I reckoned my choice would be to take the quickest route. As soon as Cresta landed after the post-and-rails I would have to gather him up and send him strongly up the slope to some larch rails with a drop. A quick turn left immediately on landing to face diagonal rails set over a wide dry ditch and another 90° turn right to face a very narrow stile, the last two being maximum height. Away to face a double over the stud farm rails with a second element at right angles. On to number 10, a swing gate approached by a sharp turn to the right. Immediately, a bank and a timber wagon. Nearly all the fences from the quarry were maximum height, and the twists and turns into the fences would benefit only the horses, like Cresta, who would obey the rider's aids immediately. This is where our dressage training would come in. Fences 13 and 14 appeared quickly, stone walls either side of Church Lane, we would have to get the stride length absolutely correct and keep a straight line, and then the fence which would land us out of the plantation and into the park, the devil's dyke. One look at this, and all of us stopped in our tracks.

It was becoming very obvious that this was a very demanding course! The devil's dyke was 13 feet across, approached innocently through the tall trees with tiny dapples of light. It was a very solid, black-creosoted log set back about three feet from the stone-faced edge of a big ha-ha which acted as dividing barrier between the farm part of the course and the south park. One leap over the dyke would take us from the relatively dark of the wood into the blazing sunlight.

From this point on the going in the park was extremely hard. Fence 16 was the giant's table at maximum height and with a spread of 8 foot 10 inches; it was a big wooden table with benches made of railway sleepers on either side. There were two giant chairs to either side of the obstacle. Then there was another relentless straight gallop to numbers 18 and 19, a high thorn hedge followed quickly by an angled post-and-rails. Another long run to the 20th fence, with a downhill approach to two sets of post-and-rails, each of them three rails high, starting joined together from the right-hand side and opening up into a very wide V on the left. Thus, it was a choice of jumping over the spread on the left, with the risk of the horse diving out through the wide gap or choosing the narrow end on the right-hand side, holding the horse straight in the air to prevent him having to jump an ever-increasing spread. Then there were zig-zag rails, a maximum height woodpile then a maximum height lambing pen. Number 24 was a big bullfinch going into the jubilee covert then a hidden approach to a bundle of pit props. Number 26 was a water trough, followed by a nasty cut-and-laid hedge with a drop down on the landing side of 6 feet 6 inches. A post-and-rails sited on the edge

21

of the bank of the lake, then a long splash to exit over the 29th fence, a big log to be jumped straight over to land on the bank. Then there were just two more to jump a sheep rack and a park seat, then the finish, and the run-in. We would be covering nearly 22 miles in all on the second day.

The British team was declared as: Sheila Willcox and Airs and Graces, Derek Allhusen and Laurien, Jeremy Beale and Fulmer Folly and Frank Weldon with Samuel Johnson. We were up against the Germans, who looked very fit and well-prepared, and even the Russians seemed to have perked up after their long journey. I was riding number one in team order and I was to go 15th. I was a little downcast as I knew that Frank Weldon's policy was always to send around the least experienced in the team first, so that was what they thought of me. If the first rider in the team was eliminated, then the other three members knew they absolutely had to get round and not take too many risks. If the last member of the team knew that the other three had got round safely then he could go all out for a fast time and a shot at the individual award. I had a sneaking feeling that this was to be my punishment for not training at Ascot, Weldon was making a point.

I went in to do my dressage test and all was going well until we had done our rein back and a passing wasp decided to hone in on us, in spite of our assiduous application of insect repellent. The wasp seemed to be going for Cresta's ears and if he got inside one of the ears then all hell was going to break loose. I had to do something. As soon as I had straightened up after the corner with our backs to the judges, which was the only time when all three judges would momentarily lose sight of what I was doing with my outside arm, I surreptitiously slipped the reins into my right hand and swotted the wasp in one swift movement. It went sideways, stunned and we lost it. What a relief! At the end of our test we were given our marks only 35.33 penalties.

Then Otto Pohlmann with Polarfuchs from Germany was given exactly the same score. Otto had beaten us before when Cresta had been a novice horse, but now he was ready to be ridden all out and I was determined to go for a win. I was getting used to the relentless heat and I had a picture in my mind of exactly how we were going to ride the cross-country course and I was feeling optimistic and keen.

Everything went well as we set off on the roads and tracks, and the steeplechase and we gained maximum bonus points for speed. Pat, my helper, and I went through the drill we had to prepare him for the cross-country, sponging him down, giving him some glucose, and a few other rituals that I had devised. We shot through the flags at a strong canter and leapt the first fence enthusiastically. Cresta felt terrific. As each fence loomed up, he listened to me, looked carefully at what he had to do and leapt like a stag. At fence four, we had to slither down a steep slope, making sure not to get too close to the upright post-and-rails waiting at the bottom to trap us if we did not arrive on the correct stride for take-off. Cresta took great care to remain balanced as we negotiated our way downwards on the rough ground with me keeping my eyes glued on the spot where I had decided it was best to jump, and he popped neatly over it like an old hand, immediately looking for the next element.

On we went jumping each fence out of our stride until we were approaching the devil's dyke. We galloped on through the wood, eyes straining as we landed over the second of the stone walls at the Church Lane crossing to catch the first glimpse of sunlight, looking for my marker as we approached the devil's dyke, seeing it, and with the realisation that we were already on the right stride, I tightened the grip of my legs, pushing Cresta forwards for even more speed to carry us well up into the air. The circle of sunlit blue sky appeared and we were on the last three approach strides. No time for Cresta to have second thoughts. Meeting the log he had no option but to rise in the air and our speed carried us high over the gaping hole of the ha-ha, where it joined the level of the park. The crowd had massed at the fence, knowing it would cause all sorts of problems. Cresta had a made a brilliant leap and as we landed the silence exploded into an appreciative roar from the crowd. I balanced Cresta to take the short stride back up to flat ground and, as our path was set to the next fences, I told him what a good boy he was. One ear flicked back in recognition then we focused on the giant's table.

Approaching it Cresta was enjoying himself. We met it exactly right and he soared over it, jumping beautifully out of his stride and picking up his rhythm as soon as we landed to the evident delight of another huge crowd. Next we faced the stark parallel rails, and coming in on another perfect approach, he skipped over them out of his stride and we then had to throttle back a little to make sure he had the space we needed between the angled double, first over the thorn hedge and then taking the quickest route with just two strides before jumping out over the post-and-rails, fences 18 and 19. Ahead of us lay the V fence, where I had spent a lot of time working out my exact approach line, and the speed. We were taking off on the narrow right-hand corner and I needed Cresta to concentrate and keep the line. In we came deviating not an inch, and Cresta was looking for take-off at our chosen spot. He could see what we had to do. Arriving at take-off, just where I had planned, his hind legs flexed deep at his hocks to thrust his body into the air. His forehand went up. Then, unknown to me his near-hind leg began to slip to the right. The small stud in his shoe could not get enough grip on the baked ground. The off-hind leg, following a split second later, also went sideways and suddenly there was no forward thrust. The front legs, neatly tucked up ready to clear the rails, were rendered powerless to go forward, and his body and neck and head were twisted to the left as his quarters sank further to the right still in front of the fence. Half over the first slanting rail his left shoulder had begun to rotate, and his front legs made a desperate pawing movement high in the air, way above the rails, and then any forward movement abruptly ceased. He crashed across the first rail, slid sideways over the top, and came to an abrupt stop with his front legs hanging over the far rail, hind legs jammed in a twist on the take-off side. He was well and truly stuck. I was still in the saddle as his front legs landed on the far side of the second rail and brought us to an immediate, and what to Cresta, must have been a very painful halt. Not having two spare legs to anchor me, I shot straight off at a 45° angle on to my face. For a second or so, I was knocked unconscious, then I heard an eerie screaming sound – it was actually Cresta stuck on the fence on his private parts – and I got up, knowing that whatever happened I must continue on our course for the team. I must have thought I was on Cresta, for I staggered to my feet, turned left and ran purposefully up the long stretch of the course towards the next fence. As I took off, the St John Ambulance people were still a little way from me, and they immediately set off in pursuit. Not far up the field, I collapsed unconscious again.

The next thing I knew I was in an ambulance, parked somewhere. I sat up and they told me I would have to be taken to hospital, and I went immediately into 'tidy up' mode, carefully removing Daddy's handkerchief from its pocket on the inside front of my big white number 15. Having removed the handkerchief, I broke the stitches and removed the bits of cotton. There were two first aid people with me and they watched, at first with fascination, and then with boredom as all the way to Leeds I solemnly smoothed out the handkerchief, and folded it neatly in three steps, just as Mummy had taught me when I learned to iron. Then I started all over again.

Once in the hospital, and in a large room by myself, I began to realise what had happened and told the nurses that I must go back to Harewood. No bones were broken, but my mouth had taken the brunt of the fall and with no sweet grass to cushion me, my upper lip had been badly cut and a mass of tiny stones and dirt were embedded there. I was feeling a bit peculiar, but at least I had not broken anything. I was worried about Cresta. At last Mummy and Daddy, and John arrived. Mummy was frantic with worry and I could see that John was very quiet. Finally, Daddy went away and came back and told me that Cresta was alright.

The newspaper reported that, "It looked as if the horse slipped on the slippery going and got too close to the fence," and, "Airs and Graces seemed to mistime his stride, put in a short one to correct it, slipped and came right under the rails". I was sure that we had come into take-off exactly on stride but began to doubt myself at the barrage of delighted criticism. I could not believe I would ever do this, as one of my good points was, as the show jumpers used to say about me, "She is the only one with a real eye for a stride". Then to my huge relief an amateur photographer sent me 16 sequence photographs which showed clearly that what I had said had happened, and I was absolutely correct. We did not put in a short stride, nor did I bring Cresta in on a wrong one. We were just dead unlucky to have found the very place where Cresta's foot had slipped sideways.

I asked for a strong nail brush and standing in front of the small looking glass I laboriously dug out all the bits and pieces in my face, yelping to myself at the pain. Then I dabbed my top lip with antiseptic and it healed beautifully, and I didn't need to wait for someone else to do the job. I was taken straight home the next day, without an option of returning to Harewood. I have never been so furious with myself, I felt like I had let the team down.

I told John that I had to return to Harewood and jump that fence and to continue round the course to the finish. We must find out if Cresta had lost his nerve through such a bad experience of being stuck on the fence for a considerable time until they had managed to take the fence apart and release him.

I got permission and we travelled back to Harewood. I had made a plan; warm up with some circle work, jump one small easy fence then set off for the V to see if Cresta would jump it, if he wouldn't then we would have a battle, and I had to win.

Colonel Aykroyd, the course builder, was waiting for us in the park with a Land Rover at the ready, filled with tools and a tough helper. We discussed how we were going to proceed, for the main object of the exercise was to find out how Cresta would react to being asked to jump the fence which had caused him so much pain. I said I would do a little work on the flat first, find an innocuous fence to jump and then immediately set sail for the V which had caused such disaster. If he refused, there would be a fight, and I had to make sure that I was the winner. If Cresta was allowed to get away with a refusal, I would never be able to trust him to jump again.

On the course Cresta looked around him and I could see from his expression he knew perfectly well where he was. I patted his shoulder from the saddle and off we went to find a flat piece of ground to do some limbering up dressage. That done, I returned to the spectators, and asked if I could jump a post-and-rails set in a hedge and return the same way. I adopted my jumping position and away we went. This was the first time Cresta had jumped since his fall, but he was not in the slightest bit worried and we flew over the hedge in both directions with great panache. Now came his big test. I asked the Colonel if we could continue around the rest of the course to the finish, if all went well at the V fence, and he said that was fine, the fences were still open, and that his Land Rover and Daddy's car would follow us. I did not show Cresta the V fence, but I circled near to it, using the same growl of warning that I had adopted to such good effect on Chips.

We set off from the landing side of the previous fence, the angled double, on exactly the same line of approach that we had taken on cross-country day a week earlier, holding a narrow corridor, held in by my legs and directed by the reins so that Cresta could have no doubt about the exact place where I intended he should jump. Without hesitation, he took off in immaculate style, sailing easily over the V, landing lightly, and I told him how very good and clever he was as we turned left up the big field, following the course. Turning right at the far end we hopped over the zig-zag rails, the wood pile and the lambing pen, both of us thoroughly enjoying ourselves, and approached the jubilee covert. We came in on a good line to face the big bullfinch, over which he soared and rounding the curve with three more strides to the mound of pit props. As we took off, Cresta decided he could make life easier by banking the top. The wires, which had been pulled taut to keep the pit props in place and to withstand the horses banking it two weeks ago, had loosened. As Cresta's weight landed on top, the whole fence shifted sideways, poles loosened, a wire snapped, and one hoof was momentarily held. Cresta and I somersaulted, freeing his front leg and we described a spectacular arc with me being tipped forward on to the ground just as he hit it. The force turned him over and he landed straight on to my pelvis with all his 500 kg in weight, pinning me beneath him, before he scrambled up, using my stomach as a soft cushion.

The people in the two vehicles had seen us jump into the spinney in perfect style and were swinging round its circumference to catch us coming out over the pit props on the other side. We certainly came out, but what they saw was a horse and rider describing a cartwheel to land heavily, head first on the ground. They watched horrified, as I was deposited roughly on the ground in front of Cresta and his cycle in the air landed him smack across my pelvis. They saw him use my stomach for purchase as he got groggily to his feet. After that, Cresta just stood there, seeing stars, and I lay on the ground unable to move, simply incredulous at what had happened. Everyone erupted out of the two vehicles and I could have died from sheer frustration and embarrassment. I knew that the pitprops fence had been designed to take the weight of a horse in case he banked it, the team and other riders had discussed it as an alternative, but I had intended to fly it in the championships. Now bad luck had struck again. Mummy, Daddy and John and the two men from their Land Rover rushed over to us. John dragged me away from Cresta, while Colonel Aykroyd and his helper guided a befuddled Cresta away from me.

No-one voiced the thought that was running through all our minds, "Why were the fences not checked beforehand?" But it was too late to worry about that now. For the second time within weeks at Harewood, Cresta and I were both unable to continue. I was carted off to hospital, but the cursory x-rays showed no pelvic bones broken, although I was labelled as badly bruised internally and suffered agony for the next two weeks. I did not improve and after four more weeks of increasing pain, with me constantly telling myself not to be so feeble, I noticed that one hip bone was sticking out at a funny angle, and I could not walk properly. Something else must be wrong, and I went by train to London to see a medical wizard.

After examining me, he said that my pelvis was very badly dislocated and it was no wonder that I was not getting better. He told the nurse to put me in one of the tiny treatment rooms on a flat surface where I lay waiting for him, and I was rendered unconscious before I realised

28

what had happened. He manipulated the pelvis and was so quick about this that when I came round he had disappeared and I was convinced that he still had not dealt with me. I began to feel rather annoyed. Then I noticed a small square cushion stuck between my legs, that had not been there before. He came back in, told me the pelvis was back in place, and said I could go home. Pain gone! It was like a miracle. On the way home, I fairly muttered away about the incompetence of the medicos who had missed what should have been a clear possibility. Cresta had recovered and was back to normal in a few days after our fall and, all the time, I was having to endure Mummy going on and on at me over the telephone that I must give up eventing. It was too dangerous, she said, but I dismissed this, saying that I had to have some bad luck some of the time, and it would pass.

Chapter Three – No more eventing!

After this Harewood debacle, the Waddingtons and the Willcoxes joined forces, and while I was held captive in my bed of pain, I was told in no uncertain manner, that I must stop eventing. I became more and more upset. Their argument was based on the fact that I was now married and should have different priorities. I was no longer master of my own destiny. I should realise that there were other things in life, like babies, and I owed it to John to stop riding in such a dangerous sport. I was told that I was selfish and uncaring. I listened to all this with dread in my heart. If it had not been for eventing, I would never have met John. I did not dare to point out that he was rather taken with what eventing had done for me. My parents, also, would never have had the same enjoyment from my job, for this is what it was, if I had achieved Mummy's pinnacle for me of becoming a secretary, no matter how accomplished in that line I may have become. Both Daddy and Mummy had thoroughly enjoyed my three years of eventing, apart from when Mummy was suffering from her nerves when I was going around the cross-country courses, and they would never have met the people who had become firm friends of the Willcox family. After a week of this continuous nagging, with everyone against me, I gave in.

A voice inside me still kept muttering that there must be something wrong with this world of 1959 where, from the moment a girl is married she is demoted and becomes second in status to her husband. And when a baby comes along, she drops another notch. This might seem beyond belief to those of you reading about this time of the late 1950s, whilst in the twenty-first century a woman enjoys the right and the opportunity to go to the top in the world of business, to take on the men as an equal in all sorts of ways. You have no idea how very lucky you are! In 1959, however, I was faced with the fact that I was going to have to comply.

With the greatest reluctance I agreed that I would give up eventing, but I refused to give up riding and training and taking part in competitions. I sold Cresta to Karen Mackintosh in the USA. I would try Grand Prix dressage instead. That should satisfy them. I had already heard on the grapevine after Badminton that the Olympic Committee men in Switzerland were still not prepared to change their views barring women from competing. Certainly not in time for me to go to the Games being held at Rome in the summer of 1960.

It had occurred to me whilst I was still eventing that I should buy a trained Grand Prix horse on which to learn the intricacies of this level of work and I had started by searching the circus rings in England for my potential dressage horse. I can imagine that this idea might seem rather astonishing to contemporary dressage riders! I went to see Bertram Mills as I remembered those beautiful grey horses that I had seen at the circus in Blackpool. They had performed passage, an elevated, slow motion trot, and piaffe, a march on the spot with the forelegs lifted high and quarters lowered, and I realised that it would be an enormous asset to start with a horse already master of these arts. Unfortunately, none of the trained horses were for sale.

At this point, I was constantly in touch with Ted Marsh, my old lover, and he had offered to buy a top dressage horse from abroad so that I had a chance of making the British team for the Rome Olympics in 1960. But I was worried about the price he would have to pay, so I flew to Holland, where, as in Germany, they excel at this high level of dressage. I found a French Thoroughbred which I thought I could improve. This meant that I was to enter dressage competitions at a lower level, hoping to work my way up. I failed to understand that several of the women in dressage at both committee and judging level were rather resentful of me and intended to thwart me at every turn. The horse that I had bought in Holland was called Grace and Favour. Ted told me that I should have bought a horse that was proven and successful in dressage. Then, at least it would have been harder for the dressage fraternity to mark me down. In retrospect he was absolutely right!

Now, I was determined to aim for the top of the dressage field. Henry Wynmalen came to stay at Long Acre and helped me with Favour's training. He told me that my advanced dressage work was 'very good' and I trusted his judgement as he wouldn't have said this if it were not true. John and I enjoyed the tales of his youth which he related over the dinner table. He had been a very successful sportsman, racing cars and airplanes all over Europe with distinction. Captain Edy Goldman also helped me. I had absolute respect for both of these men.

Then I had one more extraordinary and totally unexpected offer of help from the Frenchman, Colonel Margot, whom I did not know personally. He came and stayed at Long Acre for a week. He was the Commandant of the famous French Cavalry School in Saumur and he gave me some invaluable help towards my aim of training Favour towards Grand Prix level.

I had decided that my competition début would be in the spring of 1960 in Berlin, as there I would be judged without prejudice. However, that week the weather was very bad, and the ferry crossing was too dangerous. So, I had to wait for the Ascot Horse Show and there I was to put my head smack into the lion's mouth.

Diana Mason with her small mare, Tramella, was also competing in dressage. She had previously been eventing but as the fences became increasingly higher little Tramella wasn't coping, so they had turned to dressage. She had been accepted into the elitist circle of dressageurs, as she was from the same background. I began to realise that I was just never going to be welcomed.

When we went to Ascot the Wynmalens were there to check on how we compared with the rest of the competitors, including the Olympic contenders. Our début in the arena for the Prix St George test was not brilliant. Favour was too full of himself. Henry Wynmalen was watching and gave me some good advice and Favour improved hugely in the second and third tests. It was incredibly irritating and upsetting that my marks for all three tests were uniformly low, when it was evident not only to myself, but also to Henry Wynmalen that the two later tests were considerably better. This was to set the pattern for the future. The dressage coterie did not want me to do well at advanced dressage and they would block me at every move, but I would forge on and hope that by sheer persistence I would be able to overcome this prejudice against me. However, there were not many competitions at this level and I realised with a heavy heart that there was no way I could qualify for the 1960 Rome Olympics.

I felt that it was better to have a baby and please both sides of the family. This was a hard decision to make as I was not at all a baby person. In fact, I was not at all keen on babies. I hadn't had much to do with any and felt no burgeoning maternal longings. I imagined that I would be alright when I actually gave birth. So, from that point on John and I dedicated ourselves to this aim, making love at anytime and anywhere. This was all rather exciting. However, I fell pregnant almost immediately and this came as a terrific shock. Somehow, I thought it would take much longer. Both sets of parents were extremely happy, especially Mummy who kept repeating, 'At last! At last!'. No doubt John's parents, who were also pleased, were hoping that this was going to be the end of my inappropriate obsession with competing in equestrian events.

I absolutely hated being pregnant. I felt invaded. I put on weight, which upset me, and promptly ate more to make myself feel better. I had dreadful morning sickness and muttered away under my breath with disgust. I sank into a slough of self-pity. I felt no urge to look at babies in prams and I began to fear there was something wrong with me.

Favour had been sold and I would sit on the landing and look out over the empty looseboxes across the gravel and feel bereft. I tried to hide my unhappiness from my husband and the two sets of parents, but I was very depressed. I felt as if my dog Fang was my only friend and we went for long walks. I didn't notice when he slipped away, and his primal instinct took charge and he killed two lambs. The farmer insisted that he be put down and I had to telephone the vet. John was horrified to learn what had happened and we agreed that we must have another dog. I bought a cross-bred Border Collie, called Gyp. He was very intelligent and extraordinarily quick to learn and soon perfected all the tricks I could think of. As the years passed he became my greatest companion and truly the love of my life.

John's friends were urging him to learn to ride so he could hunt with them on Saturdays and he took to this idea enthusiastically. He began hunting on a quiet and sensible horse, that he had borrowed. I said that after the baby was born I would train a better horse for him and teach him to ride properly.

Ted had kept in touch, but he went very quiet when I told him I was pregnant. John had no idea that Ted and I had ever been sexually involved. Then Ted told me that he wanted to get married again as in his position he needed a wife. There were two possibilities one was Lady Anne Cowdray, and the other was Elizabeth Green who had been his mistress for a number of years. Ted asked my advice over which he should marry. I gave this some consideration and

33

eventually decided that although Lady Anne was higher up the social scale it was Elizabeth who really cared about him.

Ted stayed in touch and he was the only one with whom I could discuss all my fears and hopes, without being castigated. He promised to send his horse, Bilko for me to ride and school after the baby was born. This cheered me up immediately. It began to dawn on me just how upset I was to be banned from eventing by my parents and parents-in-law. John was hugely enjoying hunting and I think he began to realise how the horses were such a big part of my life.

My son Charles was born. At last I could see my legs after nine months of lassitude and indolence and I couldn't wait to get out of the hospital and back to Long Acre. I was terribly nervous of the new baby, not at all a natural mother. I felt no urge to pick him up and the sound of his crying seared right through my entire being. It made me feel totally inadequate, exceedingly depressed and very guilty. I was plunged into even deeper depths when John said that our nurse had decided that in the circumstances she would not be able to stay the agreed weeks as she was promised to an 'old customer' who was more important than us. Everyone rallied round and made the effort to come and see us at Preston but underneath my sunny face I was horrified by the situation of being cooped up in a hospital room with Charles crying for his milk, and the smell of disgusting dirty nappies. I thought the whole process abhorrent. Clearly, I was an utterly hopeless mother!

All the grandparents were thrilled and discussed which relative he resembled. I thought he was very red and crinkly and definitely not like anyone that I knew. Only Robert, my brother-in-law, agreed with me and said he looked 'all screwed up'.

I was panicking not knowing the first thing about how to look after a baby and fortunately Nurse Riley took charge and I was relieved of the responsibility. I began to cheer up, finally I was home again. At his christening Charles behaved well and stopped his piercing yells. I thought this was a good omen. I was a very good Catholic at that point in my life and referenced all sorts of daily occurrences within a framework of religious belief.

I had asked Ted to be a godfather, but he said that he couldn't bear the thought of me having a child with another man. Although when we had planned on being together and getting married, he had said he didn't want any more children and he wanted me to himself. But he did keep his promise and he sent me his horse, Bilko, to train and improve. I was hopeful that I would be eventing by autumn and in preparation for getting fit enough to ride and school a big, quality horse I walked and ran a lot and used my skipping rope. My spirits lifted, and the world began to look a better place.

I spent a lot of time with Bilko in the stable, 'banging' him with a square of soft linen cloth, in the same manner of wisping. Ultimately, it produced a noticeably better outline and I used it with all my horses over the years. It felt so good to be back in the saddle and doing dressage work. He was short-coupled with strong loins, but his mouth needed work and although he had a good walk, he had an appalling choppy and uncertain trot. Then I took him over to Holmes Chapel to Captain Edy Goldman. He was one of the few people whose opinion I valued. I was delighted when he told me that Bilko was 100% straight and showing impressive length bends on the circles and in the corners, and that his paces were very good. We jumped a show jumping course and Bilko put his head down and bucked, and I came off.

I hurt my back, and I was too sore to ride the next day. When I was x-rayed I had fractured the first vertebra of my lumbar spine. I was told to stay in bed for a week to see if it would improve. The parents and parents-in-law were horrified and there was talk of reinstating the ban on eventing. After the first week of bed rest the doctor declared that I had to stay in bed for a second week.

My mother was concerned at the time that I showed no aptitude towards mothering. She blamed horses for this and was convinced that if there were no horses then I would become what she called 'normal'. There was a great deal of pressure on me to give up eventing forever, and then after two years to do only advanced dressage.

I resigned myself to this situation and consoled myself with the idea that I would work to the top in Grand Prix dressage. I wanted to buy a German horse that had been specifically bred for dressage. As there was no way I could afford this I started going to Ascot sales to find a two- or three-year-old that might be suitable.

I began riding Spark, the horse that I had bought for John to go hunting. I entered her at the show hunter class at the prestigious Royal Lancashire Show at Blackpool and I was thrilled when she won third prize. John was going to cut a fine figure for his friends in the Pendle Forest Harriers.

In December 1962 the Olympic eventing world was considering a huge change, there were rumours that at last women were to be allowed to compete. Although the male riders in England were back in the ascendancy, Anneli Drummond-Hay was beginning to make her mark and Jane Bullen would follow on. It was the British who had put forward this proposal. Frank Weldon, Laurence Rook and Bertie Hill were retiring, and Ted Marsh was no longer in a position to continue to offer his high-quality horses to team members. Derek, was the only member of the old guard, seemingly ageless he was still going strong with Lochinvar.

However, Frank Weldon became more influential when he stopped competing. He wrote regularly for the Sunday Telegraph, reporting on the main events and in such a way as to promote the current selection committee's policy or attitude. In 1965 he became the course builder at Badminton, and in 1967 he was appointed Director of Badminton.

Chapter Four – Women Can Go To The Olympics

I was taken totally by surprise in January 1963 when the ban on women riders was lifted. Equestrian reporters in the newspaper were speculating on whether a woman was to be picked for the British team. I talked it over with my husband, John. Now he was hunting he appreciated the thrill of cross-country riding. We both realised that this was going to be the most tremendous challenge. But we had only two years to produce a horse ready to compete at Olympic level. It was like the culmination of all my dreams, the next great challenge to follow my success at Badminton. More than anything I wanted to represent my country again. Like in all the pony books, I wanted to ride for England! All the problems were swept aside. I was full of hope.

Bert Cleminson rang to offer to lend me a horse to school and train for a place on the British team. This was a tremendously generous offer, far too good to miss, and we drove over to pick up the horse. We were shown a seven-year-old, Up and Coming. He turned out to be a good-looking stamp of a horse, bay in colour, good conformation, an intelligent head with a bright, bold eye and a straight mover. He seemed to be a natural jumper. He had a good walk with clear over-tracking, where the hind feet step through on a longer stride than the front ones. This indicates good pushing ability of the hindquarters in order to jump substantial obstacles. His trot was short striding but steady, but he had absolutely no idea of how to lengthen his stride into extension. His transitions, from one pace to another, were not smooth but I was hopeful that with my training we could overcome these issues.

All my efforts were now concentrated on training this new horse, with the golden chance of competing in the Olympics on the shimmering horizon. John was now dedicated to hunting with Spark regularly every Saturday. My young dressage horse, Sun and Air, had completed a year's dressage training since I had bought him at the Newmarket Sales in December 1962. He was a stallion, and this meant that he showed more flamboyancy and presence than a gelding, and there was a tremendous air about him. I had made a vow not to compete at the lower levels of dressage in this country with the way that the judging fraternity was so obviously prejudiced and colluding

38

to give me low marks no matter what the standard of our performance. I regularly took him to Edy Goldman and Henry Wynmalen, and they told me that he was very promising.

So, on the horse front all was going well. Then things in my marriage began to go wrong. Whether or not I was delusional is a moot point, but I began to suspect John of flirtations with other women. He was away a great deal for the mills which were in financial trouble with the advent of globalisation and cheap products coming in from the East.

We attended a large party in a grand house and I began to feel as if people were looking at me in a pitying type of way. I checked that my dress wasn't hooked up at the back, but it was fine. Then I saw John talking to a beautiful young heiress in a very fixed and interested manner. I tried to ignore it and remain sophisticated and *insouciant* but I was not in my natural social milieu and I decided that I had to go up to him and insist that we went home. He ignored me, and I felt that the beautiful heiress was laughing at me. I insisted that we leave and when he declined I punched him hard on the jaw. I caught him a good one and he staggered back. The entire room was watching us in silence. I turned on my heel and stalked out, walking the length of the watching room. This awful memory is written indelibly on my mind, as if it were a recorded film. Our marital relationship never recovered from this embarrassing debacle. I tried my hardest at being a mother, but I was certainly not a natural. I probably didn't want to remember just how judgemental I had been of Ted Marsh's wife when she had snorted when he told me he would come to help me give Chips his last evening feed. I had felt that she was rude and ill-mannered. Now, of course, I realise that she knew what her husband was up to, and here in circumstances far more innocent - I had actually punched John's face in public.

I continued to train Up and Coming through a very cold winter in 1963. It began to snow in January which meant I couldn't do my dressage training in the outdoor arena. I had to take the horses in a trailer to the very small indoor arena at the Dickinsons at Gisburn. Twice I got stuck in snow drifts. By February the weather had improved, and Ted rang and invited me over to Dunsley where there were proper facilities. I jumped at the chance and stayed with Ted and Elizabeth for five days. I had long talks with Ted about the state of my marriage, which was now all cold politeness. I felt that I couldn't bear to stay married to someone who would openly and flagrantly flirt with another woman. However, I was strong in my Catholic faith and I knew that divorce was forbidden. How strange that I should seek Ted out as a confidant when he had been relentlessly unfaithful to all his wives. Although Ted was always discreet, perhaps one could even say sneaky, with his indiscretions. John had boorishly flirted in public at a party, and my pride couldn't take it.

I took Up and Coming to the beach at my parents' place and we galloped around, jumped the fishermen's boats and generally enjoyed ourselves. Then inexplicably he went lame. I rushed around to have him x-rayed and they couldn't be sure whether or not there was a fracture and it was suggested that he be rested for two months. This was a serious blow. The selectors were never going to be keen on a horse that suffered from lameness. I had to withdraw from the spring events.

I was having trouble keeping up with the stable work, so I advertised for help and employed a young woman called Sandra Towers from Norfolk. She was to stay with me for several years through what would probably be the most difficult period of my life. The time lines were now so short and Up and Coming went lame again, and Bert sent me over Might and Main but then his legs swelled up. Then I realised that the way Bert trained his horses there wasn't time to get them fit with slow and systematic work. I sent the second horse back and it was arranged that they would be returned to me when they were sound again.

Then I remembered a horse that I had seen in a copy of *Horse and Hound*. A photograph of a horse, Glenamoy had leapt out of the page at me. He was jumping a rustic fence in fine style to win a big working hunter class in the south of England. I had been so impressed with the look of this horse, and how he tucked up his legs – something about him reminded me of Chips. I found the telephone number of his owner, a Mrs Pat Gray, and asked her if he was for sale. She replied that she would take no less than £1500. She told me that he was a naturally careful jumper with a lovely temperament, a good straight mover. I looked at my bank book and this was nearly all the money that I had left, and I tried to decide whether I should risk it.

I travelled down to see him. He was very good. He had a lovely honest head with a small star in the centre of his forehead, and big generous eyes. When I was sitting in the saddle I had a good view of his well-shaped neck and good shoulders and behind the saddle were strong loins and muscular quarters. His legs looked clean of lumps and bumps and they felt cool. I was somewhat critical of his feet, which were slightly spread out, but this was the only fault that I could find.

He was in a completely different class to Bert's horses. He was ready to listen to me, he kept his rhythm approaching each fence, lengthened his stride when I asked for it, and as Edy Goldman would say, 'basculed' beautifully, rounding his back over every jump. I rode him in to a couple of fences at an angle, but he accepted that and made no attempt to run out or lose his stride. We got on very well together. I finished with a sharp gallop. I felt that he did not possess the speed of a racehorse, but his pace was steady and economical, and he had a good mouth. I paid the full amount for him and drove him home the next day. Now, I had a horse that was possibly good enough for the Tokyo Olympics, and this was my last chance to be selected.

The Burghley Three-Day Event was due to take place that week, in September 1963, and all the top eventers would be there to impress the selectors, trying to get their tickets to Tokyo. My new horse was only six years old. He was a gentle, co-operative soul and he had spent his working life in a cosseted fashion and probably raised no more than a slight sweat in all that time. The only expectations placed on him had been that he should behave impeccably in the showing part of the working hunter class and give the judge a good ride, then jump one round of straightforward rustic fences. Now it was a very different matter.

Bert had sent Slim back to me which meant I was riding seven hours a day; Bert's horse, my dressage horse Sun and Air and my latest acquisition, Glenamoy. Slim also had to learn how to clear show jumps.

We set off for Wylye with the two eventers and, also the stallion as there was no one at Long Acre to look after him. The cross-country course would be built of telegraph poles and railway sleepers to produce fences that would look daunting to both horse and rider. I was absolutely determined to try and qualify the horses for

Badminton next spring and in order to do this we had to complete at least two of the remaining three events of the season; Wylye, Tweseldown and Chatsworth.

They all did well in the dressage tests Slim had only 29 penalties and Glenamoy bettered this with 27.67. Then Slim went on to perform a master class in how to knock as many show jumps as possible and demolished seven of the twelve jumps. Slim had never faced a cross-country course before but he had been hunted a great deal. He went around clear with a great deal of panache in exemplary style. He would have been in the money if he hadn't decimated the show jumping course. Glenamoy was now in a position to win. He had been such a valuable show animal that he had never been sent out in the rough and tumble of the hunting field.

He probably went around the cross-country course with his eyes shut, obeying my insistent aids. We approached a revetted bank, enclosed by horizontal creosoted sleepers and topped with grass, only two fences before the finish, set in an island of mud churned up by all the horses that had gone before us. He had no knowledge of the way in which to tackle this jump, which was to leap up on to the top, change legs, and jump down the other side. This would have been easy for him. Unfortunately, he imagined it was to be jumped in one big leap, straight over the top of the flat bank, only to find rather late that the distance was too far. He came to earth in the middle of the bank, landing flat on his tummy and with all four legs tucked underneath. He was badly winded and elected to stay in the same position until he recovered.

I shot straight over his head but hung on to the reins of the simple snaffle bridle. I was brought to a sharp stop when the bridle's length ran out. The cheek piece then snapped, and the bridle disintegrated. It fell off his head. I got up at once, saw that there was nothing to stop him careering away round the Wylye Estate and quickly went to his head. A great deal of time was lost while I tried to find a way to put the bridle together whilst Glen decided he might as well rest where he was until he recovered his breath. I continued to fiddle in desperation, with the jump judge and a crowd of spectators engrossed in watching my efforts until I had to concede that there was no way the bridle would mend. We were not going to be able to continue.

It was infuriating as there were only two more fences left before the finish, both perfectly straightforward, but I consoled myself by thinking that, despite this enforced withdrawal from the field, Glenamoy must certainly have impressed the selectors with his excellent showing in all three phases.

In order to qualify for Badminton Slim had to complete one more competition, either at Tweseldown or Chatsworth. Glenamoy on the other hand had just two more chances. If he failed at either venue there would be no Badminton entry for him and any chance of being chosen for the Tokyo Olympics would disappear in a puff of smoke.

Before we left Wylye, I asked permission to take Glenamoy around the cross-country course the following day. It was continuing to pour down rain but still I persisted in my plan. I walked him around the bank, let him stand on the take-off side, in order to make him understand we were going to jump it. To give him more of a chance I started by picking up the course at the previous fence and coming into the bank on a rounded stride he hopped impeccably up onto the grass top and popped down the other side. I told him he was a clever boy, gave him a sugar lump as a reward and went back up the track to try again. This time he was almost nonchalant, and we proceeded over the last two fences with ease to finish the course. This was a very important lesson. He had learnt how to jump a bank properly and it gave him confidence in both himself, and also in me. I was due to stay with friends and then go on to the Wynmalen's place, followed by the working hunter class at the Horse of the Year Show, then the Tweseldown One-Day Event the next day.

John arrived at Wembley and I was surprised as this had not been planned. He was charming and courteous to me in front of other people, and monosyllabic when we were alone. I couldn't understand his behaviour, or what had happened to our relationship, but my efforts to get to Tokyo blinkered my vision and that was all I could think of, and it was make or break at Tweselden. Glenamoy had to finish in order to qualify for Badminton. Both of the horses produced top class dressage, Glenamoy on 24.67 penalties, and Slim on 25. In the show jumping they both knocked down three fences, which was not brilliant, but we were still in the competition. They went brilliantly in the cross-country. I pushed them both for speed and we finished with Slim in second place and Glenamoy had moved up to fourth. Now Slim was qualified for Badminton and all we had to do with Glenamoy was get around and finish at Chatsworth.

We went back to stay at the Wynmalens and there was a rather grand dinner with guests. I came down the stairs and everyone clapped spontaneously at my entrance. The next morning, I went to Sunday Mass and Communion and thanked God for my good fortune. We returned to Long Acre for a few days before setting off for Chatsworth. I loved this beautiful estate with the park spreading over the valley and the river running through it. Glenamoy simply had to complete the intermediate class. Our journey there was painful, even though the horsebox engine had been checked before we left, the radiator boiled over. After a delayed journey we arrived. I left Sandra to unpack and I worked both Slim and Glenamoy near the dressage arenas, so they could become familiar with the environment.

The cross-country there is over challenging terrain and I set off to walk the course. The starting fences are sited on the way up the steep hill, before the course turns downwards and horse and rider face alarming drop fences, and sharp turns where seconds can be saved or lost before reaching the ice pond, which every year is the cause of refusals, spectacular falls and loss of time. Almost every fence presents a problem of speed or difficult approach and only a fool or a newcomer to eventing would be riding without having a deep respect for the course builder's expertise.

Glenamoy was drawn second in the dressage test, which is not advantageous as judges don't like to give the highest marks to the early competitors in case better tests are ridden later. We did well and Glenamoy led the field on top marks of 31 and Slim produced another good test in the second division of the intermediates with 25 penalties and was knocked down into second place by Anneli Drummond-Hay who scored 24.67. In the show jumping Slim improved slightly and knocked down only three fences! Glenamoy was infuriating as he also knocked down three fences and I knew he could do better than this. However, he redeemed himself by going fast and clear in the cross-country and we finished in third place.

In the cross-country Slim was jumping a brilliant round until we came to the ice pond, with so many people packed around it and astonished at the sudden appearance of a post-and-rails set in front of a long, rippling pond he found it too difficult to absorb. He nearly stopped,

44

then jumped and hit the top rail with his knees. We both landed in the water and Slim, fortunately, made no effort to run away. I remounted, soaked to the skin and we finished the course making no more mistakes.

I was exultant. In the space of just under five weeks I had qualified two new horses neither of whom had ever heard of dressage, did not know about jumping coloured show jumps and had never seen a cross-country in their lives. However, I was cursed with my implacable quest for perfectionism no matter how much inconvenience this entailed. I went over to the Secretary's office and asked if I could take Slim back over the jump in the ice pond and was given permission. We had to wait until the last competitor had gone round and dusk was falling. He sailed over faultlessly and at last we could set off for home. I was confident that he had learnt a valuable lesson.

The next day Slim's leg was swollen like a balloon. His off-fore knee looked like a football, with a cut above it. He was given anti-tetanus and penicillin injections. Glenamoy's legs were blistered and he was tied up short so he couldn't rub them. I was upset that so much damage had been done to both of them but consoled myself with the thought that they might heal quickly and it had been unavoidable if I was to impress the selectors. Even Frank Weldon, who was no fan of mine, said in the Sunday Telegraph:

> *"For most competitors, the target of competing at Badminton is the ultimate aim and quite distant enough, but with commendable singleness of purpose, to Sheila Wilcox, Chatsworth was but a stepping stone to the Olympics next Autumn. Now that the Olympic Three-Day-Event is open to girls, she is determined to have a go."*

You will note that in those days it was acceptable to call women 'girls' and men were not 'boys', but rather men. It was a sign of the times that language automatically diminished females.

This media interest included Ben Wright, reporter for the Sunday Observer and BBC Television rolling up at Long Acre, insisting that I ride for him. With the two eventers invalids I had to ride Sun and Air, the black dressage stallion to give a show, followed by an interview. Then later I took part in BBC's Look North programme.

45

It took two weeks before Glenamoy's and Slim's legs improved enough for them to be driven to my friend's farm at Wrea Green for a well-earned rest. At that time my husband, John, seemed to have taken a dislike to Spark, and I had heard that he had fallen out hunting which had hurt his pride. We were now talking but the incident at the dance and the beautiful young heiress were a banned topic. There was an idea that we should move to Cheshire. We looked at several properties and one that we particularly liked had land, so we could have fields for the horses, but it came to nothing. I wanted to stay close to my parents who loved being able to visit Long Acre easily. They also enjoyed having Charles and his nanny to stay. Spark was sent to Bert Cleminson to be sold and John was hunting on his friends' horses in Cheshire. We kept up appearances and had a great party at Long Acre. Then, at ten o'clock in the evening went on to the Hunt Ball at Gisburn.

Chapter Five – Playing Away

It was about this time that we became very friendly with a particular couple in our social circle in the Pendle Forest area. David and Joan R., who lived not far from us in the little village of Dunsop Bridge. We began to go out in a foursome on a regular basis, usually to the cinema or sometimes out to dinner.

Then I suggested that we learn judo at evening classes in Preston and David and Joan volunteered to join us. Every Thursday evening, we dressed in baggy trousers and loose tops tied with sashes in a dirty cream colour. I had the advantage of being very fit, whereas neither John nor Joan could be placed in this category. David was a sportsman, tall broad shouldered, well-muscled, dark and handsome in a devilish way. He looked like the film star, Stewart Grainger. But instinctively I didn't trust him.

At the second or third lesson, we were working on how to deal with an attack from the front. Our instructor said that David would be attacking me, and John attacking Joan. We women were shown how to step back on being attacked, with left foot going up into the air and finding purchase on the villain's stomach, at which point we were to snap straight the left leg, which should catapult the attacker up into the air and he would sail on to meet the ground in a nasty crunch landing. It sounded easy enough, the way he said it, but looking at David, so much taller and broader than I was, I doubted my ability to even get my foot in the right place, never mind snap it straight to send him flying.

But I had to try. He ran up to me, fast, and I obediently fell backwards without going out of line, my left leg bent, then straightened it up and made contact with his tummy muscles. With all the force I could muster I thrust my foot upwards and he sailed up into the air and came down onto the floor with a crash. There was a moment's stunned silence. Disbelief on the part of John and Joan and me, delight on the face of the instructor, until David sat up and clutched his foot with pain written all over his face. Our night's lesson came to an abrupt end, with David having broken a small bone. It was very embarrassing, but I could not help but be pleased that I would be able to precipitate strong men over my head if ever I was attacked. It had been the most extraordinary feeling and I expect neither David, nor

47

even Joan and John would look at me in quite the same way again. Looking back, I can see that my attitude towards men was in some way combative, and perhaps this could explain my long history of disastrous relationships. Although it didn't define my relationship with Ted which could be described as more father and daughter with the worst type of incestuous overtones.

On the first January 1964 I began training the two eventers for the spring season, which looked like being the most important one of my life. My sights were set on the two one-day events at Crookham in March and Liphook in early April to prepare both horses for Badminton. Entries were split into two divisions, Little Badminton for the less experienced horses and Great Badminton for the more experienced. There were a number of international entries; four from Ireland, one from each country Germany, France, Spain and Denmark. Both Little and Great Badminton competitors did the same advanced dressage test, the same speed and endurance and the same show jumping course. I had to show the selectors that we were Olympic material and I was determined to try my heart out.

John was away a lot, on business but I was too busy to really notice. During my long rides around the roads to get the horses fit I was often confronted by the sight of David draped on the bonnet of his Aston Martin, in the middle of nowhere. We would stop and chat, but it annoyed me, I had to work hard and not get distracted. I wasn't interested in being chatted up, but he was not to be put off. Then I found myself, rather surprisingly, a little disappointed if he wasn't lying in wait for me somewhere along my training route. I had heard that his metal business was not doing well, and I wondered why he wasn't spending more time trying to save his business. He was very attractive, and I began to wonder what it would be like to have his lips on mine.

In the end he persuaded me to let him come and see me at Long Acre. Charles and his nanny were away staying with my parents and John was at work and both David and myself knew what was going to happen. We went into the drawing room and sat on either side of the fireplace nursing our drinks. Then he asked me, 'Are we going upstairs?' Stupidly I had not really considered the practical details such as location and I thought that it wouldn't be right to go up to the bed I shared with my husband. He put down his drink and came over

48

to me. He pulled me to my feet and in a moment our lips opened as if they already knew each other and our tongues entwined.

Soon we had gone too far and now there was no stopping a red-hot love making session. Clothes fell off in all directions and we were nearly naked. I took one look at his engorged penis, standing on end impatiently and nearly had a fit. I had never seen anything so large. On the other hand, I had only seen two, Ted's and John's, and fleetingly I wondered if I could contain such an instrument.

Then we were on the floor and just about reaching the stage when we would become totally deaf to anything in the world outside, when I heard a car turn in off the lane, crunching on the gravel. 'It's John!' I cried, and we were both panicking. I picked up my scattered clothes as did David. John threw open the kitchen door and I knew that in one minute we would be discovered, then miraculously his footsteps ran across the polished parquet floor of the hall and he bounded up the stairs. We both finished dressing and by the time John came into the drawing room we were sitting solemnly in the armchairs on either side of the fireplace, ready to welcome him.

This incident served only to inflame our desire and as soon as John was away for three days David came over and we ended up in the spare room. That first time we were almost deranged with lust and it was a miracle that neither of us were marked. We could not get enough of each other, feeling, stroking, kissing to such depths that it was almost too much to bear - culminating in a volcanic orgasm. And then we did it again, this time with variations.

Following this experience, I discovered how easy it is to arrange an illicit affair and we were keen to find a way of being together for a few days. I excused myself with the idea that John didn't care anyway, and we were only doing what I was certain he had been doing.

So, in the middle of this Bert rang me and told me that he had cured Up and Coming's leg. I told him it was far too late to stand any chance of being considered for the Olympics as there was no time to qualify him for Badminton. Then I realised that there must be a buyer for Slim who was now worth much more than when he had come to me, so Slim was returned to Bert.

My affair with David continued to roller coast along and we decided that we now wanted to live together. We continued to socialise with our spouses and I was always amazed that John did not seem to realise what was happening. I thought that the vibrations between us were far too strong to miss.

So, a rather chaotic and clandestine relationship swept me along in tandem with my burning ambition to get to the Olympics. Glenamoy was now my only chance and I was determined to do everything I could to prove ourselves. I went back to Chatsworth in March to practise over the cross-country fences. I thought this wonderfully kind and helpful of the Duke and Duchess of Devonshire who even flooded the ice pond just for me. It takes days to fill the pond and I was amazed at their helpfulness. The weather was bitterly cold with flurries of snow, but we managed to jump nearly all the fences and 1 was more than satisfied.

There was one more event before Badminton, the Liphook One-Day Event in Hampshire and the bad weather continued with biting winds and showers of rain and sleet. Nonetheless, Glenamoy lay second after the dressage, knocked only one show jump and finished the cross-country in a time of only three seconds behind the well-known winner, Foxdor. Ben Jones was second on Master Bernard and we were third, snapping at the heels of the established winners.

Glenamoy was as fit and keen as I could hope for and we were drawn to compete in Little Badminton. I would have hoped to be up against the big boys in Great Badminton but consoled myself with the fact that it was the same cross-country course and the same time allowed, so comparisons would be easy. One disadvantage was that we were the last to go so it was possible that the ground would be all churned up, but at least I would have the advantage of watching some of the other competitors jump around first.

The sun came out on the first dressage day and the wind blew so with luck the course would dry out for the cross-country. The Queen was not present, but the Queen Mother and the Princess Royal (Princess Mary, the sister of the Queen's father) were there. The selectors were particularly interested in Captain James Templer with M'Lord Connolly, winner of the Burghley European Championships in 1962 and an international three-day event in Munich in 1963. Mike Bullen had also been provided with two horses by prominent members of the selection committee. The Bullens were well-known in the showing world and lived in a charming, golden, glowing stone house with stables and paddocks in the local village of Didmarton, close to the Badminton estate. The Bullen girls rode expensive ponies for rich owners and Jennie the eldest had gone on to show hacks and would later find her metier in Grand Prix dressage.

Richard Meade was also a strong possibility. He was a member of the victorious British team at Munich, riding his own Barberry. There was Captain Welch of the 5th Royal Iniskilling Dragoon Guards with Char's Choice who had already a number of wins to his name. There was also Jeremy Smith-Bingham of the Royal Horse Guards riding By Golly and Sergeant Ben Jones with Master Bernard. Most of these men had the advantage of riding the dressage test in their dashing military uniforms, making a flamboyant statement that they were members of the élite group of military men who ruled the eventing world at that time. It would be years before the dress code was changed to top hats and tails.

In those days all competitors had to weigh in at a minimum of 165lbs (11 stone 11lbs) or 75kg. We had to weigh out in the official tent, not including our whip, before starting and on the finishing phase E, the run-in, riders would dismount at the steward's order and go straight into the tent weigh in again.

The speed and endurance test covered just over 17 miles to be completed within the time of 91 minutes. There were ten steeplechase fences to be negotiated at fast speed on the second phase of nearly two and a half miles, and 34 obstacles on the cross-country course. Bonus points were given for completing the steeplechase and the cross-country in less than the time allowed, and penalty marks were imposed if horses were too slow.

Glenamoy was seven years old with only five and a half months of actual training in this discipline and I knew that this, the most prestigious competition in the eventing calendar, was asking a lot of him. I had walked the course three times since the official inspection and I would have to show my horse a clear path all the way round and he had to learn to put his trust in me, jump boldly and cover the ground with as much speed as I felt he could manage. It was like galloping as close to the edge of a cliff as possible without falling over.

51

We were the last to go and I could see some of the spectators drifting away, which made me want to cry out to them, 'Stay and watch what we can do!' I had three stopwatches strategically placed along my arms, one for emergency. At the word, 'Go', I hit the first and away we shot for Glen's introduction to a steeplechase course. We jumped fast and clear, both enjoying ourselves, and as we flashed through the finish of phase B I pressed the stop button and hit the button on my second watch so that I could judge what speed was needed on the second roads and tracks. I slowed him down and we were walking. I let him stretch and lower his neck whilst he regained his breath and then I asked him to pick up speed.

During our ten-minute break before the beginning of the cross-country Sandra and I washed him down in the box. We had a reviving routine which we went through. Then it was, 'Go,' and we shot into gear and were away to the first fence. Glenamoy had settled well and was listening to me. In the quarry he slipped nearly down the drop of six feet, 1860 cm, and leapt up the steps and out over the rail at the top to gallop on to the pit props. Two fences later and he jumped the spruce fence with a big drop on landing. On we went, over the uninviting zigzag rail with hurdles in the ditch below, through the oak plantation jumping first into it over the park railing and out over the stone wall with an ox rail on top. We came to a bank with a rail on top, which he treated now like an old professional and then we faced the vicarage ditch where I put my foot on his accelerator, making him realise that I meant business and he had to jump big. It was my job to give him no time to see the uninviting ditch below, nor to allow him to check his stride. He sailed over it and I just had time to say, 'You are a good boy,' before I turned him to the Irish bank 4 feet 9 inches high and 8 feet wide. I held him on a narrow line of approach aiming for the middle and knowing that there was little room on top and a nasty sloping exit on the other side. On to a spread of water, then the splash pond and on towards the Luckington Road duo with a stark rail from the grassy going of the park on to the peat protected road, two long driving strides before take-off on to a bank and off it, turning left, and we were on the home run, jumping an old tree trunk when I could feel him just beginning to tire, galloping towards Badminton House with time for a quick glance at the third stopwatch and we turned to jump the penultimate beer barrels and finishing the cross-country by jumping into the lake, then splashing out economically in the shallows to gallop through the flags denoting the end of phase D, and straight on to E, the run in.

Passing that finishing post, I stopped my watch and looked straight at the steward as I carefully unwound Glenamoy's pace from gallop to canter, to trot and walk, all in a straight line, keeping him balanced. The steward doffed his hat, I smiled at him, jumped off Glenamoy, giving him a pat and telling him how terrific he had been, and I loosened his girth to remove the saddle. No-one must help me. Sandra threw a rug over Glen's back as I followed the steward into the tent to weigh in.

When our marks went up on the board, Glenamoy, the last horse on the course, went into the lead in the Little Badminton division with the only plus score. In Great Badminton, James Templer and M'Lord Connolly's after dressage position had been seventh with 75 penalties to Glenamoy's 65.5. Connolly had gained 108 bonus points on the speed and endurance which gave him a second day total of plus 33. At this stage, had it been one big class Glenamoy would have been in second position with 21.3, 11.7 behind the champion. I was thrilled with Glenamoy's performance and Sandra and I were soon back in the stables ministering to him for the next day's veterinary inspection where any unsound horse would be eliminated from the competition. He was tired, but his legs were clean. He had hit no fences, nor made any awkward jumps.

The final day arrived and Glenamoy ran up in hand before the packed crowd of spectators in the stable yard and was passed 'sound' without a second look. All now depended on the show jumping which would start with the Great Badminton survivors at two o'clock. 24 of the original 33 entries would be jumping, and 14 more in the Little Badminton section. This meant we wouldn't be jumping until nearly four o'clock.

I could tell that Glenamoy was tired and we left him alone in his box to rest. In the middle of the afternoon we plaited up and went into the ring for the parade of all the remaining horses and riders who had not been eliminated or withdrawn on the second day. Glenamoy and I brought up the rear and he seemed to think he was in some sort of show class without the manners, jogging along and looking sideways at the big crowds and almost passaging – high stepping – in front of the grandstand.

Then we had a long wait ahead of us, so we put him back in his box. I think that Glenamoy had imagined that he had performed for the day and when we returned to fetch him he was lying down. He certainly did not appreciate being made to get up, nor did he seem at all keen on the idea of doing more work. I stood him where he could see the other horses show jumping so that he would know why he was there and we jumped the practice fence, so that he could feel that I meant business.

Into the ring we went, the bell rang, and we approached the first fence. Glenamoy was sluggish. I gave him a quick dig with my heels to wake him up and the next fence we had a disagreement over where he should take off, most unlike him, and we literally crashed through it. Already ten of the twenty marks we could afford to lose and still keep first place were gone and I willed myself to stay calm and to make sure that I brought him in to all the remaining show jumps on exactly the right stride. Always a difficult situation as one tends to be too careful and lose momentum. There is also the risk of time penalties. The crowd went quiet, knowing that if I hit two more, I would lose first place. We hit a second fence, just rolling off the rail and I virtually had to carry him over the remainder of the course. As we passed through the finishing posts there was a huge roar of relief from the crowd and much applause. Glenamoy perked up immediately and made his exit thinking he had done well. I was not at all pleased with his performance and then I realised that in fact it was really a miracle. Not only had he won the Little Badminton event but if he had been up against the competitors in Great Badminton he would have finished third to James Templer and Jeremy Smith-Bingham.

We went home on a high note. I now knew that Glenamoy had the guts and jumping ability to take on the best in the world. My only criticism was that he did not cover enough ground in his gallop and therefore had to work harder than the big striding free movers. It was time to make a fuss of him and he would go out in the field again for a rest.

On the 30th April the newspapers announced the names of the six riders chosen to go into training for the Tokyo Olympics. They were Michael Bullen with Sea Breeze and Young Pretender and four Army men, James Templer with M'Lord Connolly, Jeremy Smith-Bingham with By Golly, Jeremy Beale with Victoria Bridge and Martin

Whiteley with Happy Talk. The sixth was Sheila Waddington, née Willcox, with Glenamoy. We were to train on our own patch where we would be visited at regular intervals by the team captain, Lt. Colonel Frank Weldon and the team veterinary surgeon whose job it was to check the training and soundness of the horses. Three weeks before the exodus to Tokyo, the six possibles would present themselves at Ascot for supervised training and the horses and riders chosen for the team would fly to Tokyo on the 30th September. I had a long talk with Glenamoy as he relaxed in his field and told him that after all our hard work and extreme effort, we now had before us, the chance of a lifetime.

Back home at Long Acre John was away for nights on end and we weren't getting on, meanwhile my infatuation with David grew. I decided to go to France for a holiday, perhaps in a semblance of normality. I flew to Nice Airport and hired a car. My left arm hanging out of the window I drove along the coast intent on reaching Monaco where Grace Kelly had married Prince Rainier and was now living in their fairy tale castle overlooking the sea. David had said that he would join me for a couple of days. We had 48 hours of red hot lust in our sumptuous room in our hotel overlooking the Mediterranean. On the last evening we went out to La Belle Auberge and had a fantastic dinner with musicians surrounding us and serenading our love. It was incredibly romantic and our passion for each other continued unabated.

After he left I was on my own in France, extremely conflicted. My Catholic side was telling me this was adultery. My body contradicted my conscience with a stream of desire spiralling out of control. I was convinced that John was not going to fall back in love with me. I was not prepared to live with someone who didn't love me.

I went home and brought the horses in to work again. The atmosphere between John and I was poisonous and erupted into a huge row. I called my parents who rushed over from Lytham. Mummy was devastated to find out about my affair with David. I was convinced that John's behaviour with that heiress meant that I could never trust him again. Actually, he had no idea about my affair with David. John took off to Majorca alone for two weeks and I was absolutely convinced that he was being unfaithful to me. I knew that it was over. To Mummy divorce was anathema. I didn't know how I could survive financially and in the end, Daddy went over to see the

Waddingtons and it was agreed that I would be paid £13,000 and John would have sole custody of Charles.

Chapter Six – Drugging Glenamoy

I went off with the horses to train at the Goldman's. I was still concerned that Glenamoy just didn't have the speed for maximum bonus points. I went to talk to Bert Cleminson and he told me that he could do something about this. At that time, it was legal for eventers to use butazolodin, to block out pain when their horses were feeling a leg or had foot trouble. I believed this was wrong because pain is there for a purpose, to tell us that something is wrong. I would only use bute on a horse in the most extreme of circumstances. Bert and his family were heavily involved in point-to-pointing and he assured me that he had a magic powder that feeding to the horse in tiny doses for two weeks would give then miraculous extra speed. I asked about side-effects and was assured that there were none.

He sent me an envelope with explicit instructions on how to give it to Glen, finishing the course of powders with his last feed the day before the race. I can imagine you all crying, 'You idiot!' for risking such a thing, but you must remember that I had a huge respect for all Bert's pills and potions. He had enormous experience from his own long life with quality horses and even more secrets had been passed down to him from previous generations of his family. I think I saw him as a shaman who knew the secret spells of success. There were no rules to contravene in those days, so I was not breaking any laws.

Frank Weldon sent me to London to be provided with coats and breeches, and I was measured for a new black riding coat and cream breeches ready for Burghley. On to the boot makers, Maxwell's who also volunteered their services free to the team and made us each a pair of boots. They were my first custom made boots and I could hardly await their delivery. Top hats were not allowed for women and I went on to see Mrs White, the doyen of hat makers, who produced beautifully shaped ladies' hard jockey hats, worn by those with money to spare for their appearance in dressage and show jumping. I stood in front of the looking glass in a dilemma as to the choice between a navy blue one or the usual black. I decided to be brave and go for the blue. It definitely did something for my eyes. There was a lot of publicity in the newspaper as I might be the first woman to be selected for the Olympic eventing team and I sat for the top social photographer Yevonde, looking extremely glamorous with false eyelashes out on stalks, specially-styled hair and a sleeveless long green dress.

The possibles for the team were instructed to compete at Eridge in Sussex during the first week of September. Another preparation was a nasty jab against cholera, ready for Japan. I had kept Ted informed of all that had been going on with John and asked him if my stallion, Sun and Air could be turned out in one of his fields until after Burghley. He agreed immediately and proposed that I break my journey to Eridge and stay the night with him and Elizabeth at Dunsley. I was so blinded by my preoccupation with David at that stage that I wasn't considering Ted as an alternative man in my life. In the end, he was the one constant man in my life and the sexual feeling between us marched in tandem with what I saw as real friendship.

At Eridge Richard Meade won the open on Barberry, and he was to become a stalwart of the British team in the following years. He was much admired, very blonde and handsome, but I have to say not at all my type. I was enamoured of the dark and perhaps sinister looks of David. I did admire Richard's riding and his wonderful horse. At the competition Michael Bullen came second, Ben Jones third and I was fourth on Glenamoy. From the British point of view, it was a very satisfactory result to have four of the first five places occupied by the team possibles and the next day we set off for Windsor for our two-week supervised training.

Training at Windsor went well. There was the usual banter from the men, seeing Glenamoy and myself working alone for strict concentration, trotting studiously around the roads of the park for two hours every day, and showing me how much faster their horses were than Glenamoy when Frank Weldon took us for the twice weekly gallops. Just as before, work was finished by lunchtime and most of the men disappeared. I had told David that we usually had the rest of the day free and he began to collect me, and we would go somewhere where we could talk and simply enjoy each other. On his birthday, it was a beautiful warm late summer's afternoon and we decided to take a rowing boat out on the Thames. I looked at him as he pulled on the oars, and a wave of love swept over me. We were still talking about how we could be together, and David was now very positive in his determination to make this possible.

We approached an island in the middle of the river, with a big willow tree, its branches making a protective dappled green curtain, like being inside a bell. This was a chance too good to pass up and we scrambled on to the island and made love naked in the long grass, trying to keep our bodies and limbs below visibility level of all the passing craft, keeping our cries to whispers, then lying side by side, sated, hands entwined, gazing up through the canopy to the blue sky above.

There were other days and sometimes nights when we managed to steal time together as the weekly training programme came to a stop from Saturday lunchtime until Monday morning. We stayed in a lovely country hotel by the river where our feelings for each other were at such a heightened pitch that we were both near to tears after a particularly sensual session of making love. I was like two different people. First the rider, determined to show the selectors that Glenamoy and I were worth our place in the team for Tokyo, striving every day to bring my horse up to the stage of fitness which would sail him through the stiff speed and endurance test which surely awaited us in the final test at Burghley, honing our dressage to as near perfection as we could possibly manage, and working on our show jumping so that we could jump a clear round on the last day. Secondly, I was the lover, caught in the depths of feelings which were forbidden and thus all the stronger.

Then we set off for Burghley. We were all staying at the George Hotel in Stamford. My parents joined us there. The horses were stabled off the Barnack Road, in the first field through the stud farm gates of Lord Exeter's estate.

We all walked the course together with Frank Weldon putting our own ideas to him and explaining why we intended to jump which ever fence in a way that most suited individual horses. I always felt distinct antipathy towards me behind Weldon's friendly face. I knew that he, quite wrongly I believe, blamed me for the death of his horse Kilbarry at Cottesmore in 1957. I also knew that he wouldn't welcome me, as a 'girl' in the team. I was too professional, utterly dedicated in my preparation for eventing and far too difficult to beat. Having me in a team spoilt the atmosphere of a men's club. I was no gentleman! Think how galling it must have been for those men when they managed to purloin High and Mighty as a team horse for the Stockholm Games of 1956. Although the official line was that he was lame I knew for a certainty, that none of them had been able to ride him. Anyway, after all that High and Mighty continued to compete with me aboard and had been unbeatable in the following autumn.

Although there had been 51 entries only 38 were starters. Germany and Ireland had both produced three entries, taking this opportunity to try out their Olympic team probables and possibles. I was delighted to see that I had been drawn last to go.

On dressage day the weather was good, the sun shining in the awesome setting of Lord Burghley's park in a warm golden glow. Glenamoy did an excellent test and we went into equal first place on 37.5 with Ludwig Goessing on King. Ben Jones riding Master Bernard was on 41.5 and James Templer with M'Lord Connolly on 42.5. The latter was being kept in cotton wool by the selectors and was to jump only the first nine fences on the cross-country phase on the next day. Inexplicably Mike Bullen's two horses, Young Pretender was a non-starter and Sea Breeze was to undertake only the dressage and show jumping phases. By Golly was not able to start at all, apparently in need of tender, loving care. I had absolutely no idea of the reasoning behind the decision for Mike's horses not to run. Even if the selectors had decided already that he would be in the team along with the dead cert M'Lord Connolly one would have expected that Mike would be asked to undertake the dressage and show jumping. There seemed to be no logic to it.

The sun was still shining on speed and endurance day and from the minute I woke up I was in tunnel vision, determined to hold Glen's hand all the way round those 10 steeplechase fences and the 29 cross-country obstacles. The previous evening, Sandra and I had mixed the final powder into Glen's feed and I was hoping that it would do what Bert had assured me it would and then he would fly like a bird.

When we trotted up to the start he seemed to be in good form, interested in all the people milling about as we headed for the start, and listening attentively as the loud speakers broadcast how our fellow competitors were coping on the cross-country. He felt no different to how he usually felt so I wondered if Bert's magic powder was going to make any difference.

We trotted out in phase A, enjoying the sun's rays as they slanted sideways through the still autumn leaves high above our heads. We emerged from the woods and could see the steeplechase to the north with the lake and Burghley House behind, as a backdrop.

When we finished phase A I waited for the 'go' and we shot off, with me hitting the stopwatch as we went. As we jumped the big fences I could feel he was faster and freer and as we sped round the first circuit and set off on the second, I glanced at the stopwatch and I could see that we had gained maximum bonus points. The powder was working, and I was hopeful that we would do well on the cross-country.

When we started on the second roads and tracks, phase C, alarm bells started to ring. Instead of the usual gradual recovery from puffing breath to normal breathing well before the first kilometre marker, Glen didn't seem to want to go at all. He would prefer to sit on a bench and watch the rest of our competitors go by. I sat very still, waiting hopefully for his breathing to ease. Keeping an eye on the second stopwatch I could see that we were already much too far behind our time and if Glenamoy did not recover quickly we were going to lose our advantage of bonus points. I decided to move him on now and hope that once we were in the box with ten minutes rest time Sandra and I could shake him out of his lassitude. I shortened the reins, talking to him, and he stumbled forward into trot with me guiding him and encouraging him and watching the kilometre markers as we passed them. I sat like the proverbial statue, trying to be as light as possible.

Some of the competitors jump off their horse and run with them for part of the roads and tracks, but I always reckoned that jumping on and off and running alongside the horse, holding the reins at an angle was more tiring for the horse than having a rider who sat on top of him.

Glenamoy at last began to perk up as we approached the halfway marker, and we moved up into a gentle canter. Perhaps he had now recovered, but I continue to treat him like a china horse. As we approached the box, I could see the veterinary surgeon and two committee members and I trotted up to them in a straight line and someone shouted 'passed'.

We had ten minutes in the box and Sandra and I worked desperately to wake him up. I put some extra glucose into his limited mouthfuls of water, and spent time massaging his neck and shoulder muscles and his loins with the dark brown embrocation mixture in a bottle which Bert had given me. Major General Sir Evelyn Fanshawe wrote in *Horse and Hound*: "I would like to know what the final and special application was she sponged him over with. I think it was the same thing we used on our polo ponies between chukkas before the war, whatever it was she was using smelt very good". I can still remember that not only did it restore Glenamoy's breathing and relax his muscles, the rising vapours fairly cleaned out Sandra's and my nostrils and windpipes! Now it was time for me to get back on board and to face the all-important cross-country. We had gained maximum bonus points on the steeplechase.

Away we went, over the first few fences with me sitting as quiet as a mouse, just bringing Glenamoy into each fence on the right stride and keeping up a settled but good gallop. He was jumping beautifully, and I began to think that he was fully recovered from his exhaustive efforts over the steeplechase. Going into the bullpen, which was numbers 13, 14 and 15, with 14 more jumps to go, I felt him beginning to tire again, and my heart sank. I was going to have to nurse him and carry him the rest of the way. We proceeded onwards, my eyes on stalks to ensure he would arrive at each fence on the right stride, and we managed to negotiate the next five and were coming into Capability's Cutting on a good, bouncy stride to give him the chance to see that the ground disappeared sharply downwards to the narrow road below. This must have been too much for his headache and, at the last minute he stopped. Twenty penalties, I turned him round and tried again. Over he went, and we laboured up the slope the other side and into the open field to cover a good stretch before meeting the calf creeps. We managed to get to the other side, but I could feel he had no energy, and in the distance at the bottom of the gentle downwards slope the trout hatchery and I could hear the silence as we drew nearer. I was almost carrying him. I was telling him, "Three, two, one, jump!" He tried but rather slithered over the top of the tree trunk, his front legs refused to hold him up as he landed. He disappeared head first under water, re-appearing rather like a hippopotamus, with a surprised look on his face and water streaming out of his ears which he held out sideways. I, too, was enveloped by the pond as I followed his neck down into the water, steadfastly clinging on to the reins, and a photographer clicked his shutter to record the scene. It shows Glenamoy emerging and no sign of me except for a white gloved hand and arm holding onto the reins above the surface of the agitated pond in the mode of Excalibur. All the spectators were transfixed, the jump judges stared in shock, all of them appalled. Except for one small boy, who was hooting with laughter. At least I made his day.

Regaining my feet, I waded to Glen, talking to him and, drenched to the skin, sorted out his saddle and checked that the stirrups were not loose, then put the reins back over his head and was legged up into the saddle by the poor fence judge with his gumboots now filled with water. It is hard to describe what it is like to stay on a horse who is sopping wet, whose saddle is diabolically slippery, and who has to be nursed over another five fences. My clothes and boots were also dripping with water and it was almost impossible to stay on board. We passed through the finishing posts and I was devastated. I could not explain to the people around the course with so many of them wanting me to go to Tokyo why it had happened, and I cursed myself for being so stupid as not to think of the difference between Bert's straightforward two and a half mile point-to-point race and the fourteen and a half miles of a three-day event with a 10 minute break. I should have realised that he could not appreciate the huge difference between the two, and that what most certainly worked for the former would not, automatically be as successful for the latter. One thing was certain. Never again would I give pills and potions to another event horse.

Washing down Glenamoy after we had finished the course, still dripping water, it became obvious that his ducking had revitalised him. Walking him back down to the stables, he was almost cheerful, he drank his first restricted water – his own bucket would go in his stable later – ate his feed, licked his manger and settled down as soon as we had come down to the stables to see if he was hurt in any way but he appeared to be completely sound. On the other hand, it would be a miracle if I did not go down with a chill after being soaked to the skin for so long.

Final day. We ran up for the veterinary inspection and were passed without a second look. We were up at the show jumping ring for the parade at a quarter past two o'clock with Glenamoy looking the picture of health and good nature with his mane beautifully plaited

63

and a gentle, co-operative look on his face. We had dropped down to thirteenth position after we had been coming first after the dressage. I was determined that we should finish on a good note and when it was our turn to go into the ring, I told Glen that he must go clear. I had walked the course very, very carefully and when it came to riding it I brought Glen into every fence straight, on a good stride and virtually lifted him high in the air over each one. The crowd was silent as we jumped this round but, as we sailed over the last fence, they clapped and cheered.

The press were equally kind. Lionel Dawson described it as 'a copy book round'. In his article in the *Country Life* he said: "Mrs Waddington (Sheila Willcox) – seemingly exactly as we knew her when she hung up her whip in 1959, and with the flame of her genius still burning brightly - tied for first place (in the show jumping alone) with Herr Goessing of Germany" Sir Andrew Horsbrugh-Porter, writing in *The Field* said: "Glenamoy put up a first class dressage performance. And the way his rider and he jumped on the final day in the main arena was quite the most polished piece of equitation of the week." In one of the newspapers he wrote: "This year's Burghley certainly proved that Mrs Waddington is an even better rider than when she won her three Badmintons". I tried to take some consolation from the fact that Glenamoy and I had put up the best performance on two of the three days of competition, and that I knew full well that our performance over the cross-country was not Glenamoy's fault, but I knew that I had failed in my efforts to represent my country in the Olympic Games which had been my dream. Now, we just had to be patient and wait until next spring to show them what he could really do.

At Windsor, the training continued with Glenamoy looking in top condition and me still furious with myself for giving him the powders and being unable to tell anyone the reason why he had gone to pieces halfway around the cross-country. I was now in the obnoxious position of waiting for the equivalent of dead men's shoes. Richard Meade, having won on Barberry at Burghley, had joined us at Windsor and it looked as if he and James with Connolly, were certain of their team places. Sergeant Ben Jones had made a good case for his and Mister Bernard's inclusion, and then there were Mike's two horses and By Golly. Naturally, everyone, the selection committee, and all the press, had come to the conclusion that Glenamoy was just not good enough, and I felt that I had let him down badly. I knew how good he really was and how miraculous had been his progress in so short a time. I vowed silently that we would show them what we could do at Badminton the following spring. Meanwhile, I would have to stay at Windsor until the team flew to Tokyo on the 28th September. One never knew if the selected horses would remain sound, if the worst came to the worst, they might have to use Glenamoy and me.

Once again, Glenamoy and I were trotting and cantering around the park and near the Virginia Water boundary, I could see what was obviously a big film crew recording a scene where a coach with four horses came galloping along the track under the boundary trees and out into the open. We stood there watching. It turned out to be the film The Adventures of Moll Flanders, starring Kim Novak. They had 'made the final wrap' of the scene and while I was watching one of the men came walking over to me. He said they had seen me riding round the park on other days and how would I like to have an equity card? I said I didn't know what that was, and he said it would allow me to work for films. I might be good. Not realising what a compliment this was, nor that it could be extremely useful in the future, I politely declined, telling him I was still in training for the Olympics and that I had better be on my way. Later on, when I had left John and was in such dire straits financially I could have kicked myself for not taking this once in a lifetime offer.

David wrote to me again and again, and I replied in the same vein. These letters were outpourings of love and frustration, hoping for a future together and sexually blatant. However, later on I realised that David was perhaps not an ideal choice, he tried to appropriate my lump sum to 'invest' in his failing business and I realised that he was not at all reliable.

My father had met with George Waddington, my father-in-law and they were negotiating for the breakdown of our marriage. I was still convinced that my husband was having an affair with the young heiress, although to this day he vehemently denies it. I could never forget how she had laughed derisively at me when John had been publicly flirting with her. The British team were meant to go to a social event at her family's home and I just couldn't face it, so I explained the situation to Frank Weldon. Perhaps confiding in him about the sorry state of my marriage was a very big mistake. He had

65

never liked me but now behaved in a way that I found, perhaps in my innocence of the way of men, utterly perplexing. I got back to Windsor and as I was going into the hotel he saw me and said, 'Follow me'. Obediently I went up to his room thinking that he wanted to discuss a team issue. I was wearing a summer cotton frock with a high line at the back held in place by a long zip running from the cleft of my bottom to the nape of my neck.

We went up in the lift to his room. He held the door open for me and as I passed through he reached over and pulled down the zip to my dress. I turned quickly, hand behind my back clutching at the open ends of my dress and fled like lightening out of the door and back to the lift. No footsteps came after me. I knew then that I had absolutely no chance of going to Tokyo as a member of the British team. Two days later I was officially informed that I had not made the team. I managed to be sunny and congratulatory with the men, waving them off. Then Sandra and I scurried back to the relative safety of Long Acre.

Chapter Seven – Striking Out On My Own

However, my home was no longer a safe haven. John and I argued violently. I refused to enter into any type of competition for Charles' affections and it was agreed that John should have care of him. I was to be paid £13,000 to leave. In a few short months my chances of making the British team were dashed and my marriage had crashed against the rocks and splintered irretrievably. I would take Sandra, my horses and my lump sum and venture back out into the world to fend for myself. I knew that Charles would be safe at Long Acre.

I rang Ted to let him know that I was leaving, and I would tell him where I was when I settled. We agreed to have lunch soon, so I could tell him everything. I was hugely upset, it all seemed so final. By the time the press had got wind of what was happening and arrived at Long Acre, they just missed me. I had left with the horsebox, one furniture van and one small car. There was Sandra and me, school trunks packed with our clothes and belongings, and also Shaun the border collie, two horses, their tack, rugs and blankets and all the stable equipment and paraphernalia. I had moved straight from my family home to my marital home and now I was depending solely on myself.

I moved into a series of temporary rented houses, and in each one David would come to stay for a least one night, sometimes two. He also suggested that I invest the modest capital I was being given by the Waddingtons into his firm. His rationale was, "We shall be sharing everything once we are both divorced, and it will be safe with me". At the time I still believed that he loved me and everything between us was very hot and sexy. Then one morning after he had come to stay I noticed that the drawer where I kept our love letters was slightly open. I reached in to feel for the envelope, but it was not there. David had stolen my letters, I knew that he had done this beyond the shadow of a doubt.

I confronted him, and he came up with a most bizarre story, he told me that he put them in a biscuit tin and buried them under the porch of a new house being built in his home village of Dunsop Bridge. I had no way of knowing if this was the truth or yet another lie. I had to swallow the enormity of what he had done. Eventually, I came to terms with the betrayal of David and the realisation that I really was on my own, and that I was facing an uncertain future both financially and personally.

Ted and Vivian Eason were the most stalwart of friends and they introduced me to their Gloucestershire circle. My social life began to flourish, and Sir Gerald Nabarro invited me across the road to Top Farm to one of his famous drinks parties, where I met even more people. I felt as if I was being accepted as part of the scene. I was urged to join the Evenlode Riding Club, whose committee organised all sorts of competitions for the riders with their horses, also evening events to bring everyone together.

I was competing on Glenamoy again and went to the open one-day event at Crookham, where we were lucky to be invited to stay in comfort with the Fleming sisters. He finished in third place at this event and was now set to be in top form for Badminton. This was Frank Weldon's first year as course-designer and it was abundantly clear that he was displaying a new talent. We came third.

Ted had not gone away and now I was free he was back with a vengeance. I had always been fond of him and we could still talk about anything and nothing had shaken the deep friendship which existed between us. He wanted to be helpful and probably thought that our relationship might be rekindled. He wanted me to move into one of his farms and I was hopeful as we drove there. It was a considerable shock when we approached the property after climbing the twists and turns of Stanway Hill from the direction of Toddington, continued along a freezing cold stretch of the flat, open land on the road to Stow, before diving down a virtually invisible farm lane, which would be extremely hard for friends and visitors even to find with instructions. It could only be described as isolated and that was being generous. My spontaneous reaction as we came to a halt in front of the house was pure horror at its forbidding façade. It exuded a bad atmosphere and I felt that it was creepy and Gothic, and I would not even go in. Later I took Mummy and Daddy over for their view and Mummy burst out with an exclamation that it was the equivalent of putting me into a chastity belt. Those really were the days when men still thought of women as possessions!

I found that now I was single I must have come across as a 'glamour girl' and all sorts of men were asking me out. So far no-one had touched my heart. I was going up to London quite often and I always sat in the first carriage, poised to jump out fast and run to the taxi point to be ahead of the queue. There was one man in particular who seemed keen on me. His name was John Gray and when we were left alone after others had disembarked at Oxford, he would take a more personal approach until he left the train at Charlbury. I enjoyed our bantering conversations. He told me that he managed the Duchy of Cornwall Estate for HRH Prince Charles. One afternoon, he suddenly broke up the conversation saying bluntly, "What would it cost for me to have you as my mistress?" I think my jaw must have dropped, horrified that he should think of such a thing when I hardly knew him. Gulping slightly, and trying to be nonchalant, I said I was not available for anything like that. Later on, we became good friends and nothing else. I then began to realise that there were a good many married men, outwardly the epitome of high-mindedness and probity and underneath boiling with the idea of finding a regular source of extra-marital sex.

In the second week of May I went with Vivian to watch the Evenlode Cross-Country at Grange Farm. There was a good little course laid out and most of the members were enjoying themselves. Vivian and I were watching the competitors jumping two fences fairly close together, first over a hedge and then turning right on landing to go across a field and jump an innocuous small stream. Along came a dark brown horse with what to me seemed an elderly lady aboard. By now I was beginning to recognise some of the members and this was Mrs Mary Montagu. She had the reputation of buying good horses, but she was small and her legs were short. She was no match in an argument with this particular animal whom she had entered as Touch and Go. Very appropriate, for as the two of them were near to take off over the stream, the horse stopped dead and nearly deposited Mary in the water. She heaved herself back into the saddle and tried again. Same result. On the third attempt, eliminated. At the end of the class, Vivian and I noticed that Mary was taking her horse back to practise, and we followed. She had several helpers on the ground running behind him, waving a lunge whip or their arms to urge Touch and Go over the stream, but nothing would persuade him to jump and Mary Montagu took him home with him having won the battle for supremacy. A situation now existed where an intelligent horse would be encouraged to refuse to obey his rider whenever he felt like it in the future. On the way home, I told Vivian that I rather fancied this horse, he was very athletic, except that he was using it in the wrong way, and I reckoned he could become a really good eventer if he were sorted out.

Two days later, I telephoned Mrs Montagu and asked her if she would like to sell Touch and Go. She would, and I arranged to drive to her home and stables in Tetbury the next morning to try out this naughty and headstrong brown five-year-old gelding. First of all, I had a good look at him without his saddle and bridle, then watched him run up in hand so that I could see that he moved straight. He was only 15.3 hh, while most eventers were well over 16 hh. He was also not a big horse in stature and his legs could have done with a bit more bone, but he rode like a big horse, powerful and long-striding. And in his jumping, he was like a cat, light, swift and athletic.

I realised that Mary Montagu watching me ride him, might change her mind and be reluctant to sell him after all, but she was an intelligent and down to earth person and would have known that he was never going to perform for her. By the time we had finished talking I had bought him at a price I could afford, knowing that there would be battles ahead, and I re-named him Fair and Square with a stable name of Bill.

I took him back to Little Barrow Stables where I was keeping Sun and Air and began his dressage education. I wanted him to acquire automatic obedience before he started to object to the rest of his work. Everything on the flat came easily to him. Being a natural athlete, he had no trouble in learning to curve his body round my inside leg as we cornered in the small paddock. He learnt to go up a straight line, and to make smooth transitions from pace to pace. It was all easy to him, and he rather enjoyed himself.

Then as we moved on and I began to ask more of him he put up several nasty fights, and to stop him bucking me off I had to hook my thumbs immediately behind my knees, locking the reins and hands and fingers clinging like leeches round the side and on to my knee bone. I had to remember to keep my head low and to one side in case he was able to fling up his head and hit me in the face. This was the only way of stopping him erupting into bucking bronco mode. It was also extremely effective and being a very bright horse, he decided fairly quickly that it was easier to do what I said rather than fight a losing battle. Soon I channelled all his villainous ideas into co-operation. He learned how pleasant it was if he did what I wanted, he was given sugar lumps and pats and strokes, and told what a wonderful horse he was. He also discovered that he would not be asked to do anything of which he was not capable, and he need have no fear I would interfere with his mouth or his balance when we were in the air over a fence. He began to trust me, and I began to realise what a very good jumper he was.

We began to compete at the summer shows in the Foxhunter and the Grade C jumping classes and soon we were coming home after winning or being placed. All through the summer both Bill and my dressage stallion were taken round the country, up to Lancashire and Yorkshire.

I had been moving from one rented property to another when stalwart family friends Sidney and Cherry Hills came to see me, and they said they wanted me to go and live with them until I could finally manage to find my own house to buy. This was something which had never occurred to me, but it would solve so many problems. They had always treated me as a close relative. They had 35 acres of good pasture fields where Cherry's famous herd of Jersey cows were looked after as if they were beloved children. I remembered their house from when I had visited as a child. The grand piano still occupied pride of place in the sitting room, whose windows looked out over the lawn and the fields beyond.

Then I met Lt. Col. Tom Greenhalgh, who was an interesting person. His manners had been honed to perfection and he was courteous to the highest degree. A good businessman, he became very keen to establish himself in the world of eventing by doing deals for the top echelons of the committee. He was already highly respected for his work in the Church of England, acknowledged by its hierarchy as a very useful contact and fundraiser. He owned greyhounds, bred and trained especially for the sport of coursing, in which they would race after a hare over the fells of Cumberland. He was always immaculately dressed, and very well-shod, courtesy of his own business in Northampton, renowned for its leather industry. He had a round face which looked as if it had been polished and somehow, he failed to adopt the mien of a naturally relaxed man of the world. His posture was permanently stiff, like a dog on the alert.

One day in 1965 he invited me to accompany him to see Swan Lake and I was totally thrilled. I had never been to a ballet in my life. They did not go in for this sort of thing in Blackpool and John Waddington and I, and the friends we met in our London life, were usually to be found in Annabel's or another night club popular with the young for the evening's entertainment of dancing the waltz, the quick-step and the tango. Now, Tom Greenhalgh and I would be going to Covent Garden to see Margot Fonteyn dancing, and I could hardly wait. I had to think what to wear. In those days, dress was very formal and important when one went to the ballet or the opera. Long frocks, long gloves, little handbags, beautiful shoes, exquisitely arranged hair and jewels were the norm and men wore dinner jackets. Opera glasses would be carried, and one could use them to scan the sixteen private boxes with soft velvet curtains which stretched from the stage backwards to meet the long strings of the balcony seats. For me, it was a night to remember.

At the end of the evening when it was time to say good-bye, Tom pecked me quickly on the cheek and shot backwards. He was the only man I knew who took me out and never made a move, it was rather sweet and reassuring.

Then Tom began to take an interest in my horse Bill, as the reports filtered through in terms of how we were progressing in the club dressage competitions and our forays into show jumping around the country. I was also taking him to cross-country courses to introduce him to jumping at speed and using his athleticism over the strange fixed fences. Previously Tom had been interested in Glenamoy when we had looked like we might have gone to the European Championships in Moscow. However, Glen had had an accident with a hay net and it was weeks and weeks before he showed any sign of recovery and I had thought that he was never going to be able to event again. I sent him to Bert Cleminson who sold him to a keen male rider to go hunting with the Middleton Foxhounds. I took comfort that Glen would enjoy this life, where he would never have to go for maximum bonus points. He was such a lovely, kind and co-operative horse.

Bill was being prepared to enter his first one day event. We had gone to Tetbury to jump the Moseleys' cross-country course. It was well built and presented Bill with fences he had never seen before and which would be a very good test as to whether or not he was cured of his wish to be boss. I think he decided that there was a real challenge for him here and he surprised me with his attitude, really sizing up the fences, no slackening of pace, and no hint of anything but good temper and co-operation. I was immensely pleased with him.

Our first horse trials were at Eridge in the third week of August, where last year Glenamoy had competed with the rest of the prospective team members before we went on to Burghley and then back to Windsor for the final decision to be made about the selection of the team. I had no intention of trying to win - I was determined that Bill should be taken slowly. We produced a very good dressage test, one fence down in the show jumping and clear on the cross-country at a speed I thought that Bill would enjoy.

Two weeks later, we were at the Meriden One-Day Event in the preliminary section, this time shifting up a gear, and intending to go faster over the cross-country. He produced a good test in the dressage for 57 penalties and this was followed by a beautiful clear show jumping round and a fast and exhilarating gallop over the cross-country. We ended up in fourth position, only five marks behind the winner. Things were beginning to look promising. Then a tiny nick on his hind leg swelled up like a balloon and he had to be turned out for months until he recovered.

A totally unexpected telephone call from Germany, from one of the leading Grand Prix dressage riders and trainers, Frau Linsenhoff caught me off balance. She said that she had heard that I had a black stallion and she would like to come over to England to see him and ride him. I had not thought of selling him but suddenly I saw the possibilities. It was a terrific compliment for the Germans, the Swiss and the Dutch to consider buying a British horse, as they looked down at us as far below their dressage standards.

If Frau Linsenhoff was prepared to pay a good price for Sun and Air then this would be greatly advantageous for me. She would expect an indoor school in which to view him, so I arranged to take him to the Fleming sisters as they had a good, big school not too far from Heathrow Airport. When the Germans arrived, I brought out Sun and Air for them to inspect, black coat gleaming, hoofs oiled, mane and tail washed and plaited, and coat groomed to perfection. I stood him up for them, then trotted him out and back. They felt his legs, ran their hands along his spine and announced that they would like to see him ridden. I showed what he could do; collected and extended walk, collected and extended trot and the same with the canter. Flowing half passes at both trot and canter and smooth as silk flying changes of leg as we changed direction. Flying changes every four strides. A straight rein back with diagonal legs in perfect unison and counter canter, where the horse leads with the 'wrong' leg but still remains in balance. His work was very well established, and he showed how easily he could produce whatever was asked. First Herr Kuckluk tried him and asked for flying changes every three strides. He hadn't been asked for this before and I don't like to see my horses pushed by a strange rider. Frau Linsenhoff saw my reaction and called her trainer in, she was going to ride him.

She clearly liked him, and I had told her that I would accept no less than £5,500. So, it was arranged subject to veterinary inspection which he passed with flying colours. I obtained an export certificate and the deal was done. Two days later I drove him to Harwich and put him on the boat for Germany.

Living with Sidney and Cherry was an interesting experience. Cherry was into what could best be described as alternative healing. She would collect hairs out of the tails of her Jersey cows and they would be sent to Lavender Dwyer, a sort of guru, who would solemnly place them in a black box. This was meant to ensure their healing. It was rather bizarre, I tried it a few times on the principle of 'just in case it worked', but it never did work for me or my horses. It reminded me of the father of the Mitford sisters who solemnly wrote the name of an enemy down and put it in a drawer and within a year he was meant to be dead. Another thing that Cherry did was suspend a conically shaped piece of wood or glass at the end of a light chain, asking it questions. If it began to swing a circle at a fast rate to the right then this was yes, if the other way it was no. I was totally sceptical and amazed when the pendulum took over of its own accord.

Ted was contacting me more often after I had moved into my own rented house called Squirrel Cottage. I knew that his wife Elizabeth was jealous, and I wondered if Ted wasn't being a little unkind towards her. I was no longer in love with Ted but there was still a very strong bond between us. Now that I had finished with David R., Ted was obviously expecting us to pick up where we had left off before I had been dating John who I was to marry.

Even though I now found Ted's love-making rather selfish and limited in his scope and all over far too quickly I did fall back in with his wishes and we enjoyed sexual assignations when he was hunting in the Heythrop country. Then he wanted me to go out with him and Elizabeth in public and I did point out that it was a bit too much to ask of her. She knew of our past relationship and suspected that it had resumed. I suggested that he stop seeing me, but he didn't like that idea at all. But then Elizabeth was told how we were seeing each other and it was all rather awkward. Ted immediately drew back saying it was not the time for 'another upset', by that I assume he meant a costly divorce. Then finally after moving from pillar to post I found a house to buy, Shenberrow. My divorce was imminent, and it looked like a line could be drawn under my recent tumultuous past and I really could strike out on my own.

Bill, aka Fair and Square had been going well but he had pulled a tendon and he was out of work for a lengthy few months at least, with a question mark over his fitness every being totally regained. Babe Mosley rang me to tell me about Radar, one of the horses the Australian team had brought over with them that had been bought by a rider in the north and thathe might be back up for sale. I remembered him vaguely as an ugly, plain horse having a reputation of having legs like steel, brilliant across country but utterly useless at dressage and not much better at show jumping. He was a Waler and was for sale for about £350. Mummy and I drove over to Yorkshire, to a village near Ripon, to see him. His hogged mane did nothing to flatter him. I rode him and tried some *uberstreichen* where one surrenders the hand on the bit and allows the horse to move forward into self-carriage. He nearly fell over himself, he was obviously used to an iron grip on his head. His paces were very stiff, and he had no concept of length bend.

Later I talked it over with Mummy. I wasn't sure that I could buy such an ugly horse. Finally, I decided to take him on, to see if I could turn an ugly duckling into a beautiful swan and it would mean that I had a second string, not something that had happened since I had tried to train Chips and Blue Jeans at the same time when I was still living with my parents. He arrived after passing a vet inspection and I renamed him Wait and See. I set to work with him going through the basics as I had done with my other horses.

Chapter Eight – A New Obsession

It must have occurred to Ted that even before my divorce was final, someone else might appear on the scene, at any time, and it was up to him to decide whether he wanted to marry me, in which case he would have to get a divorce. It was also hardly likely that I would continue to accept being visited by him for his sexual satisfaction as and when it suited him if there were no real discussion going on about the future. There was also the permanent threat hanging over us in the current situation that someone would recognise my frequent visitor, realise what was going on, and talk. Ted could then be in deep trouble with Elizabeth and my parents would be horrified. He was also failing to take into account that sex with him was no longer as enthralling as it had been when I was a young and innocent girl. I had since discovered how much more there was to sex, first with John Waddington and then with David R., and Ted was far too set in his ways to be able to satisfy me in that department. Only a younger, vigorous lover was going to do that.

Then it happened, I became obsessed with another man. I met Keith at Slaughter Manor, the Colvilles' place. He was the first lover I had who combined an interest in horses with a calculating and brilliant brain, a self-made man with the sense to learn how to be accepted in the racing game. He was tallish, good looking, with a fine athletic physique and beautiful feet! He had presence and bright blue eyes and strong wavy hair which almost crackled under my fingers as one hand encircled his neck when we were kissing. His mouth probably was the only thing about him which gave a hint of the ruthlessness within, and he had a habit of talking out of one side of it. His top lip was a mean thin line.

I would suspect that from the time he was growing up in an ordinary small house in the little village in Wales, to the point where he had established himself and attained all his goals, he had had neither the time nor the inclination to look at girls with any real interest, especially after he had married. He was far too busy for that sort of thing. Only when he had achieved everything that he had wanted in life, and then met me, did he suddenly and surprisingly fall almost instantly in love, and become aware for the first time of what sex could be like, and the immeasurable and over-riding pleasure it could bring to two compatible people. It made him think again about his future. He also had a hard inner core. I saw signs that beneath the almost boyish good looks he could be ruthless, and this, no doubt was a very useful attribute for his trade of bookmaker. He also had his unexpected cultured side, a passionate interest in fine paintings, furniture, bronzes and books. He was also in the habit of making a sudden decision to take off and travel, especially when there was something on his mind which needed deep thought.

I was optimistic about the future as Keith was talking as if he was going to divorce his wife and marry me. One day I went up to London and we lunched together at Briganza one of the most expensive restaurants in London and he explained to me that he and his wife, Eileen, slept in different rooms. But I think most men in this situation say this to make them feel better about straying away from home. However, I chose to believe his assertion that they had not made love or slept together for a very long time. He held my hands and told me that he had simply fallen in love with me and was thinking of marrying me.

I already knew he was the sort of person who would find it very difficult to actually declare his feelings so explicitly, and it must have cost him a great deal to say these words. He would not use them lightly. I neither needed nor wanted a love affair which would only bring unhappiness in the future and my reaction to his declaration was that we were both on the edge of jumping into a fatal abyss. However, there was no denying the overwhelming attraction between us, and whilst it is easy to make a sensible decision away from temptation, it is a very different thing when the person causing all this turmoil is only a hand's move away. The electricity was very strong, and we were setting off on a bumpy road.

The next day Ted turned up at Shenberrow with his trusty handkerchief, to mop up after his withdrawal method. With my thoughts full of Keith, I found it difficult to perform in my usual way in bed with Ted. It felt all wrong. I felt pulled in two directions, I didn't want to upset Ted, but I had very powerful feelings about Keith. The fact that both of them were well and truly married was bizarrely ironic, but somehow this obvious fact eluded me.

Keith was also due to see Shenberrow for the first time. I fed him a basic supper of scrambled eggs, eating off a little cane table in the drawing room, perched precariously on the rolls of waiting carpets. We talked and talked all evening. Then at midnight we walked up the hill to the top of the escarpment with a bright full moon showing us the way. Standing in each other's arms we looked towards the Malvern Hills and the faint purple outline of Keith's Welsh hills. We went to bed and lay on our sides just looking at each other, then we moved together, and the electricity sparked to such a degree at first touch that we leapt apart. It was the beginning of our first night together and the pleasure of exploration was immense. We touched each other all over, taking our time, and this night Keith took charge of our first coupling, entering me from above and pulling my bottom closer and closer into the curve of his body until he came. We did not sleep much, and we were almost silenced by the depth of our feelings and the exquisite pleasure of truly making love, not just having sex.

When he left the next morning, I felt unreasonably sad. He told me he was going to sort everything out with Eileen and I just had to wait. He telephoned again and again for long talks and neither of us wanted to be the one to put down the telephone, and the longing grew and grew, and each time he said how much I was on his mind. I wrote several letters to him and he replied.

Keith declared that he felt more and more involved with me and he was certain that he wanted us to be together forever. Then he decided he had to get away from everyone and he flew to Zambia, ringing me from the airport to assert that he still wanted to marry me, but he had to think things out carefully.

I went out the next day to train Radar, and he was unco-operative with showing length bend around corners and threw his bony head up and hit me on the nose. I was covered in blood when I eventually rode back home. My parents had come to see my new home and my mother was horrified. However, they were thrilled with the house and the seductive beauty of the village with its little shop, the old church, the village cricket field and the big house where Sir Guy Thorold lived and had invited me to go for dinner and to meet his sister.

I was missing Keith a great deal, but my parents came to stay for Christmas. Daddy went faint on Christmas Eve and when Dr Houghton finally arrived he thought it was possibly a heart condition.

78

The only treatment suggested was that Daddy be put to bed, to rest. He was terribly weak and wanted to do nothing but sleep. It was dreadful realising that my father who had been so strong, cheerful and seemingly indestructible all his life, was now so weak and feeble. Mummy was in a dreadful state. Slowly he recovered and drove back to Lytham. He began to write me letters. He warned me to be careful with men, that I shouldn't trust them. He told me that they were full of promises that they didn't keep, and I must be able to look after myself. He would write perfectly logically and then his words would disintegrate into line after line of absolute nonsense, and I felt the cold touch of deepest worry for him. Something malevolent was taking hold.

In the New Year of 1967 I began to work Radar and Bill and I was waiting for Keith to return from Zambia. He said that he wanted 'a very serious talk with me'. Finally, he rang and told me that he would visit me at Shenberrow on the 3rd January. He told me that he had talked to Eileen who had threatened all sorts of things and he was worried about his three young sons. He stayed the night and our feelings for each other continued to overwhelm us and we decided that we would not make a final decision about whether we should continue seeing each other. In the meantime, I had to concentrate on the spring horse trials.

I was praying for my father, that he would return to his robust self. I had taken it for granted that he would always be there. In the middle of this stressful time, I received a call from Charles Harrison. He was a shrewd, self-made man, who owned a large farm in Lincolnshire where he grew all sorts of vegetables. He had made a lot of money and built a beautiful large house where he lived with Macil, his extremely attractive dark-haired wife. Tom Greenhalgh had discovered him and mentioned that I might be willing to sell him Radar if he agreed that I should continue to compete on him. He would pay all Radar's expenses, which would be a huge boost to my finances. Charles was clearly a ladies' man and was under the impression that he would be irresistible. I worked out very quickly that he thought that I would be part of the deal. I found him unattractive with bad skin and a big nose. He showed me to my bedroom at the end of the evening and made his expectations obvious. So, my father had counselled me wisely. I made it clear that I was not part of the deal and later he described me publicly as 'ruthless', which I suppose translates as not succumbing to his dubious charms.

Keith phoned me to say that Eileen was not happy to separate and divorce amicably. I was unhappy, I was 'in love', which is not a comfortable state. One does not ask to fall in love. Then Keith wrote to me and told me that I should forget him. I cried for most of that day and then he rang at eleven that night and told me that he didn't want to lose me. On top of all this emotional turbulence Daddy was admitted to Blackpool Victoria Hospital where they found 'shadows'. Then David telephoned to say that he still loved me but by now I was immune to his charms and told him to go away. And just to add to the mix Ted would arrive now and again to enjoy some sexual activity.

It was a relief to throw myself into training the horses using the same twelve-week training programme that I had developed with Chips, Cresta and Glen. It was wonderful to ride in the Cotswold countryside again and I tried to lose myself in the beauty of the countryside that has since been immortalised by Jilly Cooper in her Rutshire Chronicles. I was living the life of Jilly's characters with intrigue, adultery, clandestine love affairs and the ups and downs of competing in horse events. I was perhaps a female Rupert Campbell-Black, but without his wealth. And he had won gold at those fictitious Olympics!

I explored the countryside riding past small farms, grand houses and the odd gypsy caravan. People waved to me as I went by. Sometimes it poured with rain and the wind on the top of the hills was so strong we were buffeted on all sides. As spring approached the air was clean and cool and wild flowers were peeping out. By the end of the month the seductive smell of new mown grass cut to make hay wafted around us. Amongst the hawthorn hedges, Queen Anne's Lace grew with flat, creamy, white intricately patterned heads. Later on, wild blackberries would nod at us as we went past.

Keith was blowing hot and cold and he invited me to Braganza in London and told me that there was no way to continue to see me, or to hope that he could marry me. My eyes filled with tears and I had to find a handkerchief. Now I cannot believe that I accepted his constant vacillations. If he had been a stronger and more determined man he would have brought our relationship to a decided and definitive end. But he was always thinking carefully, as if he was weighing up the odds if he went this way or that. It was one long endless calculation for him. My justification was that we were desperately in love and no earthly force could keep us apart. It sounds as if I had fallen down a rabbit hole and found myself to be in the midst of some sickly Barbara Cartland romance.

It was six weeks until my divorce and six months after that I would be free to marry. Before I met Keith, I had decided that I was not going to get married again, certainly not in a hurry. I was ambitious to get back to the top of my sport. The bond between Ted and myself was still strong and remained until the day he died. Looking back the biggest mistake in my life was not being brave enough to ignore the ban of the Catholic Church on marriage to a divorced person. Back in 1958 I should have accepted Ted's proposal. It was rather a bizarre type of logic that had said that adultery was acceptable, but a second marriage was not.

The fluctuations between the consummate love and pleasure that Keith and I found in each other's company, then the misery of his return to his wife Eileen, and his inability to break from her, turned me inside out.

So, I concentrated on Radar and Bill bringing them to peak fitness before Badminton. There were two events before this big one, the first at Crookham, a two-day event, and then the next at Kinlet. Both Bill and Radar were entered for Kinlet. Bill and I had been eliminated there the year before when I had failed to go around a flag on the cross-country course. Although I loved this venue it had also been disastrous for me in 1965 when I had incurred 60 penalties with a fall at the Water Garden when Glen had tripped over it. I was hoping that this year it would be third time lucky. The Mexico Olympics were in 1968 and I knew that I had to impress the selectors.

Finally, Charles and Macil Harrison arrived at Shenberrow and agreed that they would purchase Radar who was almost unrecognisable as the rough and ready horse that I had purchased. He looked brilliant and was supple and co-operative. This would certainly help to solve some of my financial problems.

Then Keith disappeared off to Italy to further meditate on the pros and cons of staying married to Eileen or divorcing her and marrying me. His preoccupation with what was best for him does indicate a certain type of egotistical self-interest, so I was fortunate that my stalwart friend, Barbara Cooper had volunteered to travel with me to Birmingham for the divorce proceedings. I found the whole experience unutterably depressing. A big black line was being drawn through something that had started out so infinitely joyous and promising.

I continued to train the horses and marked out quarter miles with bamboo canes and white rags so that I could practise my galloping speeds, so I would know at exactly what pace I needed to gallop in order to get bonus points. I dismounted from Bill and ran up my stirrups to walk him around to cool him down and he jumped sideways, and the rein slipped out of my hand. He galloped off gleefully and then I saw him stumble on the far side of the field near the trees. The next day he was lame on his near-fore which had been the leg that had troubled him in the past. He was out for all the spring trials now and I was down to one horse.

Radar started out very well at the Crookham Two-Day Event. He gave a polished 'look at me' test in the dressage, and Babe Mosley and the others were astonished that this was the same ugly Radar of last season. He was going very well around the cross-country, enjoying himself and jumping cleanly. Then five fences from the finish as we approached a perfectly straightforward big, solid looking hedge I saw the stride well out and said to him, 'Three, two, one, take-off', and gave him a squeeze with my heels, which was the signal for him to lift into the air. He made no effort to jump but his impetus carried us straight on, parallel with the ground. It was as if he had not registered anything at all in front of him and then we were both turning in a slow arc, as the hedge tipped us over slowly and we came to ground sideways with a thump on the far side. I scrambled to my feet immediately and the first person I saw was Keith. I was annoyed that this had happened in front of him. I apologised profusely to Charles Harrison, but he was man enough to understand how much the horse had improved. Perhaps Babe Moseley and the selectors thought that by improving him so much in the dressage and the show jumping I had somehow confused him when he had formerly been such a good horse across country. I could only believe that something very mysterious had happened and I could make no sense of it.

82

In the following five days before we went to Kinlet I jumped as many hedges as I could find and there seemed to be not the slightest sign of a repeat performance. It was very peculiar indeed.

We went to stay at Dunsley with Ted and Elizabeth and later that night I had a private conversation with Ted. I asked his advice as to whether I should marry again. He hesitated and said that only in approved circumstances, by which I took to mean if he could still visit me. It was odd but there was something of a father-daughter relationship there, as if I had to have his approval before I entered into a serious relationship with another man.

The next day I walked around Colonel Nicholl's Kinlet cross-country course which was very pleasing with its floral decoration. It had a lot of big heavy telegraph poles which would not encourage a horse to take a risk by not jumping cleanly. Radar was very experienced across country and I now looked on our debacle at Crookham as just a momentary blip in his concentration.

I prepared him in my usual manner before we were due in the dressage arena and he was relaxed and keen to please. We did a very good test with 30 penalties, putting us in third place. In the show jumping we had one pole down but were still up close to the leader. Now everything depended on the cross-country.

We got counted down and we were off, but I found that he was not concentrating. I had to really push him. At the fourth fence he did not seem to take off and we smashed our way through. I tried to wake him up, but it did no good and I had to virtually carry him round the two and a half miles. At fence 21, an upright hedge called the bed of thorns he hardly left the ground and we parted company in the air and landed with a bump on the other side. He jumped up and took off at a gallop. We were eliminated. It was bizarre, not as if he was trying to refuse but as if something happened to him just as he was about to take off. I was utterly mystified.

I phoned Charles Harrison and suggested that he might go better with another rider, perhaps it was my fault. But he didn't agree, and he wanted me to continue on him. I had his feet x-rayed and his eyesight checked but nothing was wrong. I had to go to Badminton on my own two feet, watching my fellow competitors. I was green with envy.

Then Charles Harrison had arranged for Radar to be collected from Stanton and he was delivered to Dick Stillwell's yard in the south. He was a professional working mostly with show jumpers and was beginning to help some of the eventers to improve their show jumping. Four days after Radar's arrival, Charles telephoned me to say that, 'Hanson says the horse has been ill-treated'. I was furious about this. I had never ill-treated a horse in my life. I loved every horse I had and trained them in a manner no one could help but admire. I had transformed Radar as far as his looks, his dressage, and his show jumping were concerned without even thinking of resorting to anything nastier than telling him he was a bad boy or kicking him sharply with the heels of my riding boots when I was in the saddle if he did not listen to me in our early days. Radar had not taken off to jump at the twenty-first fence at Crookham. There must have been a reason.

At some point later on Charles Harrison gave the ride of Radar to Michael Bullen, who ran an international horse transport business and was one of the sons of the virtually professional family of riders living on the edge of the Badminton Estate. At the 1969 Burghley the following year, when I was riding Fair and Square, Radar did exactly the same thing with Michael as he had with me. This time it was a perfectly straight forward fence on the cross-country. I was at the fence when it happened and watched a perfect approach stride and no take-off. As both horse and rider scrambled to their feet, with Mike totally unhurt, he decided that something was very wrong indeed and it was far too dangerous to continue. For my part, I was sure that Radar was suffering either from blackouts or some sort of brain failure. Set off by the adrenalin of cross-country, he was suddenly afflicted and had no idea where he was or what he was doing. Mike never competed on him again. We never found out what his problem was, but I felt vindicated.

At the Sherborne One-Day Event in Dorset Babe Moseley, Tom Greenhalgh and Frank Weldon were clearly watching us, and I was amazed when Weldon, now indisputably the greatest influence on who should be chosen as a member of the British team, tried to flirt with me. He was wasting his time and I could hardly believe he would have the nerve to do this after what he had tried on at Windsor when he unzipped my dress after luring me up to his room. But then I probably never really understood the way that men think.

Keith was still vacillating over whether or not to leave his wife when Ted started talking about 'our' future. Now that I was rejected by the Catholic Church with my divorce I was free to marry anyone. Unfortunately, the man I wanted was not free to marry me. I was so obsessed with him and so frustrated by the situation then I behaved in classic 'other woman' style and drove two and a half hours to Twylch, Wales to drive past his farmhouse. I sat outside and took some photographs and returned home to Shenberrow, feeling no better.

Then my father was back in hospital. I drove straight to him and he looked ghastly and wave after wave of sadness rolled over me. He was going to die, and I had never thought of that. Life would never be the same for those of us left behind, and I could not imagine how Mummy would cope.

Daddy died some weeks later and the funeral was arranged for the Tuesday before Burghley. I knew he would want me to ride at Burghley. I was riding John Shedden's Heyday. I spoke to Ted and he kindly made arrangements for his pilot to pick me up from Pershore Airport and fly me to Squires Gare, outside Blackpool and then after the funeral to fly me back. Heyday went well, we had had no hope of winning, he was not that good a horse, but we came a creditable 10th and John Shedden was delighted and I was satisfied that we had performed well under adverse circumstances.

I got back to Shenberrow to be greeted with a phone call from Keith telling me that Eileen had taken an overdose and had been rushed to hospital first thing in the morning. It had been staged and not a particularly serious attempt. She had acquired an alarm clock to ring continuously in the morning when she was unconscious so that someone would go and investigate. Keith was very angry with her, but he had to stay at Guildford with her for the next few days.

With the 1968 Mexico Olympic Games fast approaching I began to work Bill in the second week in November. I wanted to bring him to fitness, so he could perform well in the spring season and I had set my sights on Badminton in April as our first big goal. I was very confident of his ability. He jumped like a coiled spring across country, brave and keen, and he listened to me. He was fast, quick on his feet and I believed we were a great partnership. He could have been an inch or two taller with more bone, but he was so light on his feet I did not think this relevant.

I missed Keith dreadfully, and at the same time I had Ted badgering me. I was far too much in love with Keith to jump into bed with Ted. I expect he had never been turned down by anyone in all his life. He then told me that if I had second thoughts he would like to have an 'exclusive' on me. I was too staggered to answer, he wasn't suggesting marriage, but being his mistress and available to no-one else. I told Keith all about my meeting with Ted and he became thoroughly depressed about the whole situation.

Again, I was planning to compete at Crookham and then Kinlet to lead up to what I hoped would be an impressive performance at Badminton. I had a training programme for the horses, as usual pinned on the tack room wall and I was also planning a fitness regime for myself, walking and running up the hill every day and then skipping rope. I even swallowed hot cider vinegar with a teaspoon of honey every morning.

Chapter Nine – Drugging Fair and Square

On my way to Crookham Two-Day Event the horsebox broke down. I only just made it in time and I was too rushed to ride in Bill and he 'blew up' in the dressage arena. Keith had arrived and saw all of this performance. For a moment I thought Keith brought me bad luck, as he had been at the fence watching when Bill had fallen previously. But I put this thought out of my mind.

We were getting ready for the show jumping later that day when a woman stormed up to Keith, shouting at him in spectacular fashion, and disbelieving heads turned towards him. It was Eileen, intent on confrontation. Keith took her arm, propelling her away, out of sight and earshot, and later he told me that they had the most awful row. At least this was visible proof that Keith's account of his tumultuous home life had some credibility. Not that I doubted him, I was too obsessed and too in love.

Fortunately, Bill was unaffected by Eileen's appearance and the ensuing uproar and vibes, and he jumped a beautiful clear round as his apology for having misbehaved in the dressage phase. We were friends again and I gave him several extra sugar lumps. He went well in the cross-country and I went home preoccupied with how to curb his exuberance in the dressage. With a three-day event I could work him in before the dressage but not at a one-day-event when he had to perform in all three disciplines in one day.

I talked to Len about the problem and I can hear you readers crying, 'Not again – NO DRUGS!!' after the fiasco at Burghley with Glenamoy when I had used Bert's magic powders and he had gone around the cross-country half-asleep. Len unhesitatingly said the answer which would last only for a short time was obvious, bromide. He told me that this was something the military fed to the soldiers in WWII to stop them getting 'sexy'. It had a calming and soothing influence, with no after-effects. Len said it could be bought from any chemist without prescription and would simply quieten Bill for his test. 'Trust me' he said, and I did. I should point out that I was breaking no rules. I went to the chemist and bought one little sachet of powder which was produced from a box off a shelf in full view. That was problem solved, or so I thought.

The next week we went into the dressage arena, polished, smart and beautiful and Bill performed a formidably good test, smooth effortless, terrific extensions, great precision at the markers and all with an air of grace. I was so pleased that I was looking forward to telling Len what a success his remedy had been.

The show jumping was on that afternoon and I put on his jumping saddle and snaffle bridle and began to warm up. We went through the start and headed towards the first fence a red and white-striped post-and-rails and it was as if he was in some lovely dream of his own. He crashed straight through the wooden top rails. I realised then, with absolute horror that the bromide was still affecting him. He was in a happy-go-lucky state and not even entirely sure where the jumps were. I had to ride him to each fence on an absolutely spot on take-off stride and try to raise him with my reins and heels into the air. I have never had to ride a course like this and it was a miracle that we got around, demolishing only one fence for five penalty points.

We had another two hours before the cross-country and I was hoping that he would have returned to his usual enthusiastic and sharp self. We went through the start and it became increasingly obvious that he was still feeling the soporific effects of his powder. From fence one it was as if he was seeing the fences through a fog and was not entirely sure what to do. As in his show jumping round, I began to count to him the last three approach strides and kicked him into the air with my heels to make him take off. We managed to progress around the course until the last few fences. I think his poor brain was unable to focus on the conglomeration of the spider's web fence. He refused once, twenty penalties, I brought him in again and he jumped over, but in his befuddled state, and with the next combination obstacle only a few strides away, he failed to lift his legs high enough and we were on the ground for 60 penalties. I caught his reins as he sat there, resting happily, and told him we had to finish, and the time the clock was ticking, and the penalty points were mounting. Bill watched by a crowd of disbelieving spectators managed to get to his feet. I jumped on and managed to complete the course.

Kinlet had once again been a disaster, but this time through no one's fault but my own. I could never forgive myself. I was responsible for giving him the powder and Len had not thought how unsuitable it would be for an event horse with the bromide lasting too long in its system. The result of this tragedy was that some of the selectors seized on it as an example of Bill's propensity to fall. The only good thing to come out of this debacle was that I would never ever think again of giving a horse drugs to enhance his performance. I was forever cured of interfering with nature.

Another issue was that this was the second time that Keith had come to watch me. I had now fallen off twice in front of him and considered that perhaps this was an omen. It was the way the gods were showing their displeasure at my involvement with a married man.

We went on to Badminton in 1968, hoping against hope that the selectors might still be impressed. There were two Europeans dressage judges. In those days the British were not considered to be very good at advanced dressage. It was definitely a bonus for me if foreigners were judging, as they would be sure to perceive the correctness of our work, the precision and straightness of my horse's pace and we would be marked accordingly.

Colonel Weldon had been the course designer and it was demanding. This was one of the last chances for those with Olympic ambitions to show themselves worthy of consideration for a place on the team. There was Derek Allhusen with Lochinvar, Richard Meade on Turnstone, and Mary Macdonnell on Kilmacthomas. But then Colonel Weldon had written in a special article in one of the broadsheets,

> *"It has been two years since Mary's horse was at his peak, whereas Turnstone may just be reaching his, and he will have the benefit of Richard Meade's greater international experience, while Lochinvar's performance was the talking point of the European Championships last summer. Several others, like Cornishman – who will probably be ridden by Bertie Hill, the most experienced of them all, (plus) Mark Phillips with Rock On and Jane Bullen with Our Nobby, have far from forlorn hopes but straightaway the rivalry between the sexes becomes apparent which will be a feature of Badminton. Some hold the view that the Olympic three-day event is too tough a contest for women but most girls are itching for a chance to prove them wrong."*

89

At this point I had difficulty in understanding the point that the Colonel was making. I could grasp the point about the proven horses and riders with their expertise, their experience is invaluable, as long as they are still at their peak. I could not understand what he meant by 'the rivalry between the sexes becomes apparent which will be a feature of Badminton'. It would appear that the Colonel's chauvinistic attitude towards women was being expressed when he wrote this. He seemed to be greatly threatened by the idea that a woman was an equal of man in a sporting competition. His reference to the horsewomen competing, calling them 'girls' rather than 'women' is derogatory, belittling them. He does not refer to the men competing as 'boys'.

I decided that I would ride Bill just to get around and help build his confidence. I did not want to push him too much for speed. It did not occur to me to tell the selectors what had gone wrong at Kinlet, to admit that I had drugged him with bromide. With hindsight, it might have been the right thing to do. It would have stopped them saying that Bill was a faller.

On the Thursday night before the beginning of Badminton it rained, and the going was soft, but the sun shone down upon us, and the wind blew drying the ground for perfect going on the cross-country the following day. There were 55 starters and we ended up being 9 marks behind the leader, Mike Plumb the American Olympic rider. I made a great fuss of Bill as we left the dressage arena. I brushed out his plaits and left him in his loosebox to rest up the following day. After lunch I set off to walk the cross-country again. It looked no easier upon second inspection. I refused to look down into the depths of the elephant trap. I decided to jump the giant's table smack in the middle and take the park wall in our stride before I urged him on faster to fly the vicarage ditch. I checked the striding between the two elements of Luckington Lane.

The following morning, I checked the steeplechase course and walked round most of the cross-country course, to make absolutely certain that I had chosen the best routes. We were waiting in the start box, ready to be counted down and set off at a gentle trot about the roads and tracks. Then on to the first birch fence of the steeplechase. We went around faultlessly and then started on the second part of the roads and tracks. Then I jumped off for a few minutes of our reviving routine and then we were off on the cross-country. He went beautifully all the way round until we came to the stream and the stark single pole on a slightly downhill slope.   He tried to bounce over and we came in too close and he literally chest bumped into the pole and stopped. This was a refusal. Now we had to go back across the stream and try again, this time he popped economically over the muddied water, took one neat stride and popped out over the 3 feet 9 inch rail as if it were a straightforward everyday combination. On we went, and he was full of enthusiasm and I could feel the strong propelling power in his hindquarters, he was giving me a wonderful ride and enjoying himself enormously.

We approached the trakhener tripod, its single log looking airy and uninviting suspended above the deep ditch dug out below. In 1973, Gurgle the Greek was coming in to this same fence and put on the brakes in horror. He dithered on the edge and Rachel Bayliss urged him on. He lost his grip, slipped down into the bottom of the dry ditch below and Rachel had the presence of mind to realise that the log was above them and if she ducked her head, she and the horse could emerge on the landing side. No rule at this time said that one had to go over the fences! Horse and rider must pass between the white and red flags on each side of the fence, and by going underneath the criterion had been observed. Bill and I bowled over it at a great speed, and on landing I told him how good and clever he was, and his ears flickered back in response. We continued on clear and he had given me a terrific ride, and I knew that I had a very special horse.

I knew that I had not gone flat out and I would not gain anything like maximum bonus marks for speed, and it would be sure to drop us down at the speed and endurance, whereas many of the other competitors with experienced horses would be going like the wind in order to persuade the selectors that they were worthy of consideration for a place in the Mexico Olympic team. The fastest round of the day was produced by Jane Bullen riding Our Nobby, who although only 15 hh, flew round the course. Much was made of the fact that she was student nurse at Middlesex Hospital and had been on the ward until the day before the first of the two dressage test days. She was fortunate that her elder sister, Jenny Loriston Clarke, the renowned dressage rider, kept Our Nobby at her establishment in the New Forest to school him and bring him to perfect fitness and she rode him, improving his dressage when Jane could not get away. This partnership of Jane and Our Nobby had finished fifth the previous year at Badminton and third at Burghley. But at least she was one of the 'girls' that Colonel Weldon had referred to in such a patronising manner. She was the only rider to record maximum bonus points on both the steeplechase and cross-country phases.

At the end of the cross-country phase Ben Jones on Foxdor remained in the lead, Jane Bullen on Our Nobby moved up to second. In third place was Rock On, ridden by Mark Phillips, fourth were Turnstone and Richard Mead, fifth was Derek Allhusen with Lochinvar, and in sixth place the beautiful black Ballinkeele ridden by his owner Fiona Pearson. A long way behind were myself and Bill.

I was so annoyed with myself for my stupidity to have fed Bill the bromide at Kinlet. I vowed that by the start of the autumn season, things would be different, with the proviso that God also was willing to lend a hand and keep Bill on four sound legs. I was utterly convinced that in Bill, at last, I had a horse capable of beating them all – a horse for the Olympics with the talent and guts to excel in all three phases.

The next morning the crowds flocked in as usual to watch the veterinary examination. Bill ran happily up and back again along the raked-out track with all eyes glued upon him. He was passed fit without a moment's hesitation. At two o'clock in the afternoon all the horse and rider combinations gathered. The riders walked the course and then there was a parade with commentators identifying each horse and rider with a quick potted history and informing the spectators where each horse remaining in the competition stood in the result to date. As riders we had to turn our heads and salute as we passed the Royal Box. The grandstand was already packed and humming with conversation, and people were sitting and standing several rows deep behind the ropes round the rest of the arena.

In 1968 the horse and rider combinations did not appear in number order. A new method, a great idea, was that they jumped in reverse order. The lowest placed horse jumped first and then so on up to the highest placed. It put pressure on the leaders in particular, and there was a crescendo of excitement building for the spectators who knew just how many fences their favourites could knock down and still win. No-one knew who was the winner until the last horse had completed his round.

Bill and I fell further down to finish 14th after we rolled a pole. Jane Bullen won with a clear round, Richard Meade second, Ben Jones third, Mark Phillips fourth, Derek Allhusen fifth, and sixth was Fiona Pearson.

After Badminton there was no more eventing until the autumn. Inevitably there was a sense of anti-climax. However, I pressed on. Bill was now showing the results of all our hard work. He won all three classes at one of the dressage competitions and was adjusting well to learning to clear the show jumps as we travelled all around the country, as far and wide as Lincolnshire and Yorkshire, to compete in show jumping competitions. I also took the Eason's horse, Magic who I jumped as well.

Keith and I were 20 months into our relationship and he was still vacillating. I found his inability to take decisive action upsetting, but I had stars in my eyes and I made all sorts of excuses for him. He told me that Eileen was threatening to come to Shenberrow to see me. Then he knocked me sideways by declaring that he would be away for ten days. He was taking Eileen on holiday to Rome. I could hardly believe this. If, as he said, they did not sleep together, and they were hardly speaking, except to shout, what were they going to do in Rome? There was a lot to see, he said. You ought to know I would not touch her, he told me, and the subject was closed. And even though I knew he was due back on the 4th July I didn't hear from him for three more days. Meanwhile, I told Bill that he was worth far more than any man.

Chapter Ten – Not On The Short List

The selectors had published their short list and inevitably I was not on it. I would have to achieve a fantastic result at the two remaining events if I was to have any chance of being added to it. There was Eridge on the 2nd and 3rd of August, a two-day event and then Burghley five weeks later at the beginning of September.

I walked the cross-country at Eridge and decided that it posed several challenging problems. One in particular was a leap on to a bank with a deep ditch in front. It was going to cause a lot of trouble. There seemed to be a lot going on with the shortlisted riders. It had been decided that Mark Phillip's Rock On was not to be ridden at Eridge and he been given a spare horse The Lavender Cowboy to ride at this event. Ben Jones who I considered one of the few male riders who was sympathetic in his approach, and could bond quickly with horses, had suffered the disaster that his Foxdor had collapsed and died two weeks before the event. Two other horses were found for him but neither of them seemed ready for the Olympics.

It was then announced that Jane Bullen on Our Nobby and Richard Meade with Turnstone would only be appearing in the dressage and show jumping phases. No cross-country for them. The same was going to apply to Lochinvar with Derek Allhusen but he had had a fall from one of his other horses as he rode in the novice class and was therefore rendered unable to ride Lochinvar in the show jumping. This was a mini disaster as this phase was his Achilles heel and he needed all the practice he could get.

In the dressage Judy Bradwell on Drumree, produced a very good dressage test which put her in the lead. She was a pupil of Edy Goldman and was very capable. Bill was in second place, one point behind her. However, in the show jumping the next day Judy and Drumree had three fences down and Bill jumped clear. I was filled with hope. Then we started the road and tracks. The sun was blazing down and there was not a hint of a cooling breeze. Spectators were scattered all around the cross-country course.

I knew there was only a slim chance of being put on the short list, I would have to beat all our rivals by a distance to be convincing. We set off on the steeple chase and the cross-country and I was determined to gain maximum bonus points. The sun continued to beat down and by the time I'd finished the roads and tracks my face was a bright red beacon and both Bill and I were sticky with sweat. I leapt off and the saddle was loosened, Bill was thoroughly sponged down and given a glucose and water sponge to chump in his mouth. Pointed studs were screwed into his shoes and then there was just time to set his saddle carefully in place and girth it up before the starter was counting us down.

We took off, and I kept up a relentless speed except for the more difficult combinations where it was necessary to place him exactly for take-off. He jumped the bank combination as if it were simple. His ears were forward, his eyes scanning in front for the next fence and after a cracker of a round we flashed through the finish posts without have made the semblance of a mistake. It was like old times, when Chips had been at his best. We had won by a comfortable margin of 26 points. Burghley was in four weeks and five days and this would be our only chance to get onto the short list.

I did everything I could in those five weeks to get Bill ready for his best effort. We travelled around the country entering show jumping competitions, did training gallops twice a week, continued with our dressage. The selectors were all there, Babe Mosely was the Chairman, and the Committee included Lawrence Rook, Reg Hindley, Colonels Brackenbury and Weldon and Guy Cubitt. I asked Babe just what I had to do to gain a place in the British team for Mexico and he replied without hesitation, 'Be in the first three'.

The evening before, everyone was invited to a drinks party by Lord Burghley, the Marquess of Exeter in the sumptuous surrounds of Burghley House. Although I had ridden Bill in the morning and the afternoon I was still afraid that he might be a little boisterous, remembering how he had 'blown up', in the dressage. So, I decided to forgo the drinks party and ride him again in the evening as I didn't want to exercise him too much in the morning as it might take the edge off him. This was a black mark against me, for my 'professionalism and dedication', I was not a team player. I should have gone to the drinks party. I just never got it right when it came to 'fitting in' with the eventing group of people. It was perhaps not only my professionalism and dedication but that I was not 'the right class', as well as being what they termed a 'glamour girl'.

The dressage judges were the German, Comte E Rothkirch, Mrs R T Whitely, sister to Anneli Drummond-Hay and Sheila Inderwick, who still resented the fact that I had officially complained at her blatant marking down of Airs and Graces at Stowell in 1956. She had taken her revenge ever since by continuing this practice.

We did well in the dressage and scored 39.17 penalties, but Richard Meade on his brilliant Barberry became the leader with 36.67 penalties, followed by the American Mason Phelps on Argonaut with 34. So, we stood third 5.17 penalties behind the leader of this phase. Each of the judge's marks were shown up on the scoreboard in the main concourse and it was noticeable that two of the three had given Bill almost the same high marks and the third marked us down blatantly. This marking difference was so obvious that Welwyn Hartley Edward, not one usually to be provocative, wrote in *Country Life*, "Miss Willcox might have done even better had not one of the three judges marked her with unaccustomed severity, and to the observer in a way inconsistent with the general pattern."

Overnight, Richard Meade's second ride, Turnstone, owned by Lady Hugh Russell and placed at the disposal of the team was withdrawn, so Richard would be riding only one horse, his talented and experienced Barberry. A second horse, in addition to Our Nobby, had also been quickly found for Jane Bullen, True Flash. It would appear that whatever happened, the selectors wanted Richard and Jane to go to Mexico, and unless Derek Allhusen and Lochinvar made a nonsense of the cross-country – highly unlikely – as it was his forté he was also a certainty despite the show jumping being a problem for him and Lochinvar. Therefore, it looked more and more likely that Bill and I would be ignored. Mary Gordon Watson's father had given the big, beautiful Cornishman V to Ben Jones. A second Cornishman, which was owned and ridden by Mrs Bridget Park had also been lent by him to the team.

We were drawn number 34 of the 43 starters. The spectators were out in force, many with dogs on leads. They would walk the course and sometimes imagine jumping it on their own horses. They would decide which fence in particular was going to provide the most entertainment. Usually, the trout hatchery produced the biggest number of falls where horse and rider had to continue, thoroughly wet. The onlookers enjoyed watching the competitors disappear under water.

The going was officially categorised as 'holding' which meant it was even more important not to go too fast on the cross-country and have a tired horse when facing the most difficult obstacles from the trout hatchery onwards. I didn't push him too hard around roads and tracks and the steeplechase as I didn't want to tire him out. Then came the cross-country and we took on the birch fence, the saw bench, the ditch and sleeper wall, the waterloo rails with drop, over the boxed in rails, faced Capability's Cutting with its rails in front of a bank. Through the dairy farm, keeping up a sensible speed in the knowledge that a lot of energy would be required towards the end of the course. We continued on over the slab wood with its drop on the landing side, over the echelon rails, the timber wagon and the crossed poles. At every jump we managed to come in on a correct stride for take-off. At jump number 13, the hanging log, I throttled back cautiously. Next came the bull pens and I set up Bill some way out, as he had to realise that he was to jump the first post-and-rails at a 45° angle, land and immediately bounce back into the air over the second rails to take them at a second 45° angle. As we landed over the second element of the bounce we half-circled to number 15 the sunken wall which we flew.

We picked up speed on the next long run then throttled back to a shorter stride for the upright gate and then pushed on. Approaching the maltings we popped over a post-and-rails, the first element of the trout hatchery was approached downhill and I could hear the hum of excitement as we appeared in view. Bill jumped neatly and without hesitation over the big log, splashed through the water as if he did it every day, and popped out over the tree trunk to dry land. There was a burst of applause at our smooth as silk transit.

Then there was the birch palisade and the tractor tyres both of which Bill took in his stride. We galloped through the coppice which led to what had become the bogey fence of the cross-country course. Horses were refusing, falling and being eliminated one after the other. I stuck to my plan and emerging from the little wood I set Bill on a straight line aiming for the second post in from the right-hand side which would give us the best take-off from the top of the bank. Fleetingly, I saw skid marks where horses had recoiled in horror, as I rode into the fence. My legs were wrapped tightly to Bill's sides as I warned him he had to fly from the edge and land way out from the upright post-and-rails. He did not even hesitate and sailed away in a soft landing from this fence which had become the downfall of so many, among them the immensely successful Barberry and Richard Meade. This experienced partnership took a crashing fall with the horse hurting his back very badly. Cedric the Saxon had to be put down, and there was a great deal of mayhem, with all manner of refusals and falls for those who elected to come in slowly, for the horses had no chance of reaching the far side.

On galloped Bill, still full of running and keen to jump. Now we were on the sward of old turf and I was looking well ahead, intent on turning precisely at the right moment towards the left-hand corner of fence 24, and aiming to jump the corner even though there was wide, open space to the left indicating the lure of a run out for any but the most co-operative horse. Bill turned immediately to take up our 45° line and we were on a good stride. He didn't hesitate, and we sailed into the air with Bill's legs tucked up neatly behind him. We landed fast across the sloping ground and turned at once.

Picking up the track in its loop to the next fence 25, we sailed over the heavy bags of hops laid horizontally with a pole above them. Now we were approaching number 26, the double rails, deep rough heavy timber planks in the shape of a show jumping double oxer with its line curving left on the last three strides. Between the front timbers and the back ones was a spread of 1.63 metres, 5 feet 4 inches, and the height of the obstacle was 1.15 metres, or 3 feet 9 inches. As we turned to face the fence I realised that we were between strides. I had to make a lightning decision to lengthen or shorten. I moved Bill out a fraction to the right and still we were too close for a clean take off. His left knee hit the highest plank. I do not know how I stayed on unless it was sheer pig-headedness. I heard the gasps of the crowd, but was back safely in the saddle and now urging Bill to pick up speed over the next two fences, 27 and 28, a rustic arch and a rustic bench, jumping them easily out of our stride and then, with the last fence in sight, I took care to arrive smack on stride at the wattles and flashed through the finish.

I unsaddled and went to weigh in. Bill was very pleased with himself, nudging me hard with his nose, as if to say, 'Didn't I do well'. He was allowed just a few sips of water and all the time there were calls of congratulations from all sides. I had no idea of how those before me had done, and it would be some time before the last horse had completed the course and the marks went up on the big scoreboard on the concourse of the main ring. But I focused on Bill, no horse could have done better and I was thrilled with his performance.

By the end of the day Derek Allhusen and Lochinvar had gone into the lead with a score of 29.93 and we were second on 27.23 - just 2.7 marks behind. Third placed Peri was on 19.87. Barberry was out, limping away from fence 23 with a bad back, the Frenchman was fourth and Jane Bullen with Our Nobby was fifth. Only eight horses had completed the cross-country without jumping penalties and one of them had a fall on the steeplechase.

I knew that Lochinvar was not a good show jumper so we had a fair chance of winning, it was in the lap of the gods. Then to my horror when we ran Bill up we found that he was lame on his near fore, it was at the point of the shoulder. We began applying fomentations and I telephoned my vet, Peter Thorne and asked what we could do to remove the pain, he said he would be at Burghley at 6.30 in the morning on the next day to see what he could do. I told him the Veterinary Inspection began at 10 am the next day. Alison stayed up all night applying fomentations but I had to go and sleep as it would be no good for me to be too tired to ride properly in the show jumping the next day, if Bill was no longer lame.

At 11.30 pm that night we gave him Butazolidin, as a painkiller and this was repeated at 4 am. We ran him up first thing the next morning and to our relief he was sound. Word had already gone round like wildfire that Bill was lame and there were many more people than usual gathered round the running up area, for the veterinary inspection.

I decided that I should run him up myself. I led him to stand in front of the judgement panel and whilst the three men walked round peering hard at his legs. Nothing untoward was to be seen. As I turned around I allowed the rein to slacken so that it was obvious I was not helping Bill. You could have heard a pin drop as we did this and then there was a burst of applause. He was declared sound.

To my astonishment Derek Allhusen asked permission from the selectors to withdraw from the show jumping. Apparently, the horse 'had rapped himself'. I could hardly believe it. It occurred to me that Derek, of all people knew how unreliable was Lochinvar in this discipline and if he really messed up then he would look terrible. I was a bundle of nerves now I was standing first and I had to watch my competitors jump in reverse order.

Only 19 of the original 50 starters on the first day were left, and a further two were withdrawn as they failed to pass the veterinary inspection. Three more horses, including Lochinvar, were withdrawn before the final show jumping.

The rising atmosphere of excitement was tangible, I could almost reach out and touch it. With 16 riders to jump before me, we had a wait of about one hour and ten minutes to get through. I was standing in the collecting ring watching the others jump before but it made me too nervous and Alison, Bill and I walked away to a quiet spot. I couldn't see the ring but I could hear the 'oohs' and 'aahs' as fences were knocked down. I was finding it very hard to remain calm and confident. Finally, the time came to mount and do the practice jump. I allowed Bill to rap it and then growled at him. Telling him he was naughty and he must pick up his front legs high and go clear. The steward called us in to stand at the ready by the entrance to the ring. Susan Neil and Peri were now lying in second place and they were jumping. There was a groan as they rolled off the poles on what I learnt later had become the bogey fence, giving us a leeway of ten points.

There was dead silence as I began my round. We went round the 12 jumps, coming in to each fence on a perfect stride. The oxer, number 3, which had caught out most of the competitors rattled slightly. We just touched another and the crowd held its breath. Then we landed over the final fence with a clear round and half a time fault. We had won, and the crowd erupted! Back in the collecting ring I jumped off and friends and strangers alike came up to us, beaming with pleasure and congratulating us. Then we were called back into the main ring for the prize giving and as Bill and I went forward it was announced over the loud speakers that we had won, there was a huge outbreak of clapping. The National Anthem was played and the hairs at the back of my neck and into my head stood on end, a most peculiar feeling. Lastly, we exited from the ring and did our lap of honour, with my fingers on one side, stroking my horse's neck while the crowd cheered. They assumed that I had now done enough to earn my place on the British team for the Mexico Olympics.

Chapter Eleven - Training at Ascot

The games were now only four weeks away. The selectors went into a huddle after the show jumping and they announced that the short list would consist of: Derek Allhuen on Laurien, Richard Meade riding Cornishman V, Ben Johns on The Poacher. Jane Bullen would ride Our Nobby. Sheila Willcox with Fair and Square, would now join the team in training at Windsor. Having been given this news I had to stay on at Burghley until Sunday afternoon so Brigadier James Grose could fill in the mountain of necessary forms for my inclusion.

When we drove back to Shenberrow someone had decorated the wide entrance gate with flags galore and messages. That evening the telephone rang constantly, kind people wanted to congratulate us on our win, saying that it was about time that the selectors came to their senses!

Bill was still getting his shoulder treated and I was to join the others at Ascot as soon as I was sure that he was completely sound. We were all staying at the Kingswood Hall of Residence which was empty except for the team members. When I arrived I walked around not knowing where the dining hall was situated and eventually I found the others already seated and eating. The other team members were, with the exception of Ben, very frosty, not knowing what to say to me. I was certainly not welcome. They resented me and had closed ranks.

Alison and I heard the others clattering around the next day and when I went out to ask where they were off to they told me they were going to Ascot racecourse. Alison and I tacked up Bill and I set off, hoping I could find my way, as they others had left without me. The next day I came across Jane on Our Nobby, all plaited up and she was wearing her best black coat. I asked her why she was so dressed up and she said that the press were waiting for us up at Smith's Lawn as they were announcing the four riders in the team and the reserve and taking photographs. Nobody had mentioned this to me.

I was in my everyday jodhpurs with a lightweight sweater and a headscarf. I decided we had better continue back to the stables where Colonel Lithgow told me I should go up to Smith's Lawn even if I were in scruff order. I arrived there in the car just in time to hear the announcement that the British team would consist of : Richard Meade riding Cornishman V, Derek Allhusen on Lochinvar, Ben Johns on The Poacher and Jane Bullen on Our Nobby. They were having their photographs taken. As an afterthought, the press was told that Sheila Willcox was to be the reserve rider.

The press wanted a photo of me jumping a horse so I was given The Lavender Cowboy and was distinctly unimpressed with him, his lack of answering the aids, with no good paces or presence. I set off towards a brushwood with poles above it and there was the noise of clicking of cameras with all the photographers happy with what they had snapped. As we landed I patted Cowboy and told him, 'At least you have a jump in you.' Bill Lithgow came to talk to me, confirming that I was to go as reserve with Fair and Square. He also made it perfectly clear that in the event of any one of the four team horses falling by the wayside, that horse's rider would take over the ride on Fair and Square. The last straw was the ultimatum that Fair and Square would not be allowed his groom, Alison, who knew him so well and could be counted on to look after him properly. One of the other grooms looking after the team horses would resent finding time in Mexico to see to Fair and Square. It was too awful even to contemplate. I could just imagine what would happen, for he would certainly be considered an unwelcome additional workload by the grooms who would have enough to do looking after their own rider's horse. Can you imagine how I felt?

Soon I was on the telephone to Keith. In August, we had discussed what would happen if I were chosen to go to Mexico and he had said, categorically, that on my return he would have left Eileen and would come to live at Shenberrow. I began to think that, at last, he was determined to take the big step and keep his word. When I told Keith over the telephone that I had refused to go to Mexico because I would allow no one else to ride Bill and because Alison was not allowed to look after him. I went back to the hostel and Ben knocked on the door of my room and tried his utmost to persuade me that I ought to go to Mexico with the team. I was terribly upset and did not settle until well after midnight.

The next morning, I was up at Smith's Lawn with Bill and found Bertie Hill watching one of the team work his horse in dressage. I stood nearby, thinking that the work was not good enough, I suggested to Bertie that he should have a ride on Bill, to get the feel of him. He was used to racing before he took up eventing and he was accustomed to riding big, thoroughbred horses. He clearly thought that Bill was not his type. Ever the gentleman, he climbed into the saddle, and immediately exclaimed in astonishment, 'He feels like a big horse'. I urged him to try him out. He could not get over the way Bill answered his aids and how strong were his paces, with the equivalent feel of a much bigger horse. He said that he wished he had known this earlier.

Although Babe Mosely said that I would have a place on team if I came in the first three at Burghley and I had come first by a considerable margin they had offered me the reserve in such a loaded manner that they knew I would refuse.

After my announcement that I wouldn't go to the Mexico Olympics as a reserve rider there was a great deal of press coverage discussing this and I began to think I should give way. The very thought of it made me sick at heart.

Pamela Macgregor Morris wrote in The Times: "There seems little justification for Miss Willcox's attitude. She won from a decimated and largely uncompetitive field at Eridge,.." Michael Williams, correspondent for *Sporting Life* commented: "The Badminton form now seems a long way off, and not even Jane Bullen, who won there on Our Nobby can be 100 per cent of her place in the plane to Mexico. Sergeant Jones who, at one time looked fairly sure to be selected with Mrs R T Whiteley's Foxdor, has been singularly unfortunate, as this horse collapsed and died after a training gallop a fortnight ago, and although two others have now been put at his disposal, neither of them looks ready for the Olympics. As for Barberry and the Poacher, these two horses have not made a public appearance since assisting to win the European Championship at Punchestown last August. The Eridge Horse Trials, which were held at the beginning of this month and might have been expected to provide a reasonably serious test for those on the shortlist, failed to do so for the simple reason that they were not allowed to compete. True, Turnstone and Our Nobby were down to take part in them, but for some strange reason neither horse was asked to tackle the cross-country. The two Olympic 'possibles' who did go the full distance at Eridge, Cornishman and The Lavender Cowboy, were both second string horses at the time; and the former did little to advertise his prospects by stopping twice across country. The Lavender Cowboy went much better and finished fourth. But neither he nor any of the others was anything like as impressive as the winner, Miss Sheila Willcox's Fair and Square, for whom a place has still not been found on the Olympic shortlist. This seems to me to be the height of folly, because Miss Willcox is to Horse Trials what Harvey Smith is to Show Jumping. Whether or not the Selectors will be prepared to look beyond the short list after Burghley, I don't know. But one thing I do know is that Sheila Willcox and Fair and Square are going to take a lot of beating. And if they embarrass the selectors by winning it is all right by me."

Colonel Weldon pronounced me in the *Light Horse* to be "a stupid young woman" for declining the offer of going to Mexico as Reserve. Right up until the day before they were due to fly to Mexico the press continued their assault. Michael Williams, writing in the *Sporting Life* on September 19th wrote: "A cold wind has been blowing through the ranks of Olympic Selectors. Almost on the eve of departure, one embarrassment has followed another. ..... the discomfiture of their three-day event colleagues who yesterday named the rider they had been ignoring for so long in the face of claims which seemed so obvious and received a polite but firm snub. The rider in question is Sheila Willcox, winner of the Eridge Horse Trials and the Three-Day Event at Burghley. A triple winner of the Badminton Horse Trials, Miss Willcox is in a class of her own, and why she was not picked for the Olympics in the first place is a mystery. To pick her at this late stage as a reserve was only adding insult to injury, and who can blame her for declining the invitation? To have kept her horse hanging around in Mexico with little chance of competing would have taxed the patience of a saint."

The Editor of *Horse and Hound* devoted a column to the situation soon after the result at Burghley: " .... But, one cannot wonder just why Sheila Willcox and Fair and Square, after their performance at Burghley, did not commend themselves to the selectors as an automatic choice. Many people who saw the fluent manner in which the pair jumped last week to finish easy winners were quite confident they would be nominated at once. Miss Willcox is a former European Champion, she has the unique distinction of being Badminton Champion three years in succession and possesses far more international experience than the vast majority of people in the sport. No one can question her will to succeed. Her horse, too, is anything but a novice having been second two years ago in the Advanced class at Eridge, which they won again last month in convincing style. Fair and Square may be written off by some as having insufficient experience of an Olympic type course, but at Badminton this year, which was advertised as having the biggest ever cross-country, they did not fare too badly by finishing 14th. At Burghley, in which Miss Willcox attended to her horse to freshen him up in the ten minutes spent in the Box, the enclosed ring for rest and veterinary examination between phases C and D. Few were so thorough in her horsemastership methods."

The Letters to the Editor page in *Horse and Hound* were occupied completely with the general eventing people's reaction to the situation. The shortest, and the one I liked best was from a Douglas Kerr from St Andrews in Fife. He wrote: "Sir, one does not send a team to run a mile and keep Roger Bannister in the wings; one does not mount a promising apprentice in the Derby and keep Lester Piggott twiddling his thumbs – nor does one play bridge sitting like a ton of bricks on the ace of trumps!" Second best, also short, came from Mrs D Scott-Gall: "Sir, After Sheila Willcox's magnificent win at Burghley recently and her past successes, it seems incredible that such a habitual winner has not already been selected for Mexico. Why can't the Selectors recognise a girl with this winning streak?"

Third of the seven letters for which space was made came from M E Mackenzie and ran as follows: "Sir, As a keen follower of Eventing over the years I must congratulate the Observer on hitting the nail on the head when he wonders why Sheila Willcox and Fair and Square after their performance at Burghley, did not commend themselves to the Selectors as an automatic choice. I assure you, a lot of other people wonder why too! I have followed Sheila Willcox with patient and keen interest ever since she was pipped at the post in 1956, and then won the three Badmintons (1957 to 1959) for it did not take great perception to spot she is head and shoulders above anyone who has represented Britain since the war. She should have been first choice (with all respect to those already selected), for above all she has the ultimate asset, the winning psychology, as proved by her achievements. Being second in the advanced class at Eridge two years ago makes nonsense of this novice label stuck on Fair and Square. She says, I believe, that she has never had a better horse under her, and that is saying something! I was shattered when they did not take Sheila to Tokyo, for if ever this generation of riders threw up a potential Olympic medallist it's her. Oh why did they not use her? I feel the Eventing public will be utterly disgusted. Marrying horses and riders at this late stage is ridiculous and we all know it."

Colonel Weldon, a member of the selection committee and also correspondent for one of the leading newspapers, and Pamela Macgregor Morris writing for The Sunday Times were firm friends, and they clearly joined forces to persuade the general public that Fair and Square and I were not Olympic material. This alone was bad enough, but the fact that Weldon was a member of the Committee and could be putting forward their private views for public consumption in this way, was not to be countenanced. People began to stand up and say this was incorrect. Sometime later a new rule crept into being. In future, no one would be allowed to be both newspaper correspondent and a member of the selection committee. Weldon would have blamed me yet again!

The result of this furore was that it fired the chosen team to even greater efforts than in normal circumstances. Apparently, *Horse and Hound* and the newspaper were available to them in the three weeks plus they were in Mexico to acclimatise, and they were very well aware of the depth of public feeling over my not having been chosen as a team member. It must have been galling, but it almost certainly would have given them that extra kick to producing, not just their best, but more than a little bit extra.

As speed and endurance day arrived, there was dry heat to contend with as the competition began and then, on the actual day there was torrential rain. Several of the horses on the cross-country had to wade or swim to reach the other side of a particular fence, at one point the river had risen above the height of the bank and Barberry had trouble in making out where he should take off. The three men excelled themselves in the difficult going, and it was their ability to adapt to these appalling conditions which gave them the edge over most other teams and contributed hugely to their success. On phase C of the roads and tracks Jane Bullen dismounted to run alongside her horse after the steeplechase on a steep stretch of ground where she managed to drop his rein and nearly lost him altogether, only just managing to grab his tail as he moved away from her and was then dragged to the top! On phase D, the cross-country, Jane rode into one of the water fences fed by the Montana Brook which had become swollen from the rain. The partnership fell to earn sixty penalties for the fall and more for loss of time. Her score was duly discounted for the team. The three men were then in a position which meant they must all finish. This they did magnificently, and at the end of the speed and endurance, the British team were nearly 50 marks ahead of their nearest rivals, the United States, with the latter having a further 60 in hand over the overnight leaders, the Soviet Union. Next day, the British became Olympic Champions, and the press at home, quite rightly, made the best of the news and joined in the congratulations.

Meanwhile, Fair and Square and I competed at The Horse of the Year Show for the Spiller's Championship Combined Training class and won. In *The Field* magazine of 17th October Andrew Horsburgh Porter devoted much of his column to the Olympic situation as follows: "The Spiller's Championship for Combined Training was won by Sheila Willcox and Fair and Square. There has been a tendency in the Press and elsewhere to belittle his victory achieved by this pair at Burghley and at Wembley. Continual disparagement of achievement is likely to make this talented young woman give up the three-day-event. Many of her contemporaries and rivals would welcome such a course, just as many jockeys would be glad to hear that Lester Piggott was hanging up his boots. Complete concentration on winning and exceptional ability in the saddle are qualities by Miss Willcox and Piggott. A study of Rudyard Kipling's poem "If" may dissuade Miss Willcox from premature retirement."

Chapter Twelve – The Rocky Road of Love

My love life was following much the same rocky road as my eventing career. Keith continued to vacillate. He was worried that he could not afford to keep his wife and three children and me. One moment he was saying it was impossible, but he couldn't keep away from me. Out of the blue, five days before Christmas, Ted Marsh appeared on his way home from hunting. During the summer I had stayed with him and Elizabeth several times on a strictly 'don't touch' basis when I needed cross-country practice and a good show jumping course for Bill. I told him all that was happening with Keith. This was the amazing thing between the two of us throughout our lives. We could talk about anything and everything without getting upset or embarrassed. I was never again going to believe that he had lost interest in me for when I asked him, without really meaning it, if he would like to look after me financially, he agreed at once. Mummy, worrying about me and, in particular, about my long affair with Keith, was constantly telling me that I was getting no younger, coming up to 33 and that I needed either to marry again or find someone who could be relied upon to look after me financially.

In the days I am talking about, a wife expected to be looked after in all monetary departments by her husband, but in my present circumstances I had to rely on my ability to train horses and to win prize money. Ted, clearly, was the only one I could rely on to look after me, but the price he would expect in return was something I could not bear whilst I was still deeply in Keith's thrall. Someone should have waved a magic wand over me to bring me to my senses for it was now two years and two months since that fateful meeting with Keith. Part of me was becoming resentful of Keith's continuous failure to keep his word in coming to live with me. I reckoned I had been patient enough, and common sense and other people told me that perhaps he would never be able to take the final step. But as soon as I was with him all good intentions disappeared out the window.

I continued to compete on Bill and went to Kinlet, where I had managed to make a mess of things every year. This year was different, I won! The Engelheart circular wrote about this:

> *"Sheila Willcox is a fascinating, brilliant and sometimes controversial figure. Kinlet, from the start, was her bogey*

course. In her first year, Glenamoy fell at the water garden. Such was her stature that we modified the jump and dug away, by hand, 50 tons of soil on the landing side. She obliged us the following year by going the wrong side of a flag and being eliminated. The year after, she fell off at the bed of thorns, the horse (Radar) went spare and she was eliminated on time. Last year, she fell at the spider's web and had a refusal later on Fair and Square. Lesser people might, in these four years, have blamed the course, the horse, the fence judges, the course builder or the organisers. Not Sheila. She simply laughed and said she was coming back next year. A few days ago, she wrote saying: "I should like you all to know how much I enjoyed this year's event, the more so, obviously, because at last I managed to win! And I really meant what I said to you on Friday, that I should like to win the Kinlet Trials almost more than any other Event. I include 'almost' so as not to tempt fate for Badminton. Please thank everyone concerned for their help and a wonderful day". "Well, we know how Fate reacted."

Back at Shenberrow, there was a message from a certain David S. asking me to telephone him. I did, but he said it was something he had to talk about face to face, and he would come to see me at Shenberrow at five o'clock on the following Wednesday. I could not imagine why he needed to speak to me. Then I suddenly remembered that when he and his wife had shown me round their beautiful house, I had fallen in love with it. I had told David that if ever they wanted to sell to please let me know. If this was what was on his mind then I was in for some embarrassment as I didn't have that sort of money, in fact |I had hardly any money at all.

At five o'clock on the dot on the Wednesday David's car swung into the drive and stopped outside the main door. I opened it and we sat down in the drawing room. It then became the most astonishing day of my life. He knelt on his knees in front of me, and amidst tears, said that he had fallen in love with me when we had met at a dinner party at the Easons. I could only faintly remember this, and my recollection was that I thought he looked down on me. Now he was declaring that he wanted to marry me, that his wife and he were no longer compatible, and he was getting a divorce. I had difficulty in stopping my jaw from dropping. He had even brought with him a

110

bottle of champagne, ready for the possibility that I might accept him at once!

I told him that I hardly knew him and could not marry anyone without being sure it was the right person. He was a good-looking man with a fine physique, fit, well-spoken, well-tailored, interested in horses, with property in Spain, a beautiful house and one would assume, not short of money. Like Ted, he was also a JP and a pillar of society. David made a point of saying that he fully intended to get a divorce from his wife and that this would not be a problem. I was still in shock.

He persuaded me to have dinner with him and throughout a long meal we talked about all sorts of things. Shocked as I was by this unexpected revelation, I could see that an offer like this was serious enough to demand very strong consideration. Certainly, David seemed one hundred per cent genuine, and it would be a strange man who would do this for fun. That night I lay in bed worrying about what I should do next.

I told Keith on the telephone and he rushed over and was sulky, then took me to bed and was rough in his love-making, as if he were marking his territory. The following day I went to visit the Easons who had known David S. for years. I described what had happened. Vivian was stupefied. Then when she thought about it she was very much in favour, it would solve all my problems with money. No-one had a bad word to say about David as a man, he was always reliable, helpful, charming, ran his estate well and was generous in the community. There was also the fact that this situation would finally put an end to Keith and his failure, time and time again, to keep his promise and leave his wife. Perhaps it was time for me to face the cold facts and come to the conclusion that we might go on like this for years.

I was so preoccupied that I missed going to the Woburn Abbey Trials but then there were just four days until Badminton and I had to clear my mind. It was imperative that I shut out all thoughts of Keith and David and concentrate my energies on producing a brilliant display from Bill throughout the competition.

At the end of the dressage the five leaders were only separated by 18 points. To my huge surprise Mrs Inderwick, who had always

111

blatantly marked me down seemed to have suddenly decided that we have improved enormously and marked us only two behind Mr Pot, the Dutchman. Perhaps she had had a fit of conscience and was trying to do the right thing.

In the cross-country everything was fine until the third fence, the huntsman's close, with its three sloping rails and a formidable drop on the other side. We met it exactly as I had planned when I had spent so much time on my own two legs running back and forth from the previous fence, finding the right striding, and I could almost hear Bill's pleasure in his own ability as he sailed over the top rail exuberantly.

As he landed I felt a flicker of a stumble. We came to the gaping elephant trap and as we took off, perfectly placed, to jump the post-and-rails back into the park I felt Bill sag in front as his hind legs propelled us into the air and I had one horrified moment when I realised that his off fore front leg was unable to stand the force of the thrust upwards and had simply given way.

Instead of clearing the 3 feet 6 inches of the top rail with his knees, he hit it with his forearms and turned us over in a somersault onto the landing side. He fell straight on top of me, pinning me in the bottom of a furrow. He just lay there. The fence judge and helpers arrived, trying and failing to persuade him to get up. My chest began to hurt with the weight on it and I began to think I could not stand much more. Luckily Bill eventually gave a heave and stood upright, quivering on three legs, and I was pulled to my feet to stand beside him. I knew this was no ordinary fall for him and my heart sank. Horses on the course had to be stopped and the loudspeakers went dead. Apparently, there was no horse ambulance anywhere near and I was saying stupidly that I was alright and managed to stagger back towards the stables with Bill beside me. Eventually, a Land Rover and trailer pulled up beside us and we were carried back to the yard. These days anyone who falls is ministered to immediately by a doctor and a horse ambulance is near to hand. In 1969, I could hardly believe our bad luck. I realised that something serious must have happened to Bill's off-fore leg as we landed after his magnificent jump over the rails and drop but it was some days before I knew exactly how he was injured.

Later on, I watched Cherry and Sidney's film of the jump and you can clearly see that as he lands his right hind leg came forward and struck through the back of his protective boot into the tendon on his off-fore. We had found a slit in his boot when we took everything off back in the stable. I could not forgive myself for not realising what had happened. A less brave horse would never have attempted to jump the next fence. In that split second, all my dreams were gone.

Geoffrey Brain, my vet, came to assess the damage and announced that the off-fore tendon had taken a terrific strike. It was almost certain that it would have to be fired in the hope of producing tight skin all around the tendon, thereby restoring its strength so it would work again. It meant that Bill would be out of action for many, many months.

I had broken two ribs. Keith came to see me and told me that I should accept David as the difficulties that kept us apart seemed insuperable. Despite this, the love between us was very apparent although it was the first time we didn't have sex. Ted said that he would send his box to collect Bill and he would see to his treatment. I accepted his kindness with great relief, acknowledging that Ted was certainly the best and most reliable friend I could ever have.

David took me out to dinner at Chez Ruba, a Russian restaurant in London, and gave me his assurances that he was going ahead with his divorce and a private detective had been arranged for him to get evidence that his wife was committing adultery. In retrospect, it is obvious that wanting to marry me was a rebound reaction on his part. Mummy met David and was utterly charmed. Both she and the Easons were keen to get Keith knocked right out of my life and marriage to David seemed the answer. David and I solemnly agreed that we should go somewhere for a weekend in order see if we were sexually compatible.

Surreptitiously we booked into a Travel Lodge hotel which made me feel sordid. In bed I discovered that he liked to be smacked, preferably with a whip, which shocked me considerably. I had never slept with a man who needed this to make him come. It occurred to me that he had probably conjured up a picture in his mind of me standing, in black leather, legs akimbo, cracking a whip. It might do things for him, but not for me. There was no way I was going to play that sort of game, just to get married to a man the world respected.

113

I drove off and went to Keith's house in Guildford and sat outside in the car, tears streaming down my face. I felt so guilty. I then went back to my weekend with David. We spent our second night together and I couldn't resist giving him a huge slap on his bottom when he was about to come, and it made him jump. Then he was taking me back to Shenberrow and his driving was so infuriating that I had to ask why he progressed in leaps and bounds. He was surprised that I had noticed this and added that his family had always told him the same thing.

Almost as soon as I got back to Shenberrow, Ted rang and said he wanted to meet me at Aspreys to buy me a belated proper birthday present and he gave me the most gorgeous gold, diamond and sapphire brooch. I loved it and have always treasured it.

After the debacle at the Travel Lodge with David I was missing Keith even more, and I knew that I could never marry a man just for money. Bill was out of action, being treated at Ted's and I was bored. Ted had redoubled his efforts to claim me and was buying not just one new horse for me to event but a new Vincents horsebox as well. This cheered me up a little. The outlook for Bill was very bleak. Soon I was driving all over the country seeking a worthy successor to him.

We found the horse I wanted at the brother of Sir Thomas Beecham's, the maestro conductor. Sir Thomas had for many years been the *de facto* husband of Nancy Cunard's socialite mother, Maud Cunard. Adrian Beecham bred a foal every year from a good three-quarter bred hunter mare put to a Premium stallion. He was a big, black gelding whom they called Milky Way. He sire was Starlata. His one fault, as far as I was concerned, was a broad wandering blaze running from the star on his forehead. It was very uneven, and the judges would think he was tilting his head in the dressage test. He was a class horse, standing nearly 16.3 hh with good enough conformation to be near the top in county lightweight hunter classes. The only fault I could spot, beside the blaze, was that he could have a little more length of rein – a longer neck. But he had presence, the 'look at me' factor which was always a great asset.

I rode him and became more and more interested. He was a kind and co-operative horse, unspoilt and I judged that he would learn very quickly. He had natural balance in his turns even though he had no idea of how to curve around a corner. I asked to observe him galloping and could see that his raking stride would spell maximum bonus points on the steeplechase and cross-country. He had a long striding trot that promised good extension and a light and airy canter. He was known as Jolly and Ted wrote out a cheque and he was mine. He would be renamed High and Dry for his eventing career.

Then I had possibly the worst time in my life. It had become obvious that Bill was never going to come right. I realised that I had to face the fact that things could not go on as they were. Chips, my original High and Mighty had grown old and with a feeling of dread I realised that both he and Bill were going to have to be put down. With a heavy heart I made arrangements. The executioner came to Shenberrow with a big horsebox to take away the bodies. I shut the top door of Jolly's loosebox so he would not be upset by what was going to happen. I then insisted that neither horse should realise what was going to occur. The first body was to be covered with a large sheet before the second horse was done.

I was fighting hard to keep the tears at bay. Bill was first. I held his lead rope feeding him sugar cubes in the palm of my hand and he stood happily on the gravel. I stroked him as the man gently put the gun in position. There was a soft thud and he crumpled to the ground, dead. His body was covered by a big sheet in front of the truck. Next it was Chips' turn. I very nearly cried out, 'Stop!' I told myself it had to be and then the slight click, another thump, and he too dropped down dead. This was too much for me. I burst into tears and fled, sobbing my heart out. Vivian Eason had to take over. The man told her that he had to bleed the horses at once and she came in to tell me. I absolutely refused to allow him to bleed them and insisted that he take the bodies away intact.

So, life went on and I concentrated on Jolly and trained him to be a worthy successor to Chips and Bill. With both those there had been a fight to establish that I was the boss. Jolly was different - he was totally genuine and co-operative. He graduated on to show jumping and as he was six years old we were ready to compete in the lightweight hunter show classes, and then the working hunter classes where he would be j udged first as a show horse and then jump a quite demanding round of mostly rustic fences. We also competed in Grade C show jumping.

Ted kept his promise of buying me a horsebox and had one made by Vincents of Reading, the most exclusive firm in the business. I became the proud owner of a very high-class affair. It was finished externally in cream with a navy line running along the sides. There was space for storage over the cab. The floor was raised over the back wheels where I could spend my nights on a very thin mattress. There was also a light over the horses' stalls and another in my part of the box. I would no longer need a torch when I wanted to read. Along the back wall there were two small gas rings for boiling a kettle, simple cooking and a drainer beside the little sink with a cold tap. I would be able to boil water and have a proper wash down before I wriggled into my sleeping bag at night. There was even a small refrigerator. And there was a full height cupboard for clothes, total bliss after my old horsebox where everything hung on hooks and the horses would occasionally sneeze all over the mackintoshes and coats.

Jolly was not nearly fit enough to do anything but be nursed around his first few events. After seven weeks work I took him to a BHS novice event with his white blaze carefully dyed blue-black with a product I had acquired through my London hairdresser. He produced a good dressage test just two points behind the leader, one fence down in the show jumping and no jumping penalties in the cross-country. We finished in 5th place out of 29 runners and I reckoned this to be something of a miracle with so short a time of training.

He continued to go well, and we qualified to enter Chatsworth. There were 61 horses qualified for these Novice Championships and of these 40 appeared to compete, including Princess Anne and Doublet, who was trained by Alison Oliver. The Queen, also attended the event to support her daughter and this added delight to the enormous crowd who were not to be put off attending just because the weather had turned nasty.

The day before the event began I decided to ride out and have some practice jumping into water. I looked for a bank where there was solid take-off and found that in the area near Queen Mary's Bower there was a suitable place. The river was very wide, and swift flowing, but I would turn and slow Jolly as soon as we landed in. The bottom was scattered with small stones which glinted and gleamed. I circled him on our approach and he seemed to think this was fun and he jumped up and outwards to land perfectly on the river bed. He took another stride and suddenly I felt we had lost a hind leg. The momentum sent us still further on and I felt a jerk. Jumping off I held Jolly's rein and stopped him. He was caught in a wire round his near-hind and I had a terrible time manoeuvring him backwards to loosen the pull and then picked up the hind leg with his head turned round to give him the longest rein length. By sheer luck I freed him, and we walked out of the river. I cursed myself for not seeing this wire and then realised that it had been tucked out of sight deliberately under the small stones. There was a high loud speaker not far away which would be broadcasting the commentary when the cross-country began the next day and this wire was part of the communications equipment.

I led Jolly back to the stables and a vet was summoned. He recommended that I poultice his leg and I spent a worried night dreading how stiff or lame he might be the next day. He was run up in the morning and miraculously he was sound.

After the dressage Princess Anne and Major James Templer with Off Centre were both on 25 penalty points. Bertie Hill riding Class Chips was on 29 as was Jolly. After a clear round in the show jumping we moved up into third position when Doublet had a jump down.

When we were counted down to start the cross-country Jolly felt keen to show everyone just how good he was, and we bounded over all the fences up the escarpment and negotiated the jump into space with a clever, controlled hop. Then we reached the ice pond. Water and yesterday's debacle must have been on his mind. Despite my urging, he refused. I turned him round and on the third attempt he leapt in easily, splashed through the pond and over the second post-and-rails. Several more fences and we were lining up on my chosen path to Queen Mary's Bower. I could feel Jolly's disbelief as I faced him to the moat. His fear of a repetition of yesterday's horrific shock was clearly uppermost in his mind and he stuck in his toes and stopped on the edge. The water must have looked very dark and deep and uninviting. He refused on the second attempt. I felt I could not bear the disgrace of elimination and I pushed him with all my strength and will and we virtually slithered into the water and landed safely in the bottom of the moat. A clean leap upwards and we were back safe on dry land. Jolly had no objection to the remaining fences and we jumped the final obstacle, an upright white gate, with a large army of enthusiastic spectators held back on either side by posts and ropes

117

keeping the route clear for competitors and we were galloping on through the finishing flags.

The press had soon learnt that Gamble had been caught by wire in the river the day before the Chatsworth Trials began, and that I had had to wait overnight to hear from the vet whether or not his hind leg would have recovered enough to allow him to run. They had noted how close this very novice six-year-old was to the leaders after the dressage test, plus the fact that he produced one of the few clear rounds in the show jumping. It did not take much understanding on their part to appreciate that after his experience the day before he had not been keen to jump into water. Michael Williams for *The Sporting Life* wrote:

> *"Fourteen horses refused at Queen Mary's Bower, some of them more than once, and two were eliminated for refusing three times. It was here that Judy Bradwell had a fall on Just Jack and Sheila Willcox had two refusals on High and Dry who had also stopped at the ice pond. But for High and Dry, there was every excuse. He had had a most unfortunate experience at Chatsworth the previous day, when Miss Willcox was practising jumping into the river. As he was about to take off, his legs became entangled in some communications wire that had been left hidden in the river, and he was very nearly brought down. This must surely have undermined his confidence, and it can hardly have been a coincidence that his three stops the next day were all at the water. I feel sure that this big, black six-year-old will play a promising part in next season's Horse Trials."*

I had entered Jolly in the intermediate at Downlands and I was on my way there when I bumped the top of the horsebox and ripped the bulkhead on the overhang in a petrol station. Jolly lurched backwards and forwards in his partition. I looked at the damage and it was like a jagged, open sardine tin with the storage space over the cab open to the weather, undoubtedly sending a cold stream of air over Jolly's hindquarters. I stuffed up the hole with blankets and hoped for the best.

The next day, Jolly and I practised our dressage movements as close to the arenas as was permitted. Jolly produced an excellent test to go into the lead with 24 points. In the show jumping I was thrilled when

118

he performed a classic clear round. On the cross-country, approaching the fourth fence he was enjoying himself so much that he forgot to wait for my signal to take off. Supremely confident, he said to himself, 'This is easy' and jumped a stride too early. His hind legs caught the far rails of the rough wooden fence and brought us down - 60 penalties. I jumped up, unhurt, and as Jolly scrambled to his feet and stood there, shaken, it became obvious as soon as I asked him to move that apart from the cuts and scrapes on all four legs, his off-hind was very sore.

The vet treated him and advised me to get him back home as soon as possible. All four legs were poulticed, the gap on the front of the horsebox was packed to keep out the cold wind. Jolly was diagnosed with superficial bruising of the stifle joint and he went out to the field for a rest.

Chapter Thirteen – A New Horse

Fate then played a hand. In Saturday's *Horse and Hound* there was a big advertisement advising that Hugh Sumner's steeplechasers were going to be auctioned off at the next Ascot sales. I remembered Mr Sumner as an owner of top hunters years ago in the show ring, around the time of Robert Orssich.

The advert said that the horses were to be seen at Major Holliday's training yard near Droitwich, which was not too far away. Keith and I made an appointment to view them. This cheered me up. Keith had looked up the form for each horse in his book and my job was to assess their soundness as best I could and to decide whether or not I thought they had the talent and suitable nature which would make a top eventer. I walked into the yard and stood quietly looking at the horse from a side-on view and noting his reaction to a strange person. I then asked the stable boy to move the horse over, so I could see the other side. I looked at the horse's conformation, the way his neck was set on his shoulders and the length of his back.

Eventually the last but one stable door was opened for me to inspect a horse called Ambassador's Gamble. The horse's quarters faced me and then a head with a wide, intelligent brow turned around and gazed at me intently. Something passed between us and nothing like this had ever happened to me before. I was to return the next day to ride the five possibles we had picked out.

They were steeplechasers and had never had a dressage lesson in their lives, but all I wanted was to feel whether or not their racing had spoiled the horse's naturally soft mouth. After that, I had to discover how well the saddle sat behind the withers, how each horse reacted to my asking him to show me how naturally well-balanced he was on a circle, how his paces were, and whether or not he was able to show any natural extension at the trot and to what extent I might be able to improve this. None of them had a soft mouth. But they would all be trainable, once they had forgotten they had jumped on the racecourse and learned new ways of going.

The day of the sale arrived and the advert in *Horse and Hound* had drawn a good crowd. Many of the horses would probably sell for more than Keith's one thousand pounds. Most of the horses went for a good lot higher but then it was time for Ambassador's Gamble and Keith won the bid at nine hundred and twenty-five guineas. He was ours and we dressed him in one of my bright blue competition rugs, edged with navy, and the initials SMW on both sides. He walked up the ramp and into the box without hesitation. Soon we were going to be doing battle to see who was boss.

I decided to rename him as Here and Now, and Gamble was his stable name. I began to educate him, first doing some dressage. He was a very good-looking horse with a lot of presence, but his extended trot would never be in the same flamboyant class as that of Jolly's, but his paces at walk, trot and canter were regular and straight. I was confident that by the time the autumn season opened we would be competing in the novice events.

In May Jolly was declared sound enough to begin work. What a relief this was. If my luck had changed then I would now have two horses on which to compete when the eventing season opened on the 25th July.

In the meantime, I entered Gamble in some showing classes. We went to Woodstock, in the grounds of Blenheim Palace and entered the working hunter class. The judge was the ex-jumping jockey, turned thriller writer, Dick Francis and he stood in the middle of the show ring and watched as the big class walked, then trotted and cantered and galloped round the ring. We were pulled in in third place. Our famous judge went up to the top of the line and began to study the outlook and conformation of each horse and to run a hand down the forelegs to check for lumps and bumps.

Then he commented to me that he knew my horse. I told him that he used to be Ambassador's Gamble and now he was going to be an eventer. He was intrigued and when he had ridden him and slipped out of the saddle he told me that Gamble had given him a very good ride. We jumped the rustic fences and he had one down and was moved up to second place.

We were then entered in the Foxhunter show jumping class and he must have decided that he had done enough for one day and when he was faced with a double of coloured and robust poles he refused twice. We retired, and I went back to the collecting ring and made him jump the practice jump several times. I drove home thinking that

121

we needed practice over good solid jumps, not fairly flimsy ones like mine. Gamble had to learn two lessons, first, that when I pointed him at something, he must obey me and jump the obstacle. Secondly, he had to make an effort to snap up his legs and clear the fence.

So, we had to rap him, meaning that a pulley rope was fitted to the supports at either side of a chosen fence at home and when this was pulled up as the horse jumped the rail carelessly, the pole knocked the hard part of his legs and the next time, unless the horse was very stupid, he made allowances and jumped higher. A few days earlier I had decided to rap Gamble's front legs over a show jump, and the invisible rising pole which his legs met just above the top of the jump had made a profound impression on him. Finally, he began to tuck up his legs carefully.

At about that time Mummy telephoned to say that she was going into Lytham hospital but was evasive as to the reason why. Always one who refused to make a fuss, she told me she would be there for a week or so and that she would be perfectly alright.

I made a detour on the way back from a Scottish tour and drove the horsebox in to the hospital. There must have been some quizzical looks from relatives visiting the patients that day. Mummy was lying down and looked pale as I was shown into her room. I felt a shudder of dread when I saw her. She did her best to take an interest in our Scottish tour, but I could see that it was too tiring for her to concentrate.

I told her how well the horses had performed, and how proud of them I was, and that perhaps, at last, I might make the Olympic Team and ride for Great Britain in the 1972 Games at Munich. Understandably, this sent her to sleep, and I went out in search of the nurse. I asked her what was the matter, and she told me that Mummy had been to see a cancer specialist in Manchester who coldly broke the news to her that her condition might be terminal. Now, she was having treatment to combat it. I was horrified. I knew that all her life she had been afraid of cancer, why, she had never told me. But it was one of the things she mentioned when Daddy had gone to his Green Drive Club in the evenings and she and I were in front of the fire at home, before I was married.

She left the hospital on 7th September, but the disease progressed, and she was back again on the 22nd. On 3rd October a specialist went to see her, and they said that the cancer had spread to the lymph glands. It seemed that there was nothing they could do to stop the progression of this enemy within. It was dreadful seeing her begin to waste away, but her fingernails grew beautifully, and she showed them to me proudly, saying that this was the first time in her life that she had been able to have long nails. She had bought a wig for the time when her hair might fall out and made me promise to see that when she was put in her coffin it was to be on her head. I burst into tears.

It was as if I had two lives. The horses needed me, and they took up a lot of time. They also needed to travel for practice over proper cross-country fences, for Shenberrow and Stanton had none of these facilities. It all took time and it was very exhausting.

In September Gamble and I were off to Stokenchurch and it was our first time in an open intermediate class with many of the experienced open horses. We notched up a very good dressage test and had one fence down in the show jumping. Then we were setting off at a fast pace on the cross-country. Everything went well until we came to jump some rails into shallow water. He refused – 20 penalties – I turned him round and rode him very determinedly at it again and could not believe that he refused a second time. It was our last chance and I turned him for another and he refused three times and we were eliminated. I had to walk away in disgrace, furious at Gamble.

I came to the conclusion that Gamble had decided to revert to having his own way that it was he who would henceforth decide whether or not he felt like trying. But if he thought that I was going to put up with a situation like that, then he had made a grave mistake.

I went to the secretary's tent to ask if I might be allowed to go back to this fence when the last competitor had finished the course. I was given permission and went to the fence before the judges left at the end of their day. Everyone else would be occupied with the prize giving. I rode him directly into the pond, so that he knew it was only shallow and perfectly safe. Then we walked and trotted and cantered through it, with me making a fuss of him. I rode him up to the fence from the take-off side and then the landing side and we progressed out of the pond on the line we would have taken towards the next fence had we not been eliminated. This time he had no excuse to

123

stop. He knew that the grass and the turns were safe, the post-and-rails into the water was not high and the water itself was only shallow. I also took him well back on the approach path, with its high trees on either side, turning left through the open gate as the track gave way to grass, then the right turn and a straight line up for the few strides before he was to jump the rails into what he knew was a safe pond. In my opinion, he now had no legitimate reason for refusing to jump.

I told the jump judges that I was ready to start and would come galloping down the path just as if I were in the competition. Away I went, a long way back up the track and I turned around, as if at the start, and called out a countdown which all my horses loved. We came to the opening on the green sward at balanced speed. Through the gateway, turning left, then right to face the rails and water. It felt as if he were going to jump but at the last second, he dug in his toes and we came to an abrupt halt. I had warned my helpers that I would have to hit Gamble if he misbehaved, and my short whip went quickly from one side to the other, striking him just behind my legs. I growled at him and held him facing the water.

"You totally ghastly horse," I said. I turned him round and tried again. He came to another propping halt and I hit him. The third time he did not want to go near so I had to ask my helpers to get behind and shoo him forward, but Gamble just laughed at this until I suggested they break off the bottom branches on the edge of the pasture field and run up behind us. Unfortunately, Gamble was faster on his four legs than they were on two and he carted me past the fence. It then got nasty, and I had to think what was the best way of dealing with this equivalent of a fight to the death. Gamble was trying to run away, and the winner of this battle was going to be boss from now on. I could not, must not allow Gamble to emerge the victor. By now I was bright red in the face from all my pushing efforts and Gamble was sweating and steaming. I decided to really call his bluff. I rode back to the take-off side of the rails and let him touch the fence with his nose. I walked him round the edge of the pond and through it to the other side so that he knew it was neither deep nor nasty. I rode him back through the open gate towards the previous fence for another good long run back at speed, but he tripped over a root on the woodland track and both of us went wallop on the hard ground. I got up, and climbed into an extremely slippery saddle, determined he

124

should jump that straightforward rail into the pond if I had to carry him over it.

We set off again, through the open gate, turning left, turning right, meeting the rails with the water on the other side, and after a hint of hesitation where I managed one flick of the whip he decided to jump, and we were in the pond and splashing our way out. I slowed him down, stopped, all the time telling him how good he was, such a clever boy, whilst both of us panted away. My two helpers were so relieved that it was now all over, but I told them I had to be sure and that although I, too, was exhausted, I was going to jump the rails and water again. For only then would I know that Gamble had given me his best and he would think twice before ever refusing again.

When both he and I had stopped puffing, we went back up the track and turned. This time he jumped the rails perfectly and I told him what a good chap he was, stroking him and giving him sugar lumps. I then thanked our two fence judges for their help, apologised for the fact of it being such a marathon, saying that without this lesson I would never have been able to trust Gamble not to refuse on the cross-country.

Many years later Edward P., who was one of the throng gathered over at the prize giving, had been very critical of my determination to teach my horse a lesson, even though they were the only people vaguely conscious of what was going on, and unable to see clearly as both fence and water were out of plain sight under the trees. For my part, I do not know how anyone with any knowledge of horses could criticise me for making clear to Gamble that I would not tolerate refusals at a comparatively simple fence. He was by no means being over-faced, he was simply being naughty, and he had to understand that I could not keep a horse in the luxury those at Shenberrow enjoyed if he was not prepared to demonstrate his undoubted talent as a brilliant jumper. Perhaps these critics had far more money than me, and would not mind if their horse behaved as Gamble had done, refusing to jump a straightforward fence, one for which he had been taken round the country especially to learn about jumping into water. Perhaps they would pat him and say, 'Never mind,' knowing that they had others to take his place and he could do another job. My horse had not been in the least bit frightened, he had just decided he did not feel like co-operating on this particular afternoon. A decision which, as he found out, had its price. It certainly taught Gamble a lesson, and never again did he think seriously of refusing with me in the saddle. I always rated him as my best ever cross-country horse for he had character as well as looks and a huge talent for all the facets of three-day-eventing.

Although I understood horses I am not so sure that I was always cognisant of my own behaviour. Looking back, after all these years, I realise that there can be little doubt that the issues with Keith were bound to affect my riding, even though I would have denied it at the time. I had been so sure that I was capable of balancing both loves of my life, Keith and the horses. Then Mummy was dying by inches and I railed at God, asking him why such a good person should have to suffer like this. I began to wish that she would die and be free of all this suffering. I watched her shrinking away before my eyes.

I had told Ted about my mother's approaching death, and he was kind, telephoning for news and saying he would do anything to help. He brought me pheasants, wild duck and teal which he had shot to keep up my strength, but I became more and more tired, and Cherry renewed her efforts with her pendulum and pills to make me strong again.

My mother came out of hospital for two weeks, but the cancer was progressing. The pain had moved to the top of her left leg. Mr Charnley from the Hip Centre at Wrightington Hospital near Wigan produced a steel circlet covered in soft leather which encompassed the top of her left leg and the circlet, covered in soft leather, was anchored to the iron supports of the hospital bed. I was even more horrified, it was diabolical and begged Dr Glynn to find out if there was an alternative. She had to spend the rest of her life tied down, not even able to shift her weight.

Meanwhile Jolly and Gamble were fit and well and the end to the eventing season was in sight. They were both ready to go to Chatsworth in the intermediate and advanced classes. I had great hopes for Jolly at Chatsworth. Both of them produced very good dressage tests and reasonable show jumping rounds. Then in the cross-country Gamble had a rotational fall and I was catapulted upwards and outwards. I was unconscious and then when I came to I made no sense. I was concussed. By the next day I was back to normal and still at Chatsworth decided that Gamble and I must finish the course, miraculously there was not a scratch on him after the fall the day before.

As soon as I got back to Shenberrow I shot up the motorway to Lytham Hospital. Mummy was dying by inches and I felt it to be so cruel, we would never let this happen to an animal. I talked to Dr Glynn who was also a Roman Catholic and he said that everything was in God's hands and that all he could do was to ensure that she had as little pain as possible while the cancer continued to invade her. She lasted until the 24th January 1971, although she had not been really conscious of what was going on for some time. The funeral took place with a Requiem Mass being said at our Catholic church in Lytham, followed by the internment of ashes at Ansdell Crematorium and the placement in an urn next to those of Daddy. Life was never going to be the same again.

Chapter Fourteen – My Last Three-Day Event

After the new year in 1971 I was deeply depressed and liable to burst into tears at any moment. Jolly had had a mystery illness for a while which was very worrying. Then we discovered it was due to liver fluke that had come through sheep grazing in the field. He was treated for this and recovered and by the time we were due to go to Tidworth both horses were very fit, and I was planning to go for maximum bonus points for speed. It was going to be very important for me as far as showing the selectors the leaps and bounds we had made recently. I could not manage alone with both Jolly and Gamble, so Alison was coming with us to act as groom. She was to sleep in the horsebox, parked next to our allotted looseboxes in Everleigh, and I would stay in a guest house not far from Tidworth.

After the dressage phase Jolly went into first place with 70.5 marks, and Gamble was 9th on 89. This meant Gamble was nearly 19 marks behind the leader, which was the equivalent of one refusal or one run out on the cross-country. Everything boded well for the next day. Gamble was due to start the first roads and tracks at 1.34 pm and Jolly exactly two hours later. We set off on the first roads and tracks of just under four miles in phase A. Passing through that finish marker, he saw the steeplechase fences and I stroked him and told him that there was no one else around to bump him, thinking he might remember his former career as a steeplechaser. I remember how he felt confident and trusting and clever as a cat. We had gained maximum bonus points and he had been very fast. We galloped in towards the H fence, as I called it, with the stream running beneath the single airy rail and the bad ground approach. I gave him a good look at it as we galloped towards the stream, with my legs wrapped tightly round him squeezing him onwards, my body steady and secure in the saddle and my determination that we should jump out of our stride made manifest to him. A photographer caught us in mid-flight and his picture is the epitome of how to jump a big fence. It showed determination on my part, with no restricting interference with the horse's mouth, weight distributed forwards.

Next it was Jolly's turn. We set off on the first roads and tracks, trotting along happily watching the kilometre posts to make sure we were on time. Arriving there I saw Vivian Eason and Nat Tollit waiting for us, and Vivian checked Jolly's girth before the starter called us in. Away we shot towards the first birch fence with Jolly full of enthusiasm. Just like Gamble, he jumped out of his stride without the semblance of a mistake and we passed through the finish posts and began to slow down so that both of us could take a breather. He was really enjoying himself and I checked my stopwatch and we had done what I had intended and earned maximum bonus points.

I sat light and still on Jolly until his breathing returned to normal, and then we picked up speed to cadenced trot alternating with soft canter until I was sure that we were on time according to the calculations, and then we proceeded at a steady trot until we came in sight of the box. The ground jury saw us coming again and called 'passed' as we drew level with them, and I smiled my thanks. Alison was waiting. I jumped off, and we went into our refreshing mode. Jolly was washed down, everything was checked, and by the time Alison legged me up into the saddle he was ready to face the cross-country. I reckoned that with his longer stride, he should finish with maximum bonus points, when Gamble had been so close to his time. Jolly was also far more experienced over these bigger advanced fences than Gamble. I was looking forward to my ride .

We were counted down. Jolly was keen to go, and I heard the starter say, 'Good luck' as we shot forward to jump the first fence, a rail positioned above a wide log. We sailed over it and I said, 'Good boy' as we landed. The second fence was the palisade, again a beautiful jump. Then the sleeper table which he simply flew, hugely enjoying himself and the trakhener, again out of his stride. In front of us was the challenging silage pit with its deep and wide ditch gaping at the bottom, followed by two or three strides before being confronted with a starkly upright revetted bank where we must find great impulsion, coupled with control, to be able to produce the energy and athleticism necessary to produce first a clean jump on to the bank, then take one rounded stride before take-off to clear the rail and land safely over the drop. There was a big crowd at this fence, a sure sign that everyone expected there to be trouble here in the form of refusals and probably falls. Jolly did not know this and he, like Gamble earlier, listened to my instructions as we came over the edge of the silage pit and he suddenly saw the uninviting wide and gaping hole. I closed my legs on him and held him straight. He responded immediately.

129

Our impulsion took us over the ditch in a big jump. Two strides up, and we were out of the pit and back on level ground again.

Jolly was a very obedient horse and he answered my aids, hands and body directing his route, moving forwards on a good striding pattern. He leapt up onto the bank like a cat, took one short stride and with my body poised to go with him over the rail with its drop so that I did not interfere with his mouth, he took off in a perfect curve to land safely and easily on the grass below. There was a spontaneous burst of applause from the spectators as we set off across the field to the next fence.

This was a stout hedge with two wide planks set horizontally across it on the approach side, and Jolly jumped it perfectly out of his stride. We landed in the next field, turning right to proceed on a straight line of approach and galloped on with the ground sloping slightly downhill to the next fence, parallel rails, some way away. A straightforward fence, but still to be respected. As we came in I realised that we were wrong, but Jolly's gallop was long striding and I made the decision to take off half a stride early. Jolly, out of character, ignored me and took another, and fatal, late stride. This brought him in close up to the fixed and totally unforgiving fence. As we left the ground, fast and too late, there was a splintering crash. On the way up, Jolly's forearms above his knees struck the fence hard. The world turned around as we began to somersault. 'Blast!' I thought as I felt myself literally flying through the air horizontally, 'Sixty penalties, that's done it!' I hit the ground head first at around 25 miles per hour.

Coming out of the blackness, I lifted my head. There was blood all over the ground in front of my face. I was mesmerised by the intricacy of the patterns being formed. Blood seeped over and through the thick layer of grass. Bright droplets stuck to the top leaves, and paler reds showed through as the blood settled into the layers beneath.

Suddenly, it dawned on me that I was at a competition and I must get back on the horse immediately to continue. I tried to get up. Nothing happened. I tried again. Still, nothing. I didn't panic. I just realised I was paralysed. Life was never going to be the same again. My mind dissolved into blackness.

Time passed. I was oblivious to it. Then, faintly, I became aware of a man's voice. He was swearing loudly at someone. I looked upwards and to both sides and realised I was in an ambulance. I was flat on my back on some sort of stretcher. The voice continued to rail at the driver as we bumped and swayed over the uneven ground. The vehicle jolted badly, and I hurt. There was another further tirade from the man with the voice. I simply gave up and faded once more into unconsciousness.

Thankfully, I was totally unaware of the rest of the journey and I have no recollection whatsoever of our arrival at the Tidworth Military Hospital where I was unloaded, wheeled inside and placed flat on a bed to await the inspection team and the x-ray machine. In those days, there was no such thing as a MRI scanner and no neck collar which is fitted immediately to anyone suspected of possible spinal injuries. Nowadays, a helicopter with paramedics stands ready at all major three-day-events, and fence judges are warned to allow nobody to move the body until the medicos arrive.

I woke up to find myself flat on my back on a bed. Looking to either side I reckoned I must be in some sort of holding ward. I could see a curtained partition and hear a girl moaning, wailing and crying out for attention. I recognised her voice as a fellow competitor at the Tidworth Three-Day Event, and I wondered what on earth could be the matter with her before drifting into unconsciousness for a fourth time. When next I opened my eyes, there were four faces looking down at me, and a big machine poised overhead.

A male voice enquired – "What is your name?" I automatically told him.

"Where are you?" he asked.

"In hospital," I replied.

"What were you doing today?"

"Competing at the Tidworth Three-Day Event".

This seemed to satisfy them that I was *compos mentis*, and probably not concussed. They proceeded, and the doctor in charge told me they had to remove all my clothes without moving me. They managed to cut me out of my outfit and the tears rolled down my face.

131

The next thing to endure was the x-raying. I was manoeuvred under the machine and pictures were taken of my spine. Then the doctor told me it was all over and gave me an injection. I felt the stab of a needle in my arm and then nothingness.

When I came to a doctor was standing beside me. He told me that the fifth and sixth vertebrae of my thoracic spine had been shifted inwards from the force of impact and were out of alignment, part of one of the vertebrae had broken off. These injuries meant that the spinal cord itself, instead of running freely down the entire spine was forced to make a detour inwards to the dislodged T5, down through T6 and then back sideways and outside to T7. The cord was rubbing and catching first at the point of exit at T4, again as it stretched into T5, again as it emerged from T6 and yet again as it met T7. The cord itself was damaged, and in turn I was paralysed. He then told me that they were sending me to Stoke Mandeville, which was renowned for its treatment of paraplegics. I felt sick. I was utterly appalled at the very thought of it. The doctor then asked whom he should contact for me and, here I faced a dilemma. I could not contact Keith at his home and he would not be in his office as it was the weekend; I was divorced and both my parents were dead; and I was not close to my brother who lived in Yorkshire.

I was shocked absolutely rigid. What I had taken in immediately was bad enough, but the situation was an absolute disaster. What to do about the horses? What about Shaun, my border collie? Thoughts piled one on top of the other. How on earth could I cope financially if I could not walk? Worst of all, how could this affect Keith and our relationship? It is one thing to be deeply involved with an attractive, athletic and vibrant woman, who happens to be very much in love with you. It would be an entirely different situation to be landed with a paraplegic instead.

I floated in a twilight land. Intruding, the doctor was back again. He reported that Stoke Mandeville could not have me for another 36 hours, but they had succeeded in finding a bed for me at Frenchay, a hospital on the outskirts of Bristol. The Neuro-Surgical Unit would accept me the next morning. Left alone, I meditated on all this for a while, and then a nurse appeared beside me to say that I had two visitors.

By this time, I felt totally exhausted and decidedly dopey, but I was glad to see Tom and Rosemary Greenhalgh. They had been among the first people, other than the two fence judges, to arrive at the spot where I crashed into the ground some 20 metres further on from the parallel bars. Tom and Rosemary had been watching at the previous fence and had seen Jolly negotiate the three difficult elements with tremendous aplomb. As soon as they realised we had fallen they had rushed into the next field and joined the fence judge's wife to stand over my body as I lay inert on the cross-country course. Tom and Rosemary had remained there until the ambulance arrived and I was eventually carted off.

Vivian Eason and Nat Tollit visited and explained exactly what had happened in my fall. I was famed for my stickability and I had remained in the saddle, limpet-like, until Jolly's back was at right angles to the ground, then my grip on the saddle failed and I was literally catapulted along a line horizontal with the field but with gravity taking me downwards. Had I been thrown out of the saddle earlier I would have flown through the air and landed beyond the horse. What had actually happened had produced the most disastrous of results.

They reassured me that Gamble, Jolly, and Shaun were all being looked after, and this set my mind at rest. Vivian would also speak to Keith. Throughout that evening and night, I lay immobile on my back. It was as if the whole world had closed in on me. My body was dead. I had no movement except from my arms upwards. My mind was working overtime and exhausting me. Although, I was not suffering a great deal of physical pain, I lay there in a state of dread and suspense until it was morning.

Then I began to register the smell of breakfast cooking - bacon. But not for me. I remained utterly disinterested in food of any sort. A nurse came to wash me and told me that she would be accompanying me by ambulance to Frenchay. Three men positioned themselves around me and lifted me, apparently it was imperative that my back remain absolutely flat. Then I felt the first stabs of excruciating pain. They placed me in the stretcher and then gently ferried me along corridors to an ambulance. The journey was very long and every time the ambulance came to a halt and then started again I was in total agony. The nurse sat opposite and tried to encourage me. I gritted my teeth, thinking all the time, 'Soon this must be over'.

133

Finally, we arrived and again I was wheeled around corridors at a rate of knots. The lights in the ceilings blurred and hurt my eyes, and I began to feel dizzy. Then real pain began to strike. I thought that I had been hurting beforehand but that was a breeze compared to what was hitting me now. We arrived at a giant x-ray room and by then I did not know what to do about the pain. Normally, one's first reaction is to twist and turn and try to find some relief with a change of posture. I could not even twitch my toes and the realisation of my inability to move was overwhelming. For the first time I began to take in the enormity of being paralysed. I began to panic. Finally, the x-ray pictures were taken and at last I was given a deep pain killing injection which mercifully knocked me out.

Slowly I came back into a state of awareness and found myself parked at the approach end of a very large white ward. I could clearly hear sounds of a struggle coming from the room nearest to me and I heard a nurse say urgently to her colleague, "Sit on her quickly, while I give her the injection." There was silence and two nurses came out. I asked what had happened and they told me, "Don't worry. The lady was a little disturbed, but she is alright now." I felt this was a first-class example of understatement.

The nurses went away, and all was quiet. I lay supine gazing either at the ceiling or at the blank face of the side walls. Suddenly, one of the doors began to open inch by inch. A face peered out, with hair distinctly dishevelled. Eyes looked hard at me, and I was momentarily terrified. It flashed through my mind that the woman was probably mental. Perhaps I had somehow ended up in the lunatic asylum and there was no way I could get away. I didn't shout for help. The woman gazed at me unblinkingly from the door and I shut my eyes tight. Then there was a shout, I opened one eye and the woman was creeping up the ward and one of the nurses saw her and called out. The woman turned and shot back to her room. Then there was the sound of a window being pushed open, followed by a loud thump and a cry. Somehow the woman had managed to climb through the window and had fallen on to the grass outside. She was rescued and returned to her room.

Later, the consultant and one of the nurses were discussing what to do with me. Apparently, most patients like to be on a ward for some company, but I had a pathological fear of people seeing me when I was ill. I begged them to put me in a room by myself. They decided to humour me and put me in the room where the mad woman had jumped out of the window as she had been taken away.

I was terrified at the thought of my immobility and I asked the consultant, Huw Griffiths, what was wrong with me. He confirmed that my back was broken, and I was paralysed. I would have to remain there for some time. He did not add, that he believed that I would never walk again.

I was given an injection and a button to press if the pain came back. I was told that there was no point in trying to withstand the pain. From that moment I hung on to the button as if it was my only lifeline. In the end Sister Ronikle pinned it to the sheet.

I remembered Rosemary Russell who had become a paraplegic through a riding accident. The horse was walking, and she had pitched forward onto her head. Her husband, Lord Hugh Russell had taken her home and they had installed every type of machine and aid. She even had an adapted Mini Moke on which she could speed around the estate and also go to events. So, her life had gone on. But I was on my own. With very little money, my income was dependent on winning prize money. Although I had been with Keith for four and a half years he was still married and living with his wife, I could not depend on him standing by me. I believed in our mutual love, but other friends had thought he was just using me as a convenience. I was no longer going to be at all convenient!

But I was wrong. He did stand by me. As soon as he knew what had happened he went to Stanton and made sure that everything was sorted in my absence. From there he drove to Bristol and at last was shown in to my room. By now my black eyes were at their worst and my upper lip swollen and misshapen. I felt awful and looked awful. I had a black and blue face, immobile body, a cage from knees down and a catheter bag suspended under the bed. He assured me that everything had been organised at home. The horses were alright staying at Stanway and Shaun was perfectly happy with Vivian Eason.

Then Keith, who was not normally a demonstrative person, except in bed, did something entirely out of character but which showed me how much he cared and the deep compassion he felt inside. He came around to the side of the bed and miraculously managed to balance very precariously on it alongside me. He put an arm over me and kissed my ugly face.

During the next few days I continued flat on my back for a two-hour period, then three nurses would come in and turn me to the right. After two hours they would return and turn me to the left, and in another two hours I would be returned again to being flat on my back. I couldn't eat but I had to drink at least three pints of liquid a day. I had a plastic container with a spout and I could manage small mouthfuls, but a lot spilt onto the sheets.

Every morning Mr Griffiths came with various other doctors or students. They would look down on me. They told me that if the paralysis lessened then it would be my toes that would be able to move first. They would stick a pin in me in various places and I had to say whether it was the spiky or the blunt end. The sensation of feeling was very blurred, and any touch felt as if it came through several layers of cotton wool. It was impossible to say whether or not someone had laid a hand upon me. After that he would ask me to wriggle my toes as hard as I could, first on my left leg, then on the right. I could not see as far as the bottom of the bed, but I could see all the faces and the reactions upon them. I would concentrate with all my strength and willpower, sending the strongest message from my brain, telling my foot to jolly well wriggle my toes. I was sure the results would be a veritable explosion of activity down there, but from the unflickering gaze of the onlookers I would know that I had failed. The message from my brain could not get through. This continued for days and days until it became weeks with neither foot having shown the slightest sign of a response. I became very despondent.

At first, I took little interest in my surroundings and floated through that first week on a cloud of unconcern. I was awakened into full consciousness of my situation only when the first signs of returning life appeared. My body from the armpits down, simply did not belong to me anymore. I lay completely inert and unable to move an inch. Then, slowly, I had become aware of a crushing, vice-like grip. It encircled my chest as if a steel band had been fitted to me and then pulled frighteningly tight. This was at the actual seat of the injury, T5 and T6, and the choking band was in fact encompassing my ribs where they joined the crushed vertebrae. Luckily, at this time, I had no idea that this band of pain would remain with me forever, sometimes to an acceptable degree, at others reducing me to tears. Huw Griffith and the staff were pleased when I told them of this pain. To them it meant that I could now feel something which, in the overall context, was more hopeful. I, on the other hand, was rather less enthusiastic.

I remained a prisoner in my narrow bed, immobile downwards from my armpits, outwardly cheerful and co-operating with the nurses, but inside terrified of the paralysis and desperately afraid for the future. I had to submit to the daily life of the hospital and accept that I must try to do everything I was asked. In my real life I had never taken kindly to being ordered about and my spontaneous reaction would be to get awkward on principle and take an alternative course if at all possible. I had to learn that I had no jurisdiction over what should be done to me and the quicker I accepted this, the easier it would be for me.

Then one day, as usual, in came Huw Griffith and his entourage and I was asked to move firstly, the toes on my left foot, and then the toes on my right. Trying to move my left one, I must have nearly burst a blood vessel. I could tell immediately that something had happened. All the faces were smiling, and Huw Griffiths said, "You've done it". Someone went off to find a long, tall looking-glass so that I would be able to see as far as my feet. This was set at an angle to give me a view of my left foot where it was propped up against the iron bar at the end of the bed. I went red in the face with the effort of producing the result. All I saw was the tiniest flicker of my big toe. I was hugely disappointed, but Huw explained that even this feeble movement meant that there was still a connection between the signal from my brain and the nerves, and this would have to be built on, day by day. We tried the right foot to see if it produced the same result, but there was no sign of contact.

Eventually, I managed to move my left leg, drawing up my knee so that I could see the bump appearing in my line of vision. I was truly thrilled with this achievement and I practised for hours in my efforts to keep it in the knees up position. Sometimes I tried to gently lower it, instead of moving slowly back it would take a sideways diversion and immediately fall clean out of bed. Nothing I could do would fetch it back from there and ultimately, I would have to ring my emergency bell to have the leg rescued.

My body was now a stranger to me. Although I knew I was laying on my back on a bed it felt as if the backs of my thighs were draped over a log. This feeling was extraordinarily vivid even to the point of imagining the texture of the log. I was beginning to worry about my inability to do more than move my legs slightly. The trunk of my body continued to be totally inanimate, an unresponsive and heavy hulk. I felt as I were chained down and despite all my efforts I could not get free. Just as in childish nightmares I had a recurring fear. I imagined that the hospital would catch fire or that there would be some other catastrophe. I was convinced that in the panic of getting everyone out I should be forgotten, and I could actually feel the total and abject despair of knowing I had no means of moving myself. I even allowed myself to believe I was in this situation in the hope that the rising panic would unlock whatever prevented me from using my legs. All in vain. The clear recognition of my total dependence on others made a profound impression on me and I was desperate to regain movement of my whole body.

Slowly, slowly the sensation of feeling crept back over my torso and the pain began to increase to an unimaginable degree. The necessity for pain killers became more acute and for one ghastly week I suffered from violent sickness and double vision as a side effect. The slightest movement made me want to vomit. I lay there trying not to move my head even a fraction, and I discovered that instead of one pipe running along the ceiling in line with my eyes, there were now two. Everything else, the doors, the bedside cupboard and even the nursing staff developed an identical twin by its side, and the sensation of sickness persisted. At last the attributive drug was isolated and its horrific administration halted. My double vision subsided, and the sickness left me. I kept peering at the corner of the ceiling for the peculiar shape and that was the last thing to disappear. The relief was overwhelming.

In the first week after my arrival the room became filled with flowers and cards. These came from friends, acquaintances and strangers alike. The reaction of so many people to my accident astonished and touched me, and I was grateful to them all for since I had been moved to Frenchay and they had bombarded the switchboard for information. Keith came to see me as often as he could and, inevitably we had to discuss what was to be done about the two horses. It was becoming perfectly obvious even to me after the first month I was in hospital that my eventing days were probably over. I tried very hard to accept this. Eventing is, after all, a dangerous sport and falls on the cross-country are part of the course. Whilst every rider recognises this as fact, I think we are all convinced that the terrible accident is not going to happen to us. To others, yes, possibly and there have been several fatalities to prove this point.

Keith kept making it abundantly clear that I would have to sell the two horses, and I had no alternative but to agree, but the very thought of it broke my heart. I had been so very close to fulfilling my life's ambition to compete in the Olympic Games. Never before had I had two horses to ride competitively at the same time with the qualities needed to win that gold medal – temperament, conformation, action, pace, stamina, soundness, speed, plus a terrific talent for cross-country – all these were theirs. Having to face that I must give up my horses just when all the portents had looked so good was almost more than I could bear.

It took some weeks before I could be persuaded to try to eat something. I had been surviving on fruit juices and orange squash. But I could not face hospital food, just the smell of it as the food trolleys rolled in was revolting. I arranged that my friends brought me in tins of food which were arranged on a little round table. I remember the joyful sense of achievement I felt once this little grocery and fruit store was established. I had made the first steps towards refusing to become hospitalised and I strived even harder to get better.

Keith would now visit one day a week, bringing luxurious little titbits of food to eat. I longed for his arrival for six days out of the seven and I existed from one visit to the next. I was desperate to be able to get up and walk again, I hated the thought of Keith being faced with a semi-invalid. I was told that I would be at Frenchay for another 12 weeks and in approximately eight weeks I would be slowly raised into a sitting position so that my spine would begin to be able to take my weight. It seemed a life sentence. Time passed so slowly, except when Keith was there. I always had the thought in the back of my mind that Keith would get bored with it all. I knew now that I would be very lucky to walk again.

I decided to advertise both horses in *Horse and Hound*. At that point sponsorship as exists today had not commenced and no-one had the money to buy a proven horse, not in Britain. So potential buyers must come from abroad. Within a week Klaus Wagner had flown over from West Germany and tried both horses. Jolly's freedom of movement and great stride appealed very much to Klaus and suited him admirably, and it transpired that he had decided to buy him before he had ridden 200 metres down the road from the stables. Gamble's shorter stride and more rounded action did not have the same instant appeal, but even so, he tried to take both horses at a lesser price. Keith accepted the offer for Jolly alone and within a week one beautiful horse was on his way to Germany. In the end he not only gave Klaus years of pleasure, but his three sons rode him, and he was a brilliant schoolmaster.

I tried to think of someone for Gamble and the only person I came up with was James Templer who had won Great Badminton in 1964 on M'lord Connolly. Keith contacted him, and he said he would be delighted to have Gamble at Colchester Barracks with him. We began to correspond as I explained how he should establish a rapport with the horse. I knew very well that for some time Gamble would feel wooden, unresponsive and choppy in his action whilst he was adjusting to his new rider. He did not like change and would inevitably resent it, and if James did not appreciate these quirks there would be no hope of producing a new partnership. All was agreed, and Gamble was driven to the army barracks where James was stationed.

I worried about Gamble, how would he feel at being bundled off to an unknown place and a new rider. Gamble did take his time to settle in. But after three weeks James realised what a wonderful horse he was, and they both began to prepare enthusiastically for the autumn season.

Then out of the blue the Italian Federation contacted me, because a personal friend Countess Dora von Tepper-Laski asked me how much for Gamble. She had recommended him to the Marchese Fabio Mangilli, the head of the Italian Federation. He wanted several members of the Italian team to try the horse when they were in England for the European Championships at Burghley. I had to contact James with this unwelcome news, but we had previously agreed that if this happened he would receive compensation for the work he had done on the horse. They came and rode him and were thrilled and agreed to the full asking price. Gamble went to Italy and was never heard of again. So, my accident had not only destroyed my competition career, it had also wrecked Gamble's future.

After Gamble had been sold I had nothing to distract me, I had to remain in hospital for a very long time. There were no mobile phones in 1971 so I was cut off from the outside world. I could only concentrate on forcing my body to walk again and somewhere deep inside I knew that I would be able to.

Chapter Fifteen – Learning To Walk Again

I was such an independent person, and I had never found it easy to surrender to the will of others. Now, I recognised that the best way to survive in hospital was to submit to institutionalisation. My innate fastidiousness was revolted by the catheter and the way I was treated as just another body in a line. The shame and embarrassment of my incontinence was almost overwhelming.

As some signs of life returned to my body I was sent to physio. I found that I mysteriously had gained a third leg. The first and second knees were in their normal places, but I felt a third one somewhere in the middle. Every time I tried to draw up my knees and keep them together it felt as if a third one was in the way to prevent them from touching each other. They simply fell apart. I had lost all sensation on the insides of my thighs and knees and could not recognise the touch of one leg against the other.

I was hugely afraid that I would end up a paraplegic but little by little my left leg became stronger. The right leg continued to be sluggish, weak and unresponsive. Occasionally the nurses had time to wheel me out into the garden and it was amazing to be almost back in the 'real' world. Then the next step, I was being raised up, just a few inches extra a day until I was sitting up and the view was wonderful. Not only was I no longer looking at the ceiling, but I could look my visitors in the eye and I began to eat normally. I could even set and dry my hair all over properly and apply some eye makeup. Absolutely magic! At last I began to feel like a proper person again.

The next step was that I was manoeuvred into sitting on the edge of the bed with my legs dangling over the edge. I was utterly convinced that I should have no trouble walking and was immensely impatient to begin. I thought everyone was making a great fuss about nothing, and certainly, it did not enter my head for a moment that I should have any difficulty. At last the big moment came and flanked by a nurse on each side and Sister hovering round us, I was told to wriggle myself off the side of the bed down on to my feet. A hospital bed is much higher than an ordinary one and I thought that I had allowed for the extra drop as I departed off the side. It was like judging a drop fence but this time I hit the floor far sooner than I had imagined and but for the catching skills of the two nurses, I would have collapsed straight down to the floor. Having met the floor, my feet and legs did not respond with the natural reaction of righting my balance. My feet stayed on the ground and my body lurched forwards. The nurses straightened me up. It felt most peculiar to be standing on my feet, which appeared to be rooted to the ground. As soon as I attempted to straighten my back my whole body was wracked with violent muscle spasms. I felt as though it consisted only of angles, all the joints went rigid. It was as if they were screaming in indignation. I finally managed to move one foot forward, but only a tiny bit, and that took so much effort and concentration.

In the days following my first attempt to walk again I was out of bed practising my steps at every available opportunity and, in a week, I was allowed to get out of bed by myself, as long as I hung on to something solid and promised not to fall. I felt extremely unsafe standing up and had absolutely no intention of moving far from the support of either a wall or a piece of furniture. The whole process of trying to make my legs go forward and to keep standing up was very demanding, and it was complicated by the continuing attacks of muscle spasms which were almost unbearable in their intensity, bordering on viciousness. I constantly tried to walk, and I felt it would be possible if only I tried hard enough.

Then I was allowed another privilege. I could walk to my own wash basin and wash myself. I was absolutely thrilled. If someone had told me in my pre-fall days that in the future I would value beyond price the ability to wash myself in a basin, I would have thought it too ridiculous for words. Just the act alone of washing myself was a fairly hilarious procedure as my balance was far from reliable and I tended to lurch about the corner of the room in the process. But the main thing was that I was virtually looking after myself now, and it gave me an enormous amount of pleasure and a quiet sense of satisfaction.

Each day I tried to walk a little further. It could hardly be called walking as I hauled myself along, hanging on to the wall or anything where I could gain some sort of purchase, but all the time my right leg dragged along behind, literally. Nevertheless, I was becoming more and more independent. The right leg simply refused to work properly. It was terribly slow and hesitant and, despite all my efforts it could not, or would not, march with my left leg in two time. Neither knee nor ankle would flex properly, and I had to wing the legs sideways and outwards before it would go forwards, and even then, it could not manage a complete step.

I look back down the years and realised that I should have done a lot more work in the early days to make that right leg stride forward properly. As it was, I think everyone, including myself, was so surprised and, in some cases throwing it out to the side was accepted and allowed to become my modus operandi. I might be walking in an incorrect and ugly manner but at that time it was such a joy to be mobile. It was not until I wrote my training book, *The Event Horse*, and it was made into a film, that I saw myself on screen and was horrified. I did try then to get my right leg to move forward in a straight line, but I could not keep it up for more than two strides, and in the middle of what by then had become again a busy life, it was forgotten. I was surprisingly oblivious to the ugliness of my new gait.

So back in August 1971 my first thought was to find my own way to the toilets. I managed to get out of the ward and down the corridor and turned left. I found them, and they were pretty basic, but they looked good to me. I managed to use them and return to my bed in the side ward and I was utterly exhausted.

I set myself the goal of going on exploratory walks every day and going a little further every time. After a few days, having negotiated my way through the main part of the Neuro Ward I emerged onto another much wider corridor. Over time, I learnt the geography of all the corridors. Finally, I made my way to the telephone booth determined to make a private phone call. I dragged myself there to find a man in it. I managed to prop myself against the wall until he eventually finished. I went in and there was a seat. Armed with some money, I dialled Keith's number and he answered. We had a lovely private talk, somewhat different from all the previous occasions when there was no alternative but to use the telephone brought round the wards. I managed to get back to the ward afterwards on the point of collapse, but I made it.

Fourteen weeks after the fall at Tidworth, I left Frenchay for Stanton. Keith and Peggy Eagles brought some clothes for me for I had had no need of them in hospital. I was horrified to find that I could not do up the zip of my skirt, I had put on weight. Having always been so fit and slim all my life this was ghastly, and I was immediately determined to diet.

144

It was emotional to leave, and I said goodbye to different members of the staff. By the time we got to the carpark my legs were going weak with the excitement of going home at last. It took me a while to work out how to get into the back seat of Keith's car, then he got into the driving seat and we were off, destination home!

It felt extraordinarily strange and even a little frightening to be out in the wide world again and the car seemed to be going very fast. As we approached the village of Stanton at last, I looked at it with new eyes. I was much more aware of its beauty. The honey-coloured stone of the houses and cottages as we entered the village were sheer delight to the eye. Then finally, Shenberrow which looked as beautiful as ever, but the top doors of the looseboxes were tightly closed, and no horse head turned to look out enquiringly to see who had arrived.

I struggled out of the car with the help of Keith and Peggy. And I just wanted to stand and stare for a while, to take deep breaths and to gulp in the clean country air. I thought about how much there had been to look forward to when I had set off for Tidworth all those months ago. I had wanted to do well so that I could fight for a coveted place in the British Olympic Team at Munich. I had been quietly confident with my two horses, knowing that they were both Olympic prospects. I was a person who was utterly committed to winning. I did not agree with Pierre de Coubertin, who resurrected the Olympics in 1894 to prepare for the Athens Games in 1896. *"The important thing in the Olympic Games is not winning but taking part, for the essential thing in life is not so much conquering but fighting well."* The outlook for me to finally get to the Olympics had been so good. Now looking around me at Shenberrow, I had to face the inescapable reality that, for me, one era was irrevocably over.

The next morning things began to look a little better. I began to look forward to all that I might be able to do now that I was home. I heard a car swing round on the gravel outside my bedroom window and knew that Shaun, my border collie, was being returned after four months of separation. He came bounding up the stairs in answer to my call, jumped up on the bed to lick my face and was almost demented in his excitement and enthusiasm. As ever the emotion was too much for him and he departed outside to calm down. It had always been as if he could not cope with the overwhelming pleasure or excitement and he always had to go away to recover.

145

Peggy was in and out of the house regularly in those days, and I simply could not have managed without her help and kindness. I was inundated with calls and visits from friends and well-wishers, all of which I greatly appreciated. It was marvellous to have a telephone by my side once again and I began to feel I had returned to the world and normality.

All the everyday little tasks one does without giving them a thought became a challenge to me. Dressing myself was a major operation and getting in and out of the bath was an extremely complicated exercise. The days that Keith was at Shenberrow we usually went out in the car and because of my continuing and horrific incontinence this meant that we had to design our route around toilet stops. We went to visit the stud farm where he had a mare and because of my condition I had only about 30 seconds notice that I needed to empty my bowels. I could not get up to the house fast enough and once in the bathroom I spent ages cleaning my clothes and myself and then the room itself. Eventually I re-emerged, and we left and as we drove away I burst into tears, I don't think I have ever felt so desolate and degraded. I hated my disability!

Inevitably, I began to look for a miracle cure. The medical profession was of the unanimous opinion that I had recovered to a miraculous degree and their attitude was that I should be thankful that I could at least stand up. I wasn't prepared to accept this and began to look at alternative therapies. I went to see Mr McTimoney, a well-known chiropractor, and explained to him the actual injury to the two dorsal vertebrae, the resulting pain around my rib cage, the incontinence, the loss of feeling from my armpits down and the inability to get my right leg to work properly. I stressed how I had been badly hurt by over-enthusiastic physiotherapy sessions in the hope that he would not be tempted to pull me around too much. There was no change after my first session with him but I decided that I had to give him a fair chance.

On the second visit he felt around and found that one rib on the left side of my diaphragm protruded peculiarly and he felt down on this and gave it a sharp click. He told me this would release the feeling of the steel band around my chest. He said I would feel considerable pain for the next few hours but after that some relief. On the drive back, I suffered pure agony. I thought that I must have done something very stupid. I got home and took sleeping pills and

146

knocked myself out for the night. In the morning I woke and was immediately aware of a difference. The steel band, although still there, felt much looser and less restrictive. I returned to Mr McTimoney full of enthusiasm and unfortunately further efforts resulted in my spine going into spasm and I had to give up my chiropractor in Banbury.

Next, I tried a Canadian one who was at Sudbury in Suffolk. My reasoning was that chiropractics were a recognised part of the medical profession over there and one of my friends promised me that I would wake up one morning and find the whole awful experience was just a nightmare. Dr Schofield had an x-ray machine and I was immediately impressed by the pervading atmosphere of professionalism. I was photographed extensively by a big machine, lying down, standing up and sitting on a chair. I met the doctor and was quite impressed, he was an unusual person who exuded confidence and possessed a compelling sense of urgency. He confirmed the injury to the spinal cord and told me that it would never heal. Although after Christopher Reeve's injury many years later there has been a huge amount of research that has managed to find a way of regenerating the spinal cord.

Dr Schofield seemed very confident and said treatment would consist of two periods, the first covering ten days and the second for seven days with four weeks in between. I agreed to go ahead and arranged to stay at the Bull Hotel in Long Melford. The manipulations were so light and gentle that I could scarcely feel them. The massage treatments were deep massage over my loins and down the front of my thighs, the most vigorous I have ever experienced. Later on, Dr Schofield did some internal manipulation and I did find it much easier to deal with both waterworks and bowels. Just going to the loo became less of a mission and for this I was grateful.

Chapter Sixteen – Becoming a Horse Dealer

It was now six months since my accident and I also had to learn to deal with the muscular spasms which hit my body in a wave from shoulders to toes. They were the worst when I had been sitting for a while, so I had to learn not to stand up and start walking immediately. I would fuss around with my handbag to wait for the spasms to pass. I desperately missed being able to run and jump. And I missed climbing up Shenberrow Hill with Keith to the top of the Cotswold escarpment. This used to include passionate love-making on the warm baked grass, made even more delectable by the possibility that we might be seen! It was hard for both of us to come to terms with the fact that the extremely athletic, inventive and most sensual side of our love affair was almost certainly over.

In my previous life, when I was determined to become ultra-fit for eventing, I used to put on a pair of light running shoes and set off up the winding track to the top of the escarpment. This was towards evening, when all the dressage and training work was done for the day, the horses had been groomed and fed and watered, and were relaxing in their individual looseboxes, munching on the hay stacked in the wall-racks, gazing out over the lawns and the tracks beyond, and listening to the low hum of people talking as they sat on the terrace of the village pub and looked out over Shenberrow, the village and the hills.

The empty stables were a constant reminder of all that had been in the past and quite apart from what it meant purely from the physical angle, I missed the sight, the sound and smell of the horses. Whilst I was in full training there had been momentary occasions when I had wondered if all the work involved in training and competing at top level three-day eventing was really worthwhile, but this thought had been merely fleeting, and probably only the product of a bad day. There is absolutely no doubt that I would have continued to compete with Jolly and Gamble had I not broken my back at Tidworth. At that time, I was in a unique situation because never before had I had two horses at this level, both of whom were entirely genuine, sound, talented and definitely of Olympic standard.

Now I was back at Shenberrow it began to look as if there would never be another horse in the stables. That's when I decided to do something about it. I would buy a horse at one of the sales, transform him with proper schooling and good stable management and sell him on at a profit. This would give me the interest I craved and perhaps I would make some money. I would become a horse dealer.

I needed somebody to help me and I went to see my former groom, Sandra who had been with me when I left John but had then married a farmer. She now had children and couldn't possibly travel to Shenberrow but she suggested that if I put the horse at her own place then she could look after him, and ride and train him. So, having settled this Sandra and I set off for the sales at Doncaster. Not many of the horses there were suitable, but then I came to Jamaican Tweed and I was immediately and immensely attracted to this very good-looking seven-year-old gelding. His legs were cold and clean and when we ran him up on level ground we could see that he had a good stride. Although I liked him very much I was concerned that he would be too much of a handful, too lively for Sandra who had ridden my trained eventers in the past, very different to a horse straight out of a racing stable.

Despite the logic of the argument against buying the horse, all my instincts told me that this was a good thing. He had everything I liked in a horse, the looks, the movement, the carriage and the right outlook. I wanted him, but I knew it was the wrong time. I did not know what I was going to do. The bidding started briskly and then began to labour as it approached the 1500 guineas mark. I longed to nod my head for the highest bid, but common sense for once prevailed, and I let him go. I watched him led out with certain knowledge that I had lost a really good horse. I felt immensely frustrated. In later weeks this feeling was even stronger when, quite by chance, I watched him win a two-mile steeplechase on television and he won a second race soon after that.

Sandra left the sale ring for a few minutes, and during her absence in came a five-year-old gelding, smaller than Jamaican Tweed, exceptionally attractive as far as I could see under his winter coat. He was not clipped, nor was he well-presented and must be something wrong, especially as vendors usually make an effort to have their horse looking at its best. The circumstances appeared suspicious. Nevertheless, he looked a good sort to me, and would improve one hundred per cent just with being tidied up. The horse is only led around the ring at a walk as the auctioneer reads out his particulars and then bidding starts, so I was going to have to take a risk on whether or not he was a good mover. I looked carefully at his action as he walked towards me for just a few strides around the circle. I decided, as the bidding progressed that I would take a risk – most unlike me – so I caught the auctioneer's eye for a bid and, to my surprise, he was immediately knocked down to me.

Sandra returned to find that in her short absence I had bought a horse. We went away in search of the horse's loosebox with a sense of foreboding and me muttering, "What on earth have I done?" I was convinced I had bought a man-eater or a horse with a bad leg, or one just that did not move well enough. He was trotted up for us and, to my relief, his action was perfectly straight, and he moved extremely well. He also appeared to be a sensible character and I began to think that perhaps I did not have a bad buy. Sandra and I arranged transport with one of the horsebox owners and then we set off for Gloucestershire ourselves to prepare for his arrival.

I motored over to Broadway to watch the horse being ridden for the first time. We had euphemistically named him Magic, more in hope than with conviction. We took our time with Magic, putting him on the long lunge rein so that he circled around Sandra, and discovering that he knew the commands and answered, 'walk on', 'tr-ot' and 'can-ter' without any trouble and on both reins, to left and right. He seemed perfectly sensible and did not appear to be worried by the weight of the saddle. Once he had lost his initial freshness we took him off the lunge rein and Sandra climbed aboard. He moved off round the field with aplomb and I was delighted with the way he moved. Obviously, he had no bad habits and seemed to be a perfectly genuine horse. I was well satisfied with my purchase and Sandra was happy to keep him at the farm.

In the weeks that followed Magic provided me with a great source of interest. We clipped him out, taking off his heavy winter coat, scissored the hair out of his ears and heels, and pulled his mane and tail. He looked a different horse. Sandra rode him around the farm and then ventured out on the lanes. There was nowhere flat enough which we could use as a dressage arena, so his training could not progress, and I had to think of someone whom I could trust to school him for me. I decided the perfect person was Captain Edy Goldman and he agreed that his assistant would ride him. I knew that she would do a good job. Magic stayed with them for more than two months before I realised that I was spending all the profit I might make on the eventual sale. I had been so keen to improve the horse and to tap his potential that I had lost sight of the intention to make some very necessary money. I had to learn to appreciate the difference between training a horse myself and paying someone else to do it. I realised that I could not afford to pay large training fees at a top establishment and still make a worthwhile profit. I began to recognise how valuable had been my own ability to train a horse in every aspect.

I was not cured of the desire to have a horse about the place, but I did recognise that I needed to find someone local to school him for me. Meanwhile, Sandra said that she would be happy to have whatever I bought on her farm until he was ready for more advanced work. Off I went to the next Doncaster sales and this time I bought a chestnut four-year-old gelding, another good-looking individual who appeared to have a mind of his own. He soon demonstrated that he was a great character, and Sandra and I discovered that he also had a phenomenal jump in him. This time I was anxious to make sure I could be more personally involved with the training of Rufus than had been possible with Magic in Cheshire, and I arranged for him to go to Margaret Latt at the Oriel School near Cheltenham Racecourse. I knew Margaret from my competitive days and recognised and appreciated her ability as a horsewoman. Oriel was also near enough for me to be able to supervise the training several times a week.

It seemed an ideal arrangement as Margaret was small and light, an important factor with a young horse. Rufus's training progressed from the basic dressage work, to make him both obedient to the rider's aids and well-balanced, before the start of his jump education. This last consisted of trotting over a row of poles on the ground so that he learnt how to gauge the distance between them and to pick up his feet. Rufus enjoyed these sessions enormously and was patently thrilled when he graduated to small jumps. He was very light on his feet and had the agility of a cat in the air. At times he showed the fiery red side of his character with a tendency to stand on his hind legs in the corner of the indoor school, but there was never any real nastiness about these antics. He was merely experimenting as to how far he would be allowed to go, and he soon found out that the answer was 'not far'. Margaret was very capable of squashing his attempt to gain the upper hand and Rufus decided it was easier to concentrate on his jumping. Very quickly, he was jumping fences 1.2 metres in

151

height with consummate ease. He was also very careful, a real gift for a show jumper, and it was becoming apparent that his future lay in the show jumping ring. Against him was the fact that he was a girl's horse as he stood only 15.3 hh. At this height he would not carry a heavier man, but the girl rider would have to be strong enough to be the boss. Without a rider he could respect, he would become useless.

Horses are very quick to realise the limitations and deficiencies of their riders and, if they have any character at all, they will soon exploit these weaknesses and refuse to co-operate at any time. The most important thing was for him to be bought by someone good, someone capable of bringing out his undoubted talent. To make a lot of money out of him, I would have to find an experienced show jumper who could do this. Alison Dawes, a well-known show jumper came to see him and for her he jumped most beautifully. She bought him promptly, and the next season he was an immediate success in novice competitions. Master Touch, alias Rufus, looked assured of a great future.

I had now sold two horses, and had thoroughly enjoyed the experience, but in no way did this measure up to doing the job oneself. I began to consider how viable it might be for me to ride again. Perhaps, if Keith had permanently left his home in Guildford and his wife and married me there might have been an opportunity to do something of a business nature together, and I would have felt able to give up my riding. Yet even after five and a half years of a very strong relationship, during which time he fluctuated between declaring unilaterally that he wanted to marry me and was about to leave home; and then, in a fit of guilt, that he could not leave until the children were older. He still had not made a move to divorce. Every time he brought up the subject at Guildford there was so much trouble that he gave up. I had not liked this situation but was far too much in love and involved in every way to do what I should have done - walk away. I believed in him. I believed him when he said that we would be married.

Keith knew, that as long as I was improving, I was not going to do what would have been sensible after the fall, the paralysis and those dreadful months in hospital. That is, give up the horses. They were, after all, my life, a fact which he appreciated very well. Thirty years later, I can see that this is what I should have done, but at that time I was still of an age when I believed anything was possible as long as one tried hard enough. I was trying my heart out to be physically better, not only for myself but most particularly for him.

I was due at Frenchay for a check-up visit six months after my release, and Keith and I drove to Bristol one sunny afternoon so that I could be inspected by the neurosurgeon. I was shown into a rabbit hutch of a changing room with orders to emerge in a short robe. I sighed in resignation as, once again, I had to lie on the x-ray table to have the pictures taken. Finally, it was over, and Keith and I made our way up to Huw Griffiths' consulting room. We sat on hard wooden upright chairs and waited. We waited for more than 15 minutes and my back was becoming even more painful. Finally, we went in and Huw was his usual ebullient self and he asked me to walk up and down the room while he watched my movement. Then he used the blunt and sharp test with the pin. I told him of the continuing difficulty with my bowels and also of the spasms whenever I stood up either from the sitting or lying down position. He told me that my progress far surpassed his expectations, but it was still nowhere good enough for me. He told me that I had to face the fact that I had sustained a very serious spinal injury and although there was a slight chance that some of the nerve ends might knit together in the next twelve month, but I had to realise that physically I should never be the same as before the fall. He then added that in his opinion I would never run again, and I was extremely lucky if I were able to walk on all sorts of surfaces. It was a huge body blow to have the facts stated so baldly, but I would not leave until I asked him about riding. He said that my back probably could stand the strain of being on a horse but that it certainly could not stand the impact of a fall at any speed. It was such a bleak prognosis, and as we drove back to Shenberrow I was sunk in a deep depression. I felt extremely sorry for myself and thought that life would just not be worth living. I did not say this to Keith, but he too must have felt depressed and wondered how on earth we were going to manage.

Gradually I began to recover my natural optimism and determined awkwardness and my main aim was to prove Huw Griffiths wrong. I tried and tried to run, but it was no good. The left leg ran forward happily but the right one could not pick up cleanly nor stride in front of the good leg. Then I began to want to test myself with riding. The one horse I knew who would be trustworthy enough in every way for my situation belonged to Vivian Eason. He was an extraordinarily beautiful golden dun colour with darker mane and tail and had been bought by Vivian at one of the very few sales of Russian horses. His name was Dekabr, Dek to his friends. I had ridden him many times in the past on the countless occasions I was with the Easons and was pretty sure he was sensible enough and narrow enough to be the right horse for my first attempt. He was also well-schooled for dressage and was therefore obedient. Vivian agreed that I could ride Dek on the condition that Keith came with me in case of any further disaster. He would know what to do with the body. I put on my jodhpurs and polo necked sweater for the first time in many months and Keith and I, with my saddle on the back seat of the car, and Shaun full of excitement, set off for the Eason's farm.

The girl who helped to look after the Easons' horses led Dek out of the stable and we put my saddle on him, testing the girth carefully. I had already decided that it would be a physical impossibility for me to attempt to get on from the ground. To do this would have entailed placing my left foot in the stirrup while the right one remained on the ground, then springing from my right leg to send me up into the saddle. My right side had no semblance of a bounce left in it and therefore my only way of getting into the saddle was from a mounting block where I would not have to ask the impossible from the poor right leg. I climbed gingerly up the granary steps until my feet were on the same level as the waiting stirrup. I did not trust my foot to arrive cleanly there, so I bent forwards, grabbed my foot and placed the ball of it on to the receiving platform of the stirrup. Now came the most difficult part. I had to make my 'bad' right leg lift up over the raised back of the saddle and then let it drop down on the far side of Dek. Lastly, I had to find the right stirrup with my foot. Dek was placed in position. He stood quietly while I struggled to guide my left foot towards and into the stirrup and then, drawing a deep breath, I made a huge effort to lift myself upwards and then to throw my right leg over to the other side fervently hoping that this ungainly manner of arriving in the saddle would not upset Dek. Luckily, he remained unconcerned, and Vivian took hold of my foot and placed in in the stirrup. Once again, I was back on a horse. It felt very peculiar. I was immediately aware of the lack of feeling on the insides of my legs. This was not a good thing as it is the insides of one's thighs and lower legs that give one the grip to stay aboard, and the changing position of the rider's legs and hands and weight tell the horse where

154

to go and what to do. Before the fall my legs had lain tight against the horse's sides until we were as one, but now they felt like foreign bodies with no idea of what to do, something over which I had little control.

Taking several very deep breaths, I tried to relax. I patted Dek on his neck and shoulder and talked to him. His ears flickered back and forth. I began to feel more at home and safe enough just sitting there. Summoning up some very necessary courage, I announced that I was ready to move forward at a walk. Vivian gently let go of the off-side rein she had been holding and stood away from Dek and me. We were on our own. I felt his mouth through the reins and the bit, dropped his head a little and gave him the signal to walk forward with a squeeze of both legs. We set off away from the granary and the stables, under the huge trees planted by a previous farmer long years ago to give some shelter from the wind and rain when it lashed this exposed top of the Cotswold plateau. We arrived at a wide gate which had already been opened so that I could ride straight into the big field where, before the fall, I would often ride with Vivian, she on Dek and I on Jolly or Gamble. None of those thoughts were in my mind at that moment. I was there to see if I could still ride, and I had to do just that. I began to test my ability to move in the saddle and immediately discovered that it was difficult to turn easily from my hips or waist. As soon as I reached the angle of 30°, from a start zero, my rib cage immediately thought of all those years of riding when I had been so supple, so quick to adapt to any move of the horse, to twist and turn at will. I must try harder if I really did want to ride again. I had to carry on until I found out by how much I could improve and how much my back would stand.

I decided to see if Dek would react to the influence of legs to his sides. Obediently, and immediately, he gave way to whichever leg I applied, and I was delighted to realise that I could control my legs again. Gaining confidence, I announced to my helpers that I was going to trot. It never entered my head that this should present a problem but as soon as Dek began to trot and I automatically began to rise in the saddle, I realised that all was not as it should be. I felt as if I were a complete beginner doing double bumps in the saddle against the rhythm of the trot instead of rising cleanly for the second bump. Going back into walk, I tried to assess what was happening. I reckoned that it was that right side again, and it looked as if now I had to acknowledge that it was not just the right leg which had been affected and made so feeble by the fall, but also my body all the way up to chest height. This would make sense as it was T5, T6, and T7 that had been damaged, at mid-chest height. I was clearly unable to compensate or to co-ordinate the rise and fall of my body at the trot. It was as if that right side was a good split second behind the rest of me when I was supposed to be rising out of the saddle, with the consequence of a double bump on it instead of just one rise up out of it and one momentary sit in it. The right lower leg, incapable of staying in place on the girth of the saddle was slipping backwards infinitesimally with every stride. Dangerous!

Having diagnosed what I was doing wrong, I had to make the effort to see if I could correct it, and I spent the next 20 minutes trotting round the huge field forcing myself to concentrate on the offending side and leg. I began to improve a little, but it required immense concentration and application. It was as if I was trying to hold another person in position. Then there was a shout, and it was Keith calling time. Obediently, I returned to the stable feeling that I had achieved at least something. Again, with the benefit of hindsight, I can see that here was an opportunity to give up riding and yet, Awkward Annie that I was, I was determined to see if I could continue. I was not ready to give up.

I expected to be very stiff the day after this effort, but I was just as usual and I came to the conclusion that this must be one of the advantages of not having full sensation of feeling. My appraisal of the situation was that I thought with practice my riding should improve. Keith made no objection, and whether this was because he knew I was now set on trying to ride, in which case there would probably have been an argument which was better avoided, I do not know. The result, however, was that for the next few weeks I rode Dek at the Easons nearly every day. We worked on our dressage up to and past three-day event standard and I discovered that I was regaining my old ability to 'feel' the horse, to know instinctively where his legs were under me and to be able to correct him from a degree out of the straight line. Vivian watched over me every day and I must again salute her unselfishness in allowing another person to ride her special horse over such a period of time. When I kept thanking her, she was kind enough to say that Dek was learning too, and that she was feeling and reaping the benefit of my work when she tried him out on the days I could not leave Shenberrow. She was perfectly happy to continue like this. What a good friend!

By this time, I was sitting perfectly well at the walk and was fairly good at the canter. The trot pace still caused me grave difficulties and was going to be a problem. There was no doubt that it would take a great deal of determination, concentration and application to sort it out. I could just about cope with an ordinary sitting trot, but if I asked Dek for an extended one, my legs were unable to hold me tight into the saddle and I was in dire danger of falling off. The only way I could find to prevent this was to hook my right thumb into the top front of the saddle. This immediately harnessed me into position and stopped me flying about. It was not ideal for the horse as the result was a harsher hold on the bit in his mouth, but in a choice between putting up with a rider increasingly unsteady in the saddle or feeling a little restriction in the mouth in the extended trot, Dek, or any other horse would probably have opted for me to be quiet and still in the saddle.

What had become apparent to me was that there existed only a thin borderline between safety and a fall. I was alright as long as the horse continued on his course and did not suddenly jinx out of line or misbehave. If that happened my seat was neither strong enough nor deep enough for me to stay on board. I had to try to be sensible about how much I asked both of myself and the horse. I also had to work out ways and means of coping with these difficulties. I must look on them as a challenge, and find a way, somehow to overcome them.

Riding again and feeling the horse under me made me more sensitively aware and more appreciative of the aids I gave the horse for individual movements. I needed this reminder before I sat down to write my book on training an event horse. I had learned so much without realising it over the years of my eventing career, and it seemed important that I impart the knowledge I had accumulated. I must set it all down whilst everything was clear in my mind. My riding had to stop while the writing was in progress as the book, undoubtedly, would require total concentration and I could see that it was going to be a full-time job. I was a perfectionist, such a nuisance sometimes, and this would mean I had to ensure that all my instructions were imparted with great clarity. The whole idea and the aim of my writing was to produce a book which, if the reader followed what is said to the letter, and with no short cuts, his or her horse would emerge beautifully schooled and a pleasure to ride.

Almost as soon as I started to write I found that writing the original draft in longhand was anathema to my back. The curve of my spine over the desk made it ache intolerably and I could write only for short periods. I found that the only way to relieve the pain was to lie flat on my back on the floor for about ten minutes after a writing session, and then accept the increasing spasms whenever I stood up from my work. Keith bought a small tape recorder for me to save any further time at my desk than was necessary, and I recorded the text from my longhand manuscript and sent off the tapes to Keith's secretary in the London office, to be typed. I sent the manuscript to my literary agent and George Greenfield, who was a good friend, sold it to Pelham Books and I received a welcome cheque as an advance. I did feel rather proud of myself.

Taking the photographs to illustrate the text was far more difficult than I could ever have imagined. No-one before had attempted to show the horse in a series of photographs as he performed the various basic training suppling exercises. These involved showing the horse's body at slight angles off a straight line. It took me some time to evolve a method of making clear to a spectator or reader. The answer was to lay or paint a white line along the track on one side of the arena. The photograph then showed clearly the angle of the horse's body and his footfalls in relation to the line and the boarded sides of the arena. But it was remarkably difficult to capture the absolutely correct movement of horse and rider at the correct distance from the photographer and to take a plate at the necessary split second of the required movement. The photographer and I spent two long and exhausting days, the first with a competition rider, Judy Bradwell, and the second with Mrs Molly Sivewright, owner of the Talland School of Equitation. In March 1973, *The Event Horse*, was published.

At that time Princess Anne had become very successful with her horse, Doublet, and I asked the Duke of Beaufort to enquire whether she was prepared to write a foreward for my book. I was thrilled when she agreed. The book sold extraordinarily well.

Meanwhile, other facets of my life were developing. I began to judge the dressage phase at one-day events. Then I received a letter from the committee of the Burghley Three-Day Event asking me to be one of the three judges for the first day's dressage phase. I was delighted to write back, accepting, but had to make clear with some embarrassment that I would need time to visit the loo during the breaks for morning coffee, lunch and tea. I was still prone to accidents in this department and went around terrified that I might be caught at the wrong time. I felt idiotic at having to make my position clear to the organisers, but I had long since given up any façade of false modesty in this direction, and I realised only too well that it was necessary for everyone concerned that I made my situation clear.

To their credit the Burghley officials took this condition in their stride, and I duly appeared at Lord Exeter's estate just outside Stamford in September to judge the dressage. I was placed in the hut to the left of the centre of the arena, and to my horror, as the first competitor began the dressage test, I discovered that I could not see the top left-hand corner properly from the sitting position. As I was determined not to miss a thing I had to stand up every time a competitor went around the corner in order to see if the horse was showing correct length bend from head to tail, and was not dropping its shoulder on the inside, or letting his head tilt outwards. Apparently, the competitors had soon noticed my antics and ruefully agreed that I was likely to spot, and mark accordingly, anything that they did wrong, or anything they did well. I found my experience as a competitor invaluable in my new capacity as a judge. I knew only too well the difficulties each competitor faced in the test they had to perform. I also knew all the little tricks they were likely to employ to cover up slight mistakes and, as a comparatively recent competitor, I would know exactly what, where and when this was likely to happen. Unlike many of the judges for the most important first phase of the event and, I might add, the judges in pure dressage competitions, I had no hesitation whatsoever in awarding the top marks of nine, or even the maximum ten, for one of the twenty-odd individual movements within the actual test, plus the four extra marks for the overall impression of paces (freedom and regularity), impulsion (desire to move forward, elasticity of the steps and engagement of the hindquarters), submission (attention and obedience, lightness of freedom of the movements, acceptance of the bit) and position and seat of the rider, correct use of the aids.

I was particularly keen that the competitors would understand that their marks reflected exactly what they had done. Good, very good and superb were three different things and were marked accordingly. If horse and rider performed a movement excellently, they would get ten marks out of ten. If the movement was performed very badly, they would get one mark out of ten. I tried to dismiss all thoughts of personalities and to concentrate solely on what I saw in front of me. I had to disassociate myself from any knowledge whatsoever of how each horse and rider usually performed.

The whole process was of enormous interest to me, and my job was made easier with the aid of a first class 'writer'. The writer has to take down the judge's comments plus the mark for each movement as the test progresses and, as I made both clear and critical remarks on virtually every one of the 21-odd movements, this was no easy task. We got through the two days of judging without any real difficulty and with a considerable sense of pleasurable achievement, but I am sure that my stalwart helper must have been very tired by the end of the second day. I think she was an absolute star!

At the end of the two days I felt cheered up, hoping that I could take part in some sort of normal life activities. Watching the competitors riding-in their horses and then taking part in the actual event. I could not suppress my feelings of envy. No matter how hard I tried I could not yet accept wholeheartedly that I should never be able to compete again. I could only hope that time would help me to accept the obvious. Meanwhile, I bitterly resented the unkind fate which had forced me to give up eventing before I was ready.

As soon as I finished *The Event Horse* I began to go to the Easons so I might continue riding Dek. This time I had to ride in another field as there were cattle grazing the one we had used earlier. This new field was on a slope which meant that we were moving at a slight angle. I felt an immediate difference and a piercing strain when I had to cope with the changing ground. As soon as we were going downhill my rib-cage screamed in protest and I could not bear to continue. I slowed to stop and sat still to recover. Then I realised that when I was tilted forward my damaged T5, T6 and T7 vertebrae were being concertinaed and the feeling of a crushing steel band around me at that level was simply too much to bear. My spine was still unstable, and it would take a considerable time to ossify. My heart did not want to take heed of the body's warnings, but my head over-ruled and told me to be sensible. I became very depressed all over again. Then I decided on a compromise. I would keep going a little longer and see if my back was going to accustom itself to my riding.

Two or three weeks later, after forcing myself to persevere I had to face the fact that it was doing more harm than good. The spasms were becoming harsher and the imaginary steel band around my chest had returned with a vengeance. For the second time I gave up the attempt to return to active riding, and in the back of my mind I wondered if this really was the end of me ever being on a horse. Outwardly I said that I would try again in another six months, but I knew how badly it hurt this time and secretly, I did not think I would ever be able to cope with the pain.

Once again, I turned my attention to other things. I began to take a few riders with their horses for individual tuition and I was delighted to find that I had the capacity for passing on my knowledge. I also faced a fact that had never occurred to me. I had never been taught to ride, it simply came naturally and as a result, I assumed everyone else would be the same. My family was totally non-horsy and it was only due to WWII that my family moved to Lytham St Annes. Up until that time I had never seen a horse up close. I learnt to ride on the beach ponies and it was at this time that I discovered my God-given talent for horses and riding, and also my relentless determination to be the best.

When I began teaching I began to realise that not everyone was blessed with my level of athletic co-ordination. I found that they needed to be taught how to feel every movement of the horse through their seat, and to be totally clear with their aids. Some of these pupils used their intelligence and I was astonished and pleased at the transformation of their riding, others realised that it was just too hard and gave up. I did not take to training people like a duck to water but kept on with it, not realising how this was a good training for myself when it came to working with the Canadian Olympic team in the future!

I definitely preferred horses to people! I happened to see a big young horse in Shropshire that instinctively I felt would be a good proposition and I decided to buy him. I sent him to Captain Edy Goldman for several months training in dressage and basic pole on the ground work in preparation for jumping. I called him Spy and asked James Templer if he would event him for me. He was named euphemistically Time and Again. Spy was a very strong-minded horse, by no means a show horse who has to be the epitome of beauty, but he definitely was attractive and caught the eye. He looked tough enough to do well in eventing. It was now up to James to strike up an understanding with him until they formed a harmonious partnership.

They went to several small competitions in my horsebox as I had lent it to James to take Spy from Stanton to Colchester and then it was agreed that he should keep it and use it as it was more comfortable than his own transport. They took part in a great many show jumping classes and minor dressage competitions and then the horse's first one-day event at Batsford Horse Trials. I drove to the event and watched as Spy performed his dressage test. Annoyingly, he was very unsettled and produced nothing like his best form. Then he spoilt an otherwise promising show jumping round by an unnecessary run-out at a fence on the turn. I thought I should see a little of his cross-country performance as I was incapable of running from fence to fence and I was also having great difficulty even staying upright on the tufty grass, but just as James was about to set out on the cross-country, a friend drove up in his Range Rover with an official badge displayed on his windscreen and kindly offered to follow Spy around the course. I scrambled in and was delighted to find that the Range Rover did not shake up my back as a Land Rover would have done. We watched James all around the course and I was delighted with the way Spy dealt with his debut cross-country performance, and I was looking forward to his next event.

We went up to Scotland for two different events, the first at Lockerbie. I delighted by the beautiful country when we arrived, bright green grass rolling away in every direction and ancient trees. My dog, Shaun, must have thought he had arrived in heaven. Princess Anne was there to compete on three horses and on this account the crowds were enormous. A lot of the spectators seemed to have no real idea of what was going on. Spy went well, and we decided that at the next event we would be trying to win.

I returned home for a few days and then I noticed that Shaun's urine had blood in it. I rang the vet immediately and it looked like his kidney trouble had recurred and a fall he'd had as he'd try to jump into the horsebox had ruptured something. For two days I tried to feed him glucose and water, but his natural energy and vitality seemed to be literally draining away as the hours passed. I knew that I had to make a decision, but he was my last link with the happy days of my marriage and my home at Clitheroe and I was going to play God and decide if he was to live or die. I carried him outside the main entrance door and held him upright on the blanket I had placed on the flagstones. I talked to him with tears running down my face and plopping on the floor. He was perfectly quiet and confident because I was there, and he made no objection when the injection needle was slipped into his hind quarters. His eyes began to close and then to glaze, he staggered a little and then he fell. Another needle was quickly inserted, and Shaun was dead. He was gone so quickly and there was nothing I could do to bring him back. I was devastated. I had wanted to bury him, but I was no longer capable of digging a hole, so I agreed to the vet taking him away and my final sight of my beloved dog was when he was slithered into a black polythene bag. I couldn't bear it and stumbled into the house in floods of tears. I knew I had done the right thing in putting him down, but I reckoned I should have thought of an alternative to allowing his body to be taken away in such a manner. I felt as if I had utterly failed him. He had been the most marvellous companion and such a true friend all through the very difficult times since we left Clitheroe. Now he too was gone.

I could not face the journey back to Scotland the next day but in my absence, James excelled himself and he won both events at Annick and Eglinton. I mourned for Shaun and I missed him terribly.

In August that year 1972 was the Munich Olympic Games and I tried to be patriotic, to be delighted with the performance of the British team of Richard Meade on Laurieston, Bridget Parker with Cornish Gold, Mary Gordon Watson with Cornishman V, and Mark Phillips with Great Ovation, who won the Team Gold and Richard and Laurieston who won the individual Gold Medal. In truth, I was green with envy.

Chapter Seventeen - A Different Life

The next blow came when James was suddenly drafted to Ireland with his regiment which meant I had to find another rider for Spy and I knew that this was not going to be easy. He was a big horse and most suitable for a man, or a very strong woman. Keith and I discussed it for hours and in the end offered the ride to Sorrel Warwick. She was a particularly strong woman but what persuaded me to ask her was that she had ridden a number of horses in events and always put up a good performance. She was a trier.

Sorrel worked hard to develop an understanding and to form a partnership with Spy and their first one-day event was at Holme Lacy in Herefordshire. Keith and I drove there to watch. As usual, I was anxious to see the cross-country course and off we set from the start on its one and a half miles. The fences were beautifully built and very well designed and presented and I was rather enjoying myself despite always having to concentrate on lifting my feeble right leg over the changing ground. I was admiring one particular fence as we approached it and for a moment allowed my concentration to relax. The next moment I pitched forwards on to my face on to the long grass and hard ground. A sweep of panic went over me, for all the time I lived in terror of what a fall could do to me. I was shocked by the ease with which I could find myself flat on the floor without warning, simply because of a split second's loss of concentration of how to walk. I had simply looked around me whilst I was still walking, and I was really annoyed with myself for allowing this to happen. This time, I hurt my ankle, which immediately swelled up, but I decided it was not too bad and we continued onward around the course. It was a salutary lesson for me, never to take my legs for granted. They were not to be relied on in the way a normal person walks and runs upright only if I kept my concentration and had my eyes scanning everywhere.

The season finished, and Keith and I had to decide what to do with Spy. Sorrel told us that she was leaving the Russells and this meant Wylye. She said she would like to continue with Spy, but she did not know where she was going. I had no field of my own in which to turn him out.

After much discussion we decided to try racing him, and therefore possibly increasing his value. George Hyatt, a very good racing rider was based in Stanton and Spy was by Specific, sire of the Grand National winner, Specify, and his dam was also of racing stock. George was keen to have him, and it would give me a much more conveniently placed interest as George's stables were just around the corner at the bottom of the village.

Soon George was out hunting on Spy with the North Cotswold hounds in order to qualify for his Hunter's Certificate. It was a new experience for me to have a foot in the steeplechasing world and it also coincided with Keith's professional interest in racing as a bookmaker. Then out of the blue someone approached me and asked to buy him. I was somewhat put out by this, but common sense dictated that we sell Spy when the price was good. He did go on to run in point-to-points and he was very impressive for his new owner.

All this time I was 'being sensible' and I had not been back on a horse. Several friends who didn't understand intimated that I was just not trying hard enough. They recommended all sorts of exercises and cures for me. When I made no attempt to follow their advice they assumed that I was content to stay as I was. If they actually said this to me then I made sure to tell them that the neurosurgeons and the best exponents in other fields said that the spinal cord would never re-generate.

Despite all my determination not to listen to any of these people I was stung into action by the repeated remarks of one well-known steeplechase rider, John Thorne. His twin daughters, Jane and Diana, both came to me with their event horses for dressage training and John adopted the habit of dropping in to see me on his way back in the horsebox from riding in the hunter chases at Cheltenham. He was always on the strictest of diets in the racing season and could look forward only to a small piece of poached fish for his evening meal. He always had two cups of tea, no milk and no sugar, whilst he told me how he had gone that day and all the news and gossip. He kept telling me that he had broken his back badly some time before and yet he was still riding over fences. The inference was either that I had decided it was not worth the effort or that I was not trying very hard. I was hurt to the quick.

I should have asked him exactly where was his injury, and was it one vertebra or more involved, and whether or not the spinal cord had been damaged. I should also have pointed out that I too, had broken my back in 1961, but that the L1 vertebra had quickly ossified and I had gone on to return to eventing as soon as the rule banning women taking part in the Olympic three-day event was lifted in 1962. In my agitation I forgot the common sense angle. He continued and said that he had gone to see Bill Tucker in London who was renowned for curing jockeys of their worst injuries and backs were his speciality. Before I had time to think, John made an appointment for me to see this famous man whose success in the field of curing the effects of difficult broken bones was legendary. All the racing people knew of him or had been treated by him and I decided I might as well go to see him, even if the only effect would be to stop them from making me feel I was not trying.

Keith drove me to London and taking my x-rays I presented myself at Mr Tucker's rooms off Grosvenor Square. The receptionist carried the x-rays for Mr Tucker to inspect and, meanwhile, I was ushered into a comfortable room to undress and await his examination. Eventually the door opened, and he introduced himself. Then he made me walk about the room and perform various exercises with my legs, both standing up and lying down on the surgery bed. I had been told that he would send me for further x-rays before giving his opinion, but he made no attempt to do this and sat down at his desk while I dressed. When I was ready, he asked me to tell him exactly what had happened and all the circumstances which had brought me to him, and this I did.

There was no hesitation in his reply. Whilst several people have technically broken their backs, he said, their recovery depended entirely on the seriousness of the break in the first place. In my particular case, the break was extremely bad at the T5 to T7 level and I had been 'lucky' to survive in the manner in which I had from the fall and ensuing paralysis. He said that no amount of talk would make any difference to these facts. That it was incredible that I was even able to stand up. Instead of being upset by this forceful opinion, I was curiously relieved. I had almost begun to believe that I must have subconsciously given up the fight. I went back home a great deal happier and more resigned to the fact that I had to live with my back and legs as they were, and to try to accept this situation as best I could.

But, as you can imagine I still hankered for a miracle cure, and over the years following the fall in 1971, just two people were able to restore me to normal walking mode, only for the miracle to fade away. The first was in 1972, when I presented myself to Mr Rhodes Cook at 46 Portland Place. He listened to my story, looked at the x-ray of T5 and T6 and directed me to lie down on my back in a little cubicle. He then came in with a hypodermic needle and stuck it into a vein, I open my eyes without realising I had been knocked out. I was alone, but a cushion sat between my legs. A nurse arrived, followed by Mr Rhodes Cook who told me to walk up the corridor. My right leg was normal again. Back at Shenberrow, Keith and I were able to make love just as we had before Tidworth. Our spirits spiralled, but then the leg reverted to its half circle mode and not even a second visit to Mr Rhodes Cook could restore me to normality.

As life moved on I had to adjust and it was when they made a film that followed the publication of *The Event Horse* that I saw myself and was appalled at the ugliness of my adopted gait, with my fairly useless right leg being determinedly flung outwards and forwards, making a semi-circular movement. No matter how hard I tried, that right leg would never improve, and I had to accept it and find ways of dealing with my heart-breaking disability.

Keith was stalwart in his support when I returned to Shenberrow, but what must he have thought after we had enjoyed so much in our sex life and now the situation was such that never again would I be the person he loved so much in bed. Looking back, I wonder now at my attitude to relationships with men, it was as if I was doing a dressage test and had to score 10 out of 10 for every movement in order to be loved and desired. My competitive streak, which was a mile wide, somehow got transposed onto the business of romance and I didn't really grasp the concept of loving a person for their soul and their weaknesses. Somehow everything in my life was a competition and winning was everything.

Never again would I be able to move against him or over him with lithe movements. Never again would we be able to make love with that verve and abandon that he had enjoyed so much with me before the fall. Never again would I be able to change positions like lightening – my feeble right leg was now very difficult to move – and no longer would I sit astride him, tease him to the point of ejaculation and then stop only to start all over again. Nor could I rely on my own ability not to prevent my right leg from hurling itself into spasms and shuddering if he were on top. Our loss was almost too much to bear and I was horrified by my inability to control my right leg both in and out of bed. We both longed to turn back the clock. I began to wonder if my fall was punishment for my affair with Keith. Undoubtedly his wife, Eileen, would have known of it and she would be rejoicing.

I felt lonely when Keith was not at Shenberrow so I began to look for another Border Collie. I drove to Guildford where there was a litter of five well-bred, show standard puppies and fell in love with a little male who waddled towards me and looked up into my face with blue eyes. He cost £18 which was a lot in 1972 but I paid a deposit of £1 and would return when he was 10 weeks old.

I continued to give lessons and my pupils included Lucille Woodward, Diana and Jane Thorne and also Jane Starkey. It became clear that I needed proper arenas at Shenberrow. So, Keith and I converted the next-door neighbours' chicken run into a 40 by 20 metre manège, which would make training the new horses very much easier for me. In the future we would buy good lookers with strong, sound legs and a jump in them and they would be schooled as eventers or show horses. This meant that in time I would need a decent and responsible rider who was prepared to learn my ways. Later on, we decided to extend the garage and the feed shed to construct a single-storey cottage for staff.

We advertised and there were many replies and I interviewed Jeanette Watson from Yorkshire. She had worked for Mr and Mrs Sykes turning out their top show horse Gainsborough and after she had worked for me for some time she told me that the Sykes were selling this horse. He was extremely well-bred and only five years old and had competed in working hunter classes. As well as being handsome, he was also strong with plenty of bone. We brought him to Shenberrow on trial and somehow Richard Meade had heard that he was there and came over to see him. He show jumped him over a height of 4'6" and then galloped him fast around the field. Richard loved him but didn't have the money to buy him as he was extremely expensive. I did buy him, and he went into training.

I went to the August Ascot sales and purchased a 16.3 hh, six-year-old, chestnut horse by Scintillant who had been owned by Olga Bandhari. I asked her why she was selling him and she explained that he would never be a top show horse as he lacked the depth and big quarters of a champion. I decided to call him Sunny. When we got him home we found the only thing wrong with him was that he disliked being tied up. Jeanette rode him and reported him to be very comfortable. He didn't over track at the walk, but his trot and canter were excellent, and his mouth was good.

Then he was re-shod and the farrier discovered that he had seedy toe in both front feet and then I began to wonder if this had been the real reason why he had been sold. We were going to have to take it easy while this was cured.

Sometime before, I had had another project setting up a cross-country course near the village and then came a telephone call from Buckingham Palace. Princess Anne would like to come to jump the course. Panic stations! I had to contact all the field owners and asked Mr Gaskin to come with me to make sure that all the jumps were safe. On the 20th September her horsebox rolled into the yard with two eventing horses aboard. Accompanying the Princess were her bodyguard and her trainer, Alison Oliver, who I knew. She had married Alan Oliver one of the leading show jumpers of the day. My part-time employee Mrs Duddy cooked a roast chicken and an apple pie, and she could not get over the honour of providing for a princess. She was not allowed to say a thing about the visit beforehand but afterwards the village was regaled with the story of the day.

The horses were unboxed in the yard and then Princess Anne and Alison rode them along the road towards the course. Halfway along, there must have been trouble with the drains underground, the manhole was off, and two men were sizing up what had to be done. Seeing the horses approaching one of them let out a piercing wolf whistle and watching them, I saw their expressions change from appreciative grins to puzzlement as they vaguely recognised one of the faces. Then the penny dropped, and I grinned at their astonishment. The practice with both horses over the course was a great success but it stirred up all my feelings of loss that I could no longer take part in eventing, the sport which had produced so much pleasure and disappointment for me.

On the 15th October 1973 I was due to fly to the US, to Boston where Neil and Helen Ayer had invited me to judge their FEI Advanced dressage test. One of my co-judges was Rosemarie Springer, ex-wife of the newspaper magnate, Axel Springer and one of the best Grand Prix dressage competitors of her day. She had judged me at some of the leading three-day events when I had been competing and had always given me good marks. She and I took to each other during our stay with the Ayers. She knew that I was training dressage horses at Shenberrow and she wanted to come and visit to watch my methods. I felt immensely honoured by her interest as the top German dressage riders and trainers had a very poor opinion of British dressage in those days. I made many friends on that visit. Jack le Goff, French and full of Gallic charm was the long-term trainer of the American team and was a kindred spirit in his very professional attitude to training for three-day events and he accepted me as an equal. Bruce Davidson, who was a permanent team member for years, and his wife Carol invited me to go and stay with them at her parents' palatial house in Pennsylvania and Fifi Cole and her husband, who kept their horses at the Flying Horse Stables, were very kind to me.

I got back to Shenberrow and all was well. Jeanette had done a good job, keeping the horses ticking over. Rosemarie Springer turned up and was particularly impressed with Sunny. She loved my house, which was tiny compared to her own beautiful manor house in the north of Germany. She was also entranced by the beauty of the Cotswolds and the appeal of our villages. Then Bruce and Carol Davidson came to stay and there followed an influx of eventing Americans as they arrived in England in time to attend Princess Anne and Mark Phillips' wedding on the 14th November at Westminster Abbey.

I was also invited to the wedding and my first feeling was panic that I did not have a suitable hat to wear. It was not the right weather for the sort one would wear at Ascot so I would have to go to London. I found a beautiful hat made of fur, high in the crown, silky soft to the touch with fine fronds fluttering on my forehead in a mixture of cream and conker brown. Keith's car deposited me well in time outside the Abbey, clutching my invitation, dressed in my smart suit, high heels and this crowning glory of a hat. I was ushered to my seat in a pew on the left-hand side, half-way up to the altar. I had a front seat and thoroughly enjoyed watching everyone as they were shown to their designated places, and there was a hum of expectancy as everyone whispered greetings and conversations going on, with the latecomers at last being hurried into their places. Whilst this was happening I had the distinct feeling that someone was watching me, and I finally discovered that the eyes belonged to Harold Wilson, he and his wife had settled into their places way down near the entrance to the Abbey, on the opposite side of the aisle. The Prime Minister was definitely taking an interest in me!

The following Sunday, The Sunday Times newspaper dropped on my mat as usual, and the front of its coloured supplement was filled with a view of the Abbey as Mark and Anne, now married, are walking back down the aisle, smiling happily at friends. In full view, there was me, hat looking good, right in the middle of the picture as the new bride and her husband were about to pass me on their way to be greeted by a multitudinous welcome from the waiting crowd. I was not grand enough to be invited to Buckingham Palace for the reception but George Greenfield took me to Quaglino's for lunch which I enjoyed as a pretty good substitute.

Back home, I was becoming more impressed with Sunny who was very well-mannered inside and outside of the stable, with not a nasty thought in his. He had a lovely temperament but to Jeanette he was proving to be a very big horse to ride and she was failing to keep him together. Day by day, he was beginning to lose his outline and it was going to be difficult to sell him. He was too big as a hack, he lacked the depth and substance of a show hunter, and he could not jump. His market was very limited. If things did not improve quickly, he would lose his appeal as a show horse and I would lose money on him. I could not allow this to continue.

I had not ridden Dekabr, Vivian's Russian gelding, for some time, but at least I knew it was possible for me to ride to a certain degree, and this should be enough for me to assess Sunny and know what was the best thing to do with him. I pulled on my jodhpurs and sweater and short elastic side boots, found my string gloves and went out of the house. Jeanette manoeuvred Sunny against the bank wall. Tentatively I placed my left foot in the stirrup and just about managed to lift my right leg up in the air above and over the saddle, and let it drop down on to his off-side. Jeanette hurriedly placed my right foot in the stirrup. I was back on a horse, but it did occur to me that getting off might be something of a problem. It was a long way down, but I could worry about that later.

171

I felt like a child on a lead rein on the sands at St Annes as Jeanette walked us round to the back of the house and up the slope on to the arena. I patted and stroked Sunny's neck with my gloved hand and then, drawing a deep breath, I told Jeanette to let go. I closed my legs on him, asking him to go forward. Jeanette had been right when she said that his high withers and crested neck in front gave one confidence. It was like sitting in a comfortable armchair, and we proceeded at a stately walk, right-handed, around the arena, then changed the rein across from quarter marker to quarter marker and walked round on the left rein.

Summoning up courage, I dropped his head with my reins, and we moved up into trot, going around the outside track. It was the strangest feeling. My right leg flopped about, but Sunny did not seem to mind. I gained a little confidence. We described a big circle at each end and I tested him for correct bend through the length of his body first to the right, and then to the left. He still ignored the flopping of my right leg. We managed a serpentine with good length bend on both reins and then I could feel my legs and body had had enough and we slowed down to a walk.

Jeanette's usually rosy, cheerful face looked a little pale, but its colour improved when after much discussion as to how we should persuade the right leg to heave itself over the saddle. I was slipping down against Sunny's saddle on his near side and my knees nearly buckled as I hit the ground. I just about managed to stay upright. Sunny had found his metier. He made no attempt to shy away from me. He was now my nursemaid until I improved to partnership status. I was tired, even though it had been such a short ride, but I also felt that perhaps I could do better if I persevered. I had something personal to aim for. Before long, I was riding Sunny every day and he became 'my' horse, but we had a problem as my right foot was always coming out of the stirrup which then flapped freely against my foot or Sunny's side. This could be dangerous. I went to see Mr Pike in his forge at Toddington roundabout, taking a stirrup with me, and asked him if he could insert within it a half circle of steel at the level where my foot and the top of my instep rested. This then should hold my foot in place. After a few adjustments on the position and width of the band, and wrapping it in layers of black tape to stop it rubbing the top of my boot, which sent my leg into objecting spasms, we had found a way of getting round the difficulty.

My friend Cherry heard about my riding and she arrived in one of her two Porsches and out came her pendulum, with Sunny stretching out his nose inquisitively towards it as it flew round in a circle, left or right, in answer to Cherry's questions. It told her that this was a kind horse and he would be alright with me. She thought him beautiful to look at and the pendulum had told her he had a wonderful temperament. She was back again two days later to have another session with Sunny. Things were looking up, and I began to smile inside.

Ted Marsh telephoned and asked me to have dinner with him at Dormy House, a first-class hotel perched level with the top of Fish Hill. It had a reputation for serving very good food at the time. Keith was away at Guildford with his wife, and had no objection, although realistically what right would he have to protest? Ted collected me and drove out of Broadway on the old road leading to the top of Fish Hill, taking the left turn on to very narrow roads, which eventually brought us to Dormy House.

It was always amazing that no matter how long we had been apart, as soon as we met, we would talk as if it had been only yesterday and discuss anything and everything. Clearly, he could not wait to hear how Keith and I stood now, and I explained to him how brilliant Keith had been through those long months at Frenchay. Now he was at Shenberrow for two days every week and had made it possible for me, financially, to continue with horses, though not as it used to be. Despite my physical situation and the fact that my broken back was never going to mend and that I was landed with all sort of other difficulties, we still wanted no-one else. It was just cruel for both of us that the highly charged sex between us was now severely limited, compared to what it had been. This rendered Ted speechless until he turned the conversation into safer water, wanting to know how I was managing with schooling the horses when I could not do it myself.

It had become obvious that I needed more help in the stable yard, although Sandra came as often as she could she had a busy life as farmer's wife and mother of two. I advertised, and Mandy Lawson came to our rescue. I had become braver and continued to ride Sunny, who was now named Sun and Air as a competition name. We competed in novice and elementary dressage competitions at Stoneleigh and I had decided that the two of us would work our way right up to Grand Prix standard.

I went back to Ascot sales the first week in June and there bought one of the best-looking potential event horses that I had ever seen; a bay thoroughbred with great depth, strong loins, muscular quarters and good bone. He appeared to have a good temperament and was named The Sheik (pronounced 'shake'). He had already raced over fences so for him to end up at the sales he was either not fast enough or there was something wrong with him that wasn't obvious. I also picked up an ex-racehorse called Regal Walk.

Meanwhile, Solo had started his jump training, over poles on the ground so that he learnt to round his back, bascule. He was a very athletic horse and was quick to realise exactly what we wanted him to do in these important jumping exercises. It was now time to start filming *The Event Horse*.

Jeanette was sometimes a little too keen and rushed the horse, which meant that he flattened. It was a matter of sitting still and letting the horse find his stride. This time she approached the coloured rails of the vertical jump, she suddenly threw her weight and her reins forward so that Solo increased his speed, elongated his stride, flattened in outline, and the next moment he was too close to the rails and hit the top pole above his knees. He lost his balance and somersaulted spectacularly over the fence, sending Jeanette face first onto the grassy ground. Solo picked himself up, unhurt, and began to eat grass thinking he deserved a special treat. Jeanette lay still and Robin and I and the crew carrying the cameras set off towards her inert body. I knelt down beside her as she began to move, telling her she was alright. Holding her gums, she said she had lost a tooth. I told her that I had seen something fly into the air but when I looked around, there was no sign of it. Eventually, Jeanette staggered to her feet, ready to try again, and with Solo now recaptured and waiting beside her, she climbed into the saddle for a second attempt. It is very important to do this if one's body and mind are still in working order, and this time Jeanette and Solo sailed over the post-and-rails with Jeanette riding quietly, not throwing her body at the jump, and Solo really concentrated on making sure he did not hit the fence nor trip over the poles on the ground. Having made a fuss of Solo and told Jeanette how brave she had been to jump again and win a battle for herself, I watched the two of them set off back to the stables and wondered what I should do for the best. Jeanette had to visit the

174

dentist for a new tooth, and Solo was sore for a few days, but the crew were ecstatic with the next day rushes.

After this performance, I was even more worried about Jeanette's ability to be able to ride to win on a novice horse in a BHS affiliated one-day event. Much depended on her ability to put on a good show. Privately, I thought just getting around would simply not be good enough to warrant all the time and expense it would take to produce an interesting film. As far as Robin and I were concerned, it would make a terrific ending if Solo, or Two and Two as he would be known in competition, could get into the prize money. I talked to Keith about this and he agreed with me that what we wanted was a rider with more experience. Enter Pammy Sivewright, whose parents ran the Talland School of Equitation at Siddington, outside Cirencester. She was coming over to Stanton twice a week to school Solo.

Pammy soon made it clear to Solo that she was not going to accept having his head thrown up near her face and with proper riding just twice a week the habit began to disappear from Solo's repertoire. His jumping ability, which I had seen when Sandra and I had gone to see him at Mrs Pritchard's, soon began to show with Pammy in the saddle and slowly it became clear that, after all, Two and Two might be counted on not to disgrace the Willcox name at the Bucklebury One-Day Event on the 22nd September 1974. Jeanette continued to ride Solo for his road work and she was also the one to ride his fast work in a long gallop on Cheltenham Racecourse itself, with a Land Rover matching him stride for stride on the other side of the white rail and me, stopwatch in hand, leaning out of the window dictating the pace at which Two and Two would have to travel to gain maximum bonus points on the cross-country course.

We were lucky that some of the cross-country fences which had been part of the course for our Stanton event were in the middle of the fields so we still had access to them and as Solo continued to prepare for Bucklebury we were able to use several of them to accustom him to the sort of obstacles he would face at a one-day event. Soon after our cross-country day not only did Princess Anne bring her horses for another practice, but also Lorna Clarke. Now Solo was to have his turn over the solid and imposing obstacles. We spent a lot of time at the water splash where Solo waded in, being told what a clever chap he was, and then jumped into and out of it in all directions and we added an extra jump in the middle of the pond with show jumps.

175

We also drove him in the horsebox to Eason's silage pit where he said that he could not possibly jump into and out of such an obstacle. After a battle, he decided to bow to the fact that Pammy knew best. We began to work through the list of what Robin wanted in his film. Exercising on the roads, stable management, exercising on the hill, practice at another water splash, show jumping, and cross-country further afield. The last session at Stanton was covering our packing up for departure to the one-day event at Bucklebury, loading the horsebox with everything we would need.

Meanwhile Sunny began to lose his filmstar looks with a large weight on one eyelid, which was drooping over his eye. Mr Walker a local person who dealt with such matters came and smeared a very smelly ointment all over the wart, being careful not to get it in the eye. Four days later, he was back again and rubbed in more ointment. Still no improvement. Mr Walker returned after two more weeks and this time he covered it with a white substance out of a bottle and he told me the wart should drop off shortly. Poor Sunny's eye was swollen like a boxer at the wrong end of a punch. Then the wart seemed to be hanging a little and I gave it a push and it dropped off, a solid round ball squelched out leaving a crater. Sunny's beauty was restored forever.

Jack le Goff, the American team trainer and some of his riders arrived at Shenberrow in their search for top class three-day eventers. They were interested in both the horses I had recently purchased at the Ascot sales, Le Sheik and Regal Walk. The horses were not fit and Jack decided he wanted to see them jump free, something that neither of these horses would ever have done before. Some members of Jack's entourage set up the fences down the long side of the arena and the test began. The heights were raised gradually to 1.2 metres and I was impressed that neither of them made an attempt to run out sideways even though humans stood in the gaps as mobile sentries. The Sheik was outstanding, and Regal was sent back to the stable. Then Jack decided to set The Sheik a very hard test and raised the jump to 1.6 metres and 2 metres wide, far bigger than anything an event horse would face in the show jumping phase. Sheik went towards it and basculed perfectly in the air clearing it. At this point I told Jack it was enough. I left Sheik with Jeanette putting a cooling lotion on his feet and joined Jack in the drawing room. Eventually, he agreed to my price. He was sent back to Canada and won his first four events and was tipped for Olympic honours in the 1976 Games at Montreal.

We arrived at Bucklefield and Robin Crane was there with his camera crew as we rolled in the gates. There was a large entry including Princess Anne riding Blackjack, her sister-in-law's horse. We walked around the cross-country deciding which route Solo would take. With any luck we should not disgrace ourselves.

The next morning Robin saw Princess Anne and her husband Mark Phillips talking together near one of the rings and he suggested that I ask if she would allow us to film a short conversation. It was agreed, and I was supposed to be walking along, see them and stroll over for a conversation. I went past and called out, 'Good Morning'. Robin stopped me and told me I sounded like a milkman. I was better at my second attempt.

This was only Solo's second event but still I was hopeful we would not disgrace ourselves. We were on 25 points after the dressage with Blackjack beating us by a margin of two. Both horses jumped clear show jumping rounds, with Pammy doing an excellent job. They jumped clear around the cross-country but so did Princess Anne so she was the winner, remaining two points above us. Robin was beside himself with excitement, it was a triumph and he had one hell of a good film in his canisters.

Completely out of the blue I had a real shock. I was approached by the French in order to discuss the possibility of training the Olympic French team for the 1976 Olympic Games. It would mean more than 18 months away from Shenberrow and it was agreed that I would fly to Paris and meet the committee, all male and very charming with the most divine food. I decided that I could get used to this, food was definitely the way to my heart!

They took me to Saumur and there was a lot of saluting and troops lining up. The French 'possibles' were brought out for my inspection and to my eyes they lacked the bone and depth of the British horses. Despite the surface politeness of the Commandant in charge, I felt that these men were not going to take happily to the idea of being taught by a woman. At Fontainebleau there was more enthusiasm, higher quality stables and a better atmosphere. I fell in love with the town, but that was not enough. I had been asked by the committee to

177

write a report when I was back in England and my careful assessment was that it would be difficult to train a team in the current circumstances with the intention of improving to such a degree that we would be expecting to win a medal. We would need a central eventing base with facilities for training in dressage, both indoor and outdoor arenas, first class cross-country fences, gallops, and show jumps. Returning to Stanton I wrote my report with as much tact as was possible, saying that I felt I was not the right person for the job, but I thanked them for their courtesy and loved their country.

I went to Burghley as a spectator, wishing once again that I could have a new spine. Then I received a message to meet someone down by the stables after the second day's dressage was finished. I assumed it was a member of the press. It was Alexander Scrope who had been sent to Burghley on behalf of the Canadian Team to see if I would consider training them. He cleverly made a remark which was calculated to butter me up, telling me that he had heard I was the best trainer in the world. They had secured a generous sponsor, Bruce McLaughlin, of Mississauga, on the outskirts of the sprawling city of Toronto. Bruce was in the construction business and had built one of the vast malls in the city where he was based to manage his empire. At that time the idea of malls was a new one. He was willing to supply the team with the facilities of an indoor school, stables, ancillary buildings, a clapboard house and fields of 'good riding country' and he, in the syndicate name of Hooves, was also willing to buy event horses for the team who were yet to make their mark at the international level. He rang me and offered to pay me a very good salary and with bonuses for good results in the prime competitions along the way, and especially if the team won gold, silver or bronze medals at the Montreal games. He also wanted the Canadian team to compete in the Pan-American Games in Mexico City in 1975, going to Florida beforehand to acclimatise to the heat. I was duly impressed. He said the team would need more horses and he wanted me to fly to Toronto first to see what I thought of his set up and the offer to become the trainer for Canada.

This was a very different offer to the one from the French and I was surprised that Keith was rather keen. The idea of a regular salary coming in was a far better proposition than to continue with my rather precarious business of buying and selling horses.

Now, after my paralysing fall, Keith and I still wanted to be together and we looked on this as being only a matter of time. We had, before my fall, considered pooling our resources and buying a farm where I could continue my business but with more flat land and an all-weather arena and a proper show jumping course. There was a property, Top Farm that we had had in mind and at that time it came onto the market. Perhaps if we bought it together then the work that needed to be done could be completed while I was away.

It was obvious that I must visit Canada and ascertain that it was the situation that had been described. Keith and I flew to Toronto together and were soon on our way to Blue Ridge, the McLaughlin's farm where I would be living in the stable complex. Arriving there, the first thing one saw was the large indoor arena, approached through an arrival point for visitors, and the stable complex was at a right angle to it with the looseboxes inside reminiscent of those at Badminton. The door into each loosebox and its front was constructed of strong vertical boards up to a height of about four feet topped in a continuance of the vertical line with rounded iron railings to a height which would prevent the horses from stretching their necks over to see what was going on further along the central gangway. All the horses could do to amuse themselves, except for eating the food in their manger, pulling at the hay in their racks, and drinking water out of a bucket was to gaze across the central wide passageway to the looseboxes on the other side. The designer had given no thought to the fact that horses are gregarious creatures. I could see that if I were to come here as trainer this would be the first thing that I would change.

I appreciated that the winter weather in this part of the world was bound to throw a great deal of snow at us, but I had no idea of just how cold it could be and how difficult a task it would be when the horses were due to start 'long exercise'. I was told that the snow was wonderful for roaring around in snow mobiles, but still it did not enter my head that the horses might be confined to the indoor school for weeks on end.

Bruce showed me the hay and straw and feed stores, and then we turned to the inner hall and went upstairs to the McLaughlin apartment which had a viewing space overlooking the floor of the indoor school below. Keith was appalled at the thought of living 'above the shop' but I did not mind this at all. I would be able to keep

179

an eye on everything very easily and the apartment was clearly set out at present in a manner which would be perfectly acceptable for the odd weekend but not for being there seven days a week for a very long time. Bruce McLaughlin, however had anticipated this and said that the apartment would be revamped to become a comfortable home for me, with a proper kitchen, a dining/sitting room with television and radio, and a double bedroom with a bathroom next door.

Outside, there were grass fields to one side of the property which could be used for outdoor dressage training and practising show jumping, and Bruce said that he had anticipated that it would be necessary to build international type adjustable cross-country fences such as I had designed at Stanton. I was told that the McLaughlin arable land was on the far side of the equestrian facilities. I was more worried about where Jeanette and Mandy would live, and also the riders when they were being assessed as to whether or not they and their horses were team material. All of them needed to be warm and comfortable at the end of the day for we would be working hard. I had noticed an attractive clapboard house, on the left as we drove into the property but the McLaughlins had diverted my attention from this without me noticing. When I persisted in asking where my girls and the team members whose homes were far away in this vast country, would live, they decided that there was no alternative but to renovate this house, never used in their time, to a state where it was warm and comfortable. They said that this work would start as soon as I made up my mind that I would accept their offer and come to Canada.

I was told that there were two women who were extremely keen to be trained by me, the first a successful show jumper, Liz Ashton, who had become very interested in eventing and was looking forward to being taught proper dressage and how to ride cross-country. The second, Cathy Wedge, came from the eastern side of the country and she was already riding in eventing with a very talented horse, City Fella. Then there was Jim Day, Canada's most successful show jumper, with his leading horses Mr Super Plus and Deep South, who was apparently making no secret to the press of the fact that he intended to be the first person to compete in both straight show jumping as well as the three-day event when he was at the 1976 Olympic Games. I could see nothing wrong with this as long as he was prepared to learn his new job in dressage and speed and endurance. He had absolutely no experience of competing in either of them. Next was Jim Henry, purported to be a good event rider, therefore he would know what hard work was required to excel in all three phases of our sport. He had no horse of his own. There was also Peter Howard, who was a good friend of Jim Day.

Bruce McLaughlin also said that part of my job would be to find several top horses for the team, paid by the Hooves Syndicate. He knew the Americans had bought from me and that I had the reputation for training and selling potential top-class eventing horses. It is always easy to be clever after the event, it was perfectly obvious to me from the start that it would take an immense amount of work and co-operation if I were to transform these team members into international eventing material. What I was being asked to do was to make it an accomplished fact that Canada, by 1976, was ready to take on both the Americans and the British and to have moved up in class to such a degree that they were 'possibles' for team gold medal at the games in Montreal.

They did not seem to appreciate that this was asking for a miracle. Anyone with any sense would have run a mile when just this surface information was revealed. Unfortunately, I reckoned that if the riders realised, from the start, how hard they would have to work to reach a high enough standard, as Bruce assured me they would, it could be done. It was a real challenge, and one I was going to find hard to resist if I could count on Bruce keeping his word and making sure the facilities for training in dressage, show jumping, and cross-country were at hand, and the right terrain for our road work existed around Blue Ridge. We would also need access to a steeplechase course to practice for that part of the speed and endurance test. Meanwhile, Bruce wanted me to find class horses for the Hooves Syndicate to buy, and said he would fly to England, purchase Solo and possibly Archie from me once they had been thoroughly vetted, and it would be my immediate job to seek out and buy other outstanding types capable of starring on the international scene, and then train them at Shenberrow until we all left England for Canada and Blue Ridge. It would be part of the contract that my horse, Sunny, would fly to Canada with the other horses, and that when I was returning home, Canada would pay to fly him safely back to England.

Before Keith and I flew back from Canada, salary and bonuses had been discussed and we were bound to take the offer very seriously. It would go a long way to the general funding of the purchase and renovation of Top Farm. It was also perfectly obvious to us both that Bruce McLaughlin was very serious in his desire for his country to do well in the three-day event at the Montreal Olympics, and he had the Hooves Syndicate backing him, mostly members of the country club near Blue Ridge where they all enjoyed their hunting. He said that he would be flying to England to visit Stanton as soon as he could, and it was obvious that this would be the time when I would have to make a decision.

Just eight days after our return from Canada, Bruce was in the drawing room at Shenberrow. Keith and I had agreed that I would accept the Canadian offer and I told Bruce that I was prepared to take up the role of training the Canadian team as long as I had his full support, for I felt this was a truly challenging job. There was no way it could be described as a sinecure, a job that requires little work but financial and status reward. I also made clear that I would be counting on him to keep his word that the necessities for being able to teach the possible team members would exist before I arrived in March and that I must have the facilities for working the horses properly in each of the three spheres of eventing. Bruce was tremendously impressed with Stanton and its surrounding countryside. It was a very different world from those indoor looseboxes at Blue Ridge. Bruce was shown the arenas where we worked on the dressage and show jumping training and he walked round the cross-country course with its 35 obstacles and was deeply impressed. It made him realise how much more was necessary at his Blue Ridge farm in Canada if his country's team were to stand any chance of success at Montreal.

To my surprise he wanted to buy, subject to their passing the veterinary examination, Solo – our film star, and also Gainsborough, whose stable name of Archie, who I had bought from the Sykes. He was now back in work and doing well, and Bruce decided that this horse was his particular favourite and requested that I search and find other horses with Olympic three-day event potential and they would all be flown out to Toronto when I was due to start work for the Canadians on the 14th of March, two days after my 39th birthday.

Soon after this I was at the Ascot sales as usual and spotted a horse with the conformation, paces and perhaps the right temperament to be a good addition for Canada, but if we found that this Whisky Gold was not talented enough to become an Olympic hope, he would be

182

sold on from Shenberrow without Bruce and the Hooves Syndicate having been involved.

I began to travel all around the country searching for the right sort of horses for Hooves, and those I purchased duly arrived at Shenberrow for training as soon as they had passed a very rigorous veterinary examination. It became necessary to find a second groom. Soon afterwards, Mandy Lawson answered the advert to help Jeanette, and in January 1975 both of them were given work permits by the Canadian immigration authorities.

Just to complicate matters, Glen Allen chose to put Top Farm on the market to coincide with this period. Suddenly, the reality of the situation, and my impending departure seemed to affect Keith and me. Keith and I had agreed to buy the farm together by combining our resources, and we had even sent a letter to the agent with an offer. Whilst I was in the maelstrom of buying and training horses to take to Canada I failed to notice that Keith had not gone ahead with our plan. By the time I had noticed it was too late. He placated me with an offer of extending rooms at Shenberrow so that the house was bigger, but I still did not have the acreage I needed for the horses. I said nothing and went along with the alteration in our plan.

I also had to constantly dash up to London to the film company in Soho to do voiceovers for The Event Horse film. At the end of January 1976, a large crowd of guests turned up for the premiere event, including Princess Anne and her husband, Mark Phillips. There were also the cream of equestrian journalism, Michael Clayton the Editor of *Horse and Hound*, and Dorian Williams. These two men had also contributed to the film with 'talkovers'. The men were all in black tie and the women wore long frocks. The BBC bought the rights to show it twice on television and there was a surge of sales of *The Event Horse* book.

Chapter Eighteen – Canadian Adventure

There were dramas with training the horses to be taken to Canada. First, I had to clear the decks and sold three of the horses who were taking up stables and then I went to Paul Rackham the Master of the Suffolk Hunt and purchased Game Moss and took George on two weeks' trial. I had really taken to Game Moss, who I called Gamble, with his bold, yet honest eye, his laid-back shoulder and high withers which gave one the feeling of being in a comfortable chair. He had been competing in show hunter classes and was perhaps a little set in his ways at nine years old. He had been bred at Badminton and when he was three years old he had had an accident in the stable and torn the right side of his mouth, splitting it wide open. In time it had mended, but it was the orbicularis muscle which had been sliced, rendering that side of his mouth bereft of proper feeling. I was planning to retrain him with dressage, so he got used to a very light feel on his mouth rather than the very strong pressure that had been exerted on him in the showing ring. He responded extremely well to this new treatment. I then changed his competing name to Law and Order but still called him Gamble.

Meanwhile Archie who had earlier gone lame came back after his long rest and had gone lame again. This time the vets discovered that he had two damaged discs in his spine, one under the saddle and the other behind it. They operated on him and he was declared cured and became an entirely different horse. But he needed time to recuperate which meant that the other horses would be flown to Toronto ahead of him.

I had Paul Rackham's other horse George on trial and it didn't take me long to realise that he was exactly the sort of horse that was wanted in Canada. He had an amiable temperament and learnt quickly, was very good looking with paces to match and a clever jumper. It was becoming obvious that I must find someone to school the horses in their show jumping development and practice, but that person had to be able to appreciate how the ongoing dressage training must also be used when the horses were jumping.

I began to train Peter Horton, starting with poles on the ground to make the horses look where they put their feet, and once they had mastered that we progressed to the row of poles followed by a low show jump, just as Solo had done in the film. Gamble was at first extremely affronted by these coloured jumps in an enclosed area, he was used to the freedom and scope of the hunting field. At first, he hovered over the top of the rails as if he were considering the possibility of a return to the take-off side with a reverse landing. However, when the time came to turn to cross-country jumps he was in his element.

Still I had not found the total number of horses wanted by Bruce McLaughlin for the Canadian team and I went to the next Ascot sale where there was one horse of those I had marked in my catalogue which interested me, Corrib Chief. He had run over hurdles and after that had been show jumping. I thought this experience might have made him into a very useful horse with plenty of pace for the speed and endurance, and he had already shown that he was a proven and respectful show jumper. I liked the look of him in the loosebox, bright bay with an intelligent eye, good conformation and bone. The young woman in charge of him ran him up and down at the walk and then at the trot outside the row of looseboxes and he was a straight mover with a long, supple stride. I was told that he was a talented jumper. I purchased him and he would go to Canada.

We had many preparations to make for our departure and while I was busy somehow Top Farm slipped out of my memory. Just as I was about to leave Keith said that it was best to forget it, and while I was away he would get the builders onto Shenberrow. We had never actually discussed giving up the Top Farm idea, but Keith had managed to manipulate the situation, so it was no longer viable.

Later on, I found out that when I was away Keith found my personal diaries that were hidden away in a cupboard and he could not resist the temptation to read them. He must have been thrilled reading my complimentary remarks about him after our meeting at the Colville's house in 1966, nine years ago. It must have hugely flattered his ego. However, he also read the entry where I had had a drinks party at Shenberrow. I had wanted him to attend but he had not arrived, and I had had a light-hearted flirtation with a show jumper. In my diary I made a reference to this man's performance as 'very virile'. And Keith read this in March 1975. However, this knowledge remained hidden within him whilst I was in Canada and ate away at him like a malignant tumour.

Just before I left the enormity of the task ahead hit me. However, I had huge faith in Bruce McLaughlin, even though he hadn't paid the balance of the sum for the horses I had purchased for him. Keith drove us to Heathrow Airport and I was dressed in my suede coat with fox fur running around its collar and hem, and the Princess Anne wedding hat on my head and polished knee-high boots. I turned around to wave to Keith as I went through the final gate and I had to swallow back tears.

I arrived in Canada to find Bruce waiting for me, with members of the press and two hours later I was unpacking at Blue Ridge. The weather was bitterly cold. The clapboard house had rats on the ground floor, so Jeanette and Mandy moved upstairs out of their way. The only thing that had been properly done according to my instructions was the removal of the iron bars on top of the doors of the horses' looseboxes.

The horses were in quarantine and Dr Henderson arrived to vet them for insurance purposes and made it clear that we were not allowed to take them outside. I was taken to collect our team vehicle which was the equivalent of one of our Range Rovers which had been donated by the Geoffrey Lynch Company. It was covered with all sorts of colour-clashing advertisements on every visible part of it. I was beginning to realise just how different things were over here. I never got over the embarrassment of driving such a vehicle.

The first potential horse and rider combination to arrive was Cathy Wedge with an outstanding quality horse. He was City Fella and had a temperament to match his beauty and paces. He was Cy for short. This pair was quickly followed by Liz Ashton with the grey gelding Abracadabra. These two had been successful show jumpers but Liz was keen to turn to eventing and wanted to learn the job properly.

There was no sign of Jim Henry, who had no horse of his own. The fourth rider was Jim Day, who was at that time the leading show jumper in Canada, loved by the press. He had two possible horses, Mr Superplus and Viceroy, both were quality horses. He had never in his life competed in affiliated dressage, nor cross-country, speed

186

and endurance; all three were very different disciplines from jumping in the show ring.

One of the original agreements was that all the possible horses were to be based at Blue Ridge so that I knew they were sound. I began to ask why Jim Day and his horses were not at Blue Ridge and I was told that he preferred to keep his horses at home. No doubt, that might be his preference but as the trainer of the time I had to know for a fact that his horses were sound and well and no visit to his stables would be a substitute. I began to suspect that his horses were not sound. I then discovered that no one from the Canadian equestrian team hierarchy, nor Bruce McLaughlin, were prepared to tell Jim Day that I doubted their soundness. With very bad grace he brought Mr Superplus and Viceroy to stay for two days at Blue Ridge. I watched them attempting dressage and neither the horses, nor Jim Day, produced genuine good dressage work.

I went back to basics with jumping exercises and we concentrated first on athletic jumping in the indoor school, trotting up a line of six poles on the ground, then one canter stride before take-off over coloured rails. I was looking for concentration and steadiness from both horse and rider. We progressed to doubles, in and outs, the horse jumping over the first element then having the space for two canter strides before taking off over the second element. The interim space would then be shortened and lengthened so that the rider had to tell the horse what his stride should be for a clean and a safe passage. Lastly, they would learn to bounce jump the fence, land and take off immediately. I also had them jumping narrower and still narrower fences, then with no wings, and they began to appreciate the necessity of holding their horses on a straight approach line, so that the horses could be in no doubt as to the fact that they were going to jump.

Cathy and City Fella worked hard and well. Cy was a class horse, a natural for dressage and show jumping and he soon adapted to these athletic sessions. Jim Henry arrived and I put him on Gamble (aka Law and Order). Gamble was a big, class horse. He had a ground devouring gallop for speed and endurance and beautiful paces which had earned him good marks in the dressage arena as the riders learnt to respect its benefits. He should become a superb cross-country horse.

Peter Howard arrived at last from sheltering behind Jim Day, and I put him on Corrie, (aka Crisp and Even), for this ex-show jumper had a lovely temperament, good easy paces and was very willing to learn. Peter was very young and inexperienced but out of sight and hearing from Jim Day, he was prepared to listen and learn. One day he might be really good. Presently, it was pretty clear that he had no idea of dressage or eventing as I knew it, and I could see that he was going to have to work very hard indeed. It would be a miracle if I could bring him to international standard in time for Mexico, and it was only possible if he was prepared to co-operate with me. With Jim Day as his undoubted idol, and his concrete allegiance to him, I could see problems ahead.

Even the Canadian Equestrian Committee seemed to allow Jim to do as he liked, so I must have been a great shock to him and them when I said that he must train at Blue Ridge like everyone else. If Jim had never been eventing and thought he would like to be in the eventing team as well as the show jumping team he had to learn how it should be done to a winning standard. I had been brought in by the Canadian Team Committee to take Canada to success at the Mexico Games, and I was prepared to try my heart out to do just that, but I needed backing. I needed Jim Day to realise that as he had no knowledge or experience of eventing he must be taught properly, and I was there, waiting for him. And I was working in what I considered were very difficult conditions of weather and lack of facilities, and I expected their co-operation and backing. I must have Mr Superplus and Viceroy at Blue Ridge for there was no valid reason why there should be an exception for them, and I wanted our veterinary surgeon to inspect them for soundness. It took Jim Day some considerable time to produce his two horses for just two days. Jack Chassells, who had been designated as team vet at the big competitions was now due to vet Superplus and Viceroy, and a little bird whispered to me that he and Jim Day were extremely good friends.

On the 15th of April Jack Chassells arrived at Blue Ridge to vet all the horses. They passed with flying colours. Two days later, Archie arrived from Shenberrow at Toronto on a flight which would continue on to Boston and we collected him from the cargo area. He had recovered from the operation to the two discs in his spine in February and he was now ready to start work. Following their instructions, he

188

had been lunged carefully in the outdoor arena at Stanton and been ridden on long walks around the country roads.

At Blue Ridge, we could now start light dressage work with Archie and I very much hoped that this outstanding horse with so much potential talent had now shrugged off his run of bad luck with those unfortunate wrong diagnoses which had lost us so much time and had been so worrying. The poor soul had had his leg blistered on the vet's advice, then his shoulder had been declared the culprit and turned out. Next, he was taken to Newmarket where he was anaesthetised and turned upside down, with the x-rays of the humerus, the bone running from the shoulder to the elbow, which had showed nothing untoward. Now we knew the true source of his pain, his vertebra which had been operated on and finally, with a bit of luck, he would be returning to perfect health.

Bruce had arranged an open day at Blue Ridge for the Hooves Syndicate, so they could have a good look at the horses which the money they had put in the kitty so far had bought. I don't think he actually understood that I had, so far, been the greatest contributor in terms of underwriting the funding for these horses and was still waiting to be reimbursed. The syndicate sat on chairs at one end of the arena with blankets to wrap around themselves and Jeanette and Mandy led in four of the horses, one at a time, to be stood up in front of the audience. Each horse was paraded before them. I had been given to understand that these spectators were horsy people and would appreciate that at Blue Ridge, we had a great deal of work to do if we were to perform well in top grade three-day events later in the year. We would have to work even harder to shine at the Pan-American Games at Mexico. We had only five Canadians as potential riders for their eventing team, which gave me very little choice, and one of these, Jim Day, had never competed in eventing and was expecting his two show jumpers to make a successful transition to the top when he, personally had no experience whatsoever of dressage, or speed and endurance. I had no doubt that Jim was an immensely talented show jumper, but it would take time for him to be genuinely good at eventing, and I was no fan of shortcuts.

I said all this, and more, to the syndicate and tried to impress upon them the huge amount of work and effort that was needed. I then elaborated on the work that would be needed to be undertaken specifically for the riders. I reiterated that |I was prepared to do all that I could to train them.

Finally, the snow had cleared, and we were able to ride out of the confines of the Blue Ridge stable complex, starting the same training programme which had served me so well with my various event horses. I had to make the riders appreciate that even when they were walking or trotting along the horses should remain on the bit at all times, with the riders having constant contact from hand to mouth. Going around corners and turns, length bend should become the norm, and transitions from one pace to another should be smooth and straight. Every day, the dressage lessons came first and, when the last pair of horse and rider had finished in the indoor arena, we would all go out together, with the glaring absence of Jim Day, who declared himself too busy for this programme. Soon, we would be including outdoor show jumping, and cross-country practice. There was nowhere suitable for a proper gallop and it became glaringly obvious that Blue Ridge did not have the facilities we needed when there was so much work to be done, if I were to transform my comparatively inexperienced riders and their horses into Olympic material.

Bruce told me that we were flying to Montreal to meet a new sponsor, an extremely rich businessman, who was on the verge of being persuaded to make a large contribution to the cost of easing Canada's monetary path to the games as far as eventing was concerned. We flew in Jim's private plane to the Island Airport at Montreal and we met the rich businessman at the Royal York Hotel. All went extremely well until I began to register the fact that this man had a son, who had expressed a wish to ride in the eventing team in Montreal. If he was chosen for the team Daddy would be prepared to finance the purchase or one or two very expensive horses for the team. I could see how advantageous it would be to have some very experienced eventing horses, but I had no time to train a young man who had absolutely no experience of eventing. We were being offered a bribe, and I was having none of it.

I think that Bruce could cheerfully have murdered me, but on the way back to Blue Ridge, I told him that a brilliant horse still needed a competent rider. Also, outstanding horses would be in short supply. Obviously, in other countries the outstanding horses were all being got ready for the Olympics and any outstanding horse for sale was deemed to be very suspect.

I was told that it got cold here in the winter, but I could not envisage just how cold and how much snow and how difficult this would make the horses' fittening work. By the time we were due to compete for the first time at the New Jersey Three-Day Event at the end of May. Some of the horses' legs had been strained due to jumping in a small arena and they had turned too sharp a corner or run out of space. This would never have happened had we been able to follow my usual training programme walking, trotting and cantering in the countryside around Blue Ridge. We needed two more horses and I sent a message to Shirley Clifford in Gloucestershire asking her to search for sound, top class types with enough natural talent.

The horsebox set out with the grooms on the long trip down to New Jersey. Meanwhile I had flown from Toronto to Heathrow. Shirley Clifford had called to say that she had found two more horses that the team needed. Keith duly collected me from the airport and it was wonderful to be in the car with him again, placing a proprietary hand on his left thigh as we drove along. I couldn't stop talking, pouring out the difficulties that I was facing in Canada.

The first horse to look at in Herefordshire was a six-year-old by the well-known sire Little Cloud, he was a good-looking 16.3 hh, a straight mover with good strong bone and plenty of presence. He also had a big jump in him. This horse was to be named Lo and Behold in Canada.

Our second visit was to Terry Biddlecombe's somewhat chaotic yard. Years and wives later Terry was to astonish everyone by marrying Henrietta Knight, who trained Best Mate, winner of the Cheltenham Gold Cup for three years in succession from 2002 to 2004 at her yard in East Hendred and the three of them became national favourites. Terry had been a top-class jockey and also was well-versed in training show jumpers, as well as racehorses, and any horse of his was sure to be a good jumper. What I was looking for was a quality horse with an obliging temperament, a sound horse with good looks and paces on four clean strong legs, and he must have had experience in working hunter classes, going hunting cleverly over difficult country, or able to show us as we watched him being ridden for us just how versatile he was. It would be a bonus to a find a champion worker hunter, as talented and as tractable as Paul Rackham's renamed Fine and Dandy.

The third horse to be inspected was at Carlingscott, on the way to Stratford-upon-Avon from Shenberrow. This was another six-year-old brown gelding, sired by Gallant Phoenix and an inch and a half smaller in height at his withers than the other two horses. I decided that he was not the right horse for Canada. On we went, this time as far as Ockley in Surrey, to look at a horse called Grand Lad whom the vet described as a great galloper and a high blower and found his heart and wind sound. He looked a real event horse and became Ways and Means in Canada. These two horses would be shipped by air to the Flying Horse Stables in the United States by Mike Bullen's firm, Peden's Transport, plus five trunks full of items I had been instructed to buy in England, saddles, bridles, leather headcollars to be kept polished as we did at Shenberrow with clip on ropes, as well as lightweight summer sheets and warm winter ones with arch rollers. All these from Sidney Free's saddlery shop in Cirencester.

I got back to the USA and had been missing in England for just three working days. On the Sunday we all set out together to practise the cross-country over some of the Ledyard course. This was great fun as well as being used to decide the right approach. The very next day, we would be walking the cross-country course there and hoping that the two Jims, Day and Henry, plus Peter Howard, would arrive in time.

On the 31st of May it was dressage day, our introduction to eventing in the States. We had four horses competing *hors concours*: Cathy Wedge riding Fine and Dandy, Jim Henry on Law and Order, Peter Howard on Crisp and Even, and Liz Ashton on Two and Two. They were not fit enough to risk running over the steeplechase and roads and tracks on the second day. The organisers had no issues with everyone riding over just the cross-country. After the dressage Fine and Dandy was fourth, Two and Two not far behind in 8th place, and Law and Order and Crisp and Even were well within striking distance. I spoke to the dressage judge, Louis de Lavalette, as I was anxious to know how we might improve. He told me that he knew the English horses were novices and he did not expect good tests from them and marked accordingly!

In the cross-country Fine and Dandy, Law and Order, and Two and Two were unpenalised and Peter Howard allowed Crisp and Even one unnecessary refusal. On the third day, in the show jumping, both Fine and Dandy and Two and Two dislodged a pole each, whilst Jim Henry

192

on Law and Order and Peter Howard on Crisp and Even each had two fences down. Considering what a sparse preparation we had had, it was a fairly miraculous result. I requested that the Canadians might be allowed to return the next day to practise over the cross-country course and the following morning we were occupied in jumping the more difficult fences, making sure of the right line of approach and with me on Sunny emphasising that the riders must begin to look for the next fence as soon as they landed over the last one, and that they must present their horses on a clear line of approach, so that they could not be confused as to the exact place for take-off.

It would have been so much better to stay permanently at the Flying Horse stables, rather than returning to the bitter cold of the indoor arena at the aptly named Blue Ridge stables in Canada. However, Cathy and Liz, in particular, had made great strides in their dressage work, and Jim Henry had shown that he was prepared to work hard, learning that there were no short cuts if one wanted to excel. They had all been listening to what I had said and now realised what a difference the dressage training made to cross-country riding and even the show jumping when the result was to have a horse immediately responsive to the rider's aids.

The next competition was Charlie and Fifi Coles' three-day event. All the British horses were in division one. Liz had volunteered to be guinea pig and ride the dressage test on Abracadabra before the first competitor was due in the arena at nine in the morning. This would give the judges a welcome opportunity to get their eye in before competition proper began. I had worked out for my riders how much time each individual horse needed to be worked in before he would be in just the right frame of mind to go into the dressage arena and perform the test before the judges. Crisp and Even emerged in second place at the end of the first day.

We had walked the cross-country course and I was looking forward to seeing if my riders had learnt lessons from our practice session at Essex. At the end of the second day Crisp and Even was still in second position but Law and Order as close behind him with Cathy and had had an unnecessary stop and a fall which incurred 80 penalties and put them down to 11th place. I would have expected this to galvanise Cathy to greater efforts the next time we were trying to show how we were improving. On the third day of the show jumping Crisp and Even was still in second place; Two and Two had moved up to fourth; Law and Order, despite a silly stop for 20 penalties, was fifth and Liz with Abracadabra was sixth. We all felt that things at last were looking up.

On the next day there was a press conference to attend in Toronto and after that I went straight to the airport, flying from Boston to New York and then New York to Toronto. It took nearly four hours before I saw Harry Ridgley waiting patiently in the reception area to collect me and take me to Blue Ridge for the meeting with Bruce McLaughlin. I reported all that had happened and told Bruce how much better was our work and progress since we had settled at Flying Horse Stables. I was not at all happy about the Jim Day situation for it was clear that no one in authority in the National Equestrian Federation was brave enough to stand up and tell him that if he wanted to be considered for the Canadian three-day event team for the Olympics he would have to become very good not just on the third day in the show jumping ring, but also in dressage – to which he was a total stranger – and the speed and endurance which was a totally different thing from show jumping.

Jim did not even entertain the thought that perhaps his two show jumpers, Mr Superplus and Viceroy, would not take kindly to dressage tests, or that they might object to facing a speed and endurance test over twenty odd miles which would include two sets of roads and tracks, a two and a half mile steeplechase course, and around thirty five fixed cross-country fences, the like of which they would never have seen before in their lives. Brilliant show jumping horses do not often make eventers, and vice versa. The only one I can think of was Anneli Drummond-Hay's Merely a Monarch.

One would have thought that Jim Day must have been very badly advised or very arrogant to expect to conquer the three different disciplines in eventing in just a few months. This situation put me in a very awkward position. It was too ridiculous for words, that I should have to put up with Jim's lack of co-operation, and his attitude did nothing to foster good morale within the team. Jim was intent on persuading my team that they did not need me. He had agreed to join the team at Flying Horse just before Neil and Helen Ayer's prestigious Ledyard Three-Day Event, where the British team would also be competing. Jim Day had already told the press that he would be competing and also at the Mini Olympics at Bromont.

194

I decided to put Jim Day out of my mind and concentrate on the training. The horses were now becoming fit and we had the use of proper gallops held in with running rails like those guarding a professional racetrack. Jim Henry said that Gamble was difficult to hold on these occasions, so to the team riders' horror I said that I would ride him in the next training gallop. There was no doubt that Gamble was enthusiastic, and his great stride fairly made one realise the ground he covered, but he responded and stopped pulling when I relaxed the bit in his mouth, and the team ranged alongside me saw this and learned a valuable lesson. It was not necessary to hang on to the horses' mouths, they must keep a light contact, but he was ready to give and take. We were also able to ride over the Ayers' estate and were warned to keep an eye open for holes dug in the ground by gophers. I had no idea what these could be until they turned out to be similar to the British rabbit, but larger and darker in colour and with longer ears, which was what we often saw as they felt the earth shaking from our approach and poked their head out of the vertical hole to see what sort of danger was approaching. These holes were difficult to spot because they were not like the ones at home in the field where it would appear the rabbits dug with their front legs, sending the earth out through their hind ones, like a dog, so that there was a tell-tale trail leading to the hole, easily identified. These American gophers must have been capable of diving down head first!

During this time Keith kept reminding me that Hooves still owed me £15,250 which was now supposed to be subject to accumulating interest, but beyond pushing Bruce for this, there was little I could do. I had also had to pay the telephone account for Blue Ridge and was still owed £120 for this. It was a very awkward situation.

Keith and I were totally committed to each other and the last thing I wanted was any sort of distraction. I was not in the slightest bit interested in any other man and I made this abundantly clear if any man approached me. Unknown to me, back in England, Keith had read in the newspaper that a certain team of show jumpers were now based in Canada. He convinced himself that the show jumper with whom I had had a fling years before, was now back in the picture and that I was involved with him. Instead of mentioning this to me Keith allowed his imagination to run wild. His festering anger mounted.

Jim Day arrived to join us at Flying Horse the day before the start of the Ledyard Three-Day Event. He had succeeded with the backing of Peter Howard, in convincing Jim Henry and even Liz and Cathy that they could manage without me. I decided to wait for them to come to their senses on the day before the big three-day event was due to start and concentrated instead on organising the transport of all we would need for the cross-country. Jeanette and Mandy would be in the box, ready to make sure that each of our horses' tack and leg bandages and jumping studs were as they should be before they set onto the demanding cross-country course with its beautifully built and impressive fences, some of which would be entirely new to them. I was very anxious to be allowed to ride Sunny around parts of the course where the fences were most difficult so that I would know whether or not my riders were remembering what they had been taught and were following the line it had been decided they should take.

I asked Neil Ayer to ask if this would be allowed and, as he knew I could be counted on not to get in anyone's way, I was given a bright sash to wear which meant I was not to be stopped. My Canadian team members were running in the open preliminary class as opposed to the advanced international section, and we were facing our first big test over thirty odd fairly intimidating obstacles. By now, the weather in the States was very hot and the horses would sweat profusely. The American team was accustomed to using ice to cool down their horses as they came into the box for the ten-minute revival time. The Canadian team would be copying their method and would also use it in the Pan-American Games in Mexico at the end of September.

Meanwhile, Cathy and Liz were having second thoughts about adopting Jim Day as their leader. The two of them came to find me and to apologise. Soon afterwards, Jim Henry also returned sheepishly to the fold. Jim Day and Peter Howard continued to behave as if they had nothing to do with me. Peter was to ride one of Jim Day's horses stabled for him in the Day yard, presumably to ensure that he would stay loyal to Jim. They steadfastly refused to acknowledge my authority as Canadian team trainer. This was a shame for I sensed that Peter did not embrace the situation. Basically, he was a well brought up young man. Before we walked the cross-country for a second time, the first being the official walk round with all the other competitors, I made clear to both Jim and Peter that they must behave like team members and accompany the rest of us on the team's private inspection when we would decide the approach and choice of line over each fence bearing in mind which alternative would best suit each individual horse and rider. Approach speed, line and the choice of alternative routes over some of the double or treble fences, and the rolling terrain, all had to be considered and agreed.

I spent a great deal of time discussing the options of how to ride each fence on the cross-country. The open preliminary class was over the usual two phases of roads and tracks, with the steeplechase course in between, and then after the ten-minute break the horses would face the long cross-country course in intense heat. The horses were all very inexperienced and I stressed how very important it was that the horses enjoyed their first experience of a three-day event. Fine and Dandy, Two and Two, and Crisp and Even would take on just the cross-country phase and not the speed and endurance and the steeple chasing and they, in particular, would need nursing round the course, going fast enough to have the momentum to jump all the fences, but at a speed which would not exhaust them. We had had enough trouble with leg strains as a result of having to work our horses in a small indoor arena, in a far too restricted space. I told Cathy, Liz and Jim Henry that they must make sure their horses were well awake before they set off from the box to tackle the cross-country phase. I would be tracking them on Sunny on speed and endurance day. Also, they should remember the rules governing the carrying of a whip as set out in the *Federation Equestre Internationale* (FEI) rule book, a copy of which all the riders were given when I first met them.

The British team had arrived five or six days before the competition was due to start on the 27th of June. Sensibly, they had given themselves plenty of time to recover from the flight and settle in. Here at Ledyard they had good stabling, which was a real bonus. Princess Anne would be riding Arthur of Troy, Sue Hatherly was on Harley, Lucinda Prior-Palmer on Wideawake, Janet Hodgson on Gretna Green, Mark Philips on Laureate, and Mike Tucker on Ben Wyvis. This was a very strong team for Great Britain, but so was that of the United States, with the big names of Bruce Davidson, Tad Coffin, J. Michael Plumb, Mary Anne Taskey, Tad Zimmerman and Beth Perkinds. Their trainer was Jack le Goff. Whilst we were at Ledyard, I had to list all those who were to go to the Bromont Three-Day Event at the end of July. The count was 10 horses, six riders, plus Jim Day if he decided that he would compete, four grooms – Jeanette, Mandy, Valinda and another, plus our vet and farrier then all the hay, fodder, tack and the mound of baggage which had to go with us. My heart sank at the prospect of the long journey north to Bromont which lay eastwards in Canada, across the River Lawrence from Montreal towards the Atlantic Ocean. The two Canadian reporters who had been attached to us for some time, were making a film of our progress in three-day eventing and were delighted at the prospect of returning to their French speaking part of the world and its important three-day event. Their last job would be to accompany us to Mexico, where we were entered to compete in the Pan-American Games at the close of the 1975 season.

The other teams had horses and riders competing in the advanced class and Bruce Davidson and Golden Griffin won on a final score of 57, he was also third on Royal Cor. One step below in the open preliminary class I was delighted when the winner emerged as Jim Henry and Law and Order on their final score of 45.3 points. The American riders took all the places from second to eighth and in tenth place was James Day with Mr Superplus on 70, having incurred a refusal for 20 penalties. We therefore had all three of our team placed. I felt that considering our starting point we had done well. One thing we did need to practise was using ice to cool down the horses. We would also need to install a water filter system for the horses' drinking water.

I had organised several training sessions at the cross-country course at Ledyard. On the first day Cathy, Liz, Jim Henry ad Peter were practising and Liz was having problems with striding on the top of a square topped bank with a rail sitting on the far edge which meant a drop on landing. Her horse was not big and did not possess the physique to give him the thrust and strength to land well in the middle of the bank and take off immediately to bounce up over the rail and land back on the ground, balanced and safe to gallop away from the landing side. Liz had to think of the length of his stride which was short – remember that he had been her show jumper before coming to Blue Ridge to be transformed into an eventer. I told her to come in again, this time on a short, bouncy stride so that there was room on the top for another short one before take-off. Snoopy appreciated this. He might have lost a few seconds, but he would be free of the risk of stopping at the rail out if he had tried for a bounce and breasted the rail instead. He would have earned 20 penalties for the refusal,

60 if there was a fall, and inevitable time faults whilst Liz reorganised him for a second attempt.

Cathy was riding Two and Two as well as her own City Fella, and she had a good day listening to my advice on speed of approach, and realising there were times on a course to gallop on, but in balance, and times where it was prudent to throttle down so that the horse could take in a combination of fences and realise just what had to be done. I stressed that whatever the fence, the rider must give the horse the chance to size it up and he must be presented on a straight and narrow line so that he was in no doubt as to where he was going. Peter rode Corrib Chief and again I was surprised how well this horse from Ascot jumped and what an easy ride he was. He was the type one had to 'point' and he would jump economically. He was a very good 'fall back' horse and Peter rode him well. We progressed to all the combination fences there were and paddled around in the water jump before jumping it and went home to Flying Horse very pleased with our confidence building day's work.

Three days later and Jim Day was due to arrive for his cross-country workout at an agreed one o'clock. I waited and waited. He eventually arrived at seven in the evening and I was furious with him. He had no excuse and made no apologies. Our cross-country practice would have to wait until the next morning and I had to telephone to explain that my rider had not arrived. Next day, to be fair to Jim, he was a pleasure to direct. I knew that he must have an eye for a stride, but I wondered how he would be at speed over fixed fences. There was no doubt that if he were prepared to work with me on a steady basis he would be a very useful team member. At present his Achille's Heel was on the fast approaches after a long run between fences. I hoped that he would listen to me when we were up against the American and British teams at Montreal. It would also do him a world of good to ride round Badminton. He certainly needed a genuine dressage training, for to my experienced eyes, he was producing work which might kid the judges in Canada who were influenced by his name but would not be applauded by the international judges, who, hopefully, would judge what they saw and not what they wished they could see.

On the third practice day Cathy, Liz, Jim Henry and Peter were back practising over the Ledyard fences and this time we were riding parts of the course, not just individual fences. Today they were instructed to ride at competition speed over five diverse obstacles, and both horses and riders were thoroughly enjoying themselves. We kept moving round the course so that the horses were being asked all sorts of questions. Whilst one of the riders was jumping, the rest of us stood on the best vantage point we could find. I told the team riders, grouped on either side of me, to remark on the speed and approach of which ever combination was jumping and asked them to say if he or she presented the horse correctly at each fence so that he knew exactly what he had to do.

It came to Cathy's turn on City Fella and the rest of us were on the highest part of a gentle slope from which we could see all five obstacles with ease. She counted herself down and shot off towards the first of our present five fences. They sailed over that and turned right in a half curve on a gentle downhill slope. At the bottom of this stood an 'island' fence of two substantial rounded poles, sloping upwards, the first set at 55cm and the second higher, just under maximum height of 125cm. It appeared to be what I called a 'flyer' fence, approach at a good speed, on a good stride, and fly it. On inspection it was not as straightforward, for underneath, starting under the first rail, it had been dug out to a depth of around 40 cm which made the rails looker higher and the fence rather intimidating. It was one of those in England where it was necessary to fling one's heart over first, and it was obligatory to arrive fast but on the correct stride for take-off. If one managed this, the feeling in the air would be terrific. If the approach stride brought the horse in for take-off half a stride too early or half a stride too late, it would be very nasty.

We were all watching carefully, expecting Cathy and her horse to fly it with ease. They arrived at a good pace on the slightly downhill approach. Her line was fine, but it was becoming clear that the partnership was not going to meet the fence on the correct stride for perfect take-off. I think Cathy hesitated, momentarily, and in that fleeting second it meant that she had missed the one opportunity to drive on for an early take-off. Her increased speed coming in would have made up for the half stride. It must have gone through Cathy's mind to kick him upwards, but by then it was too late, and the horse tried to put in a short stride and this was disastrous. He took off but could not clear the top rail and fell in a sprawling heap on the other side.

City Fella scrambled to his feet and walked off. Cathy stayed on the ground, clearly unable to get up and I told her to stay still. She thought she had broken a bone in her leg. There were no mobile phones in those days, so Neil set off for the house to telephone for a hospital in Boston. The rest of us went back to the stables at Flying Horse in a very subdued state and desperately sorry for Cathy. I was driven to the hospital, hardly able to believe that this could have happened. As far as I was concerned, Cathy was my most promising all-round team rider, and City Fella was a very talented horse. They had made just one mistake in arriving at the fence with just that moment of hesitation yet nine times out of ten over a fence like this, the horse would have taken off earlier in a powerful jump and all would have been well. I had to telephone Cathy's parents, her father was a judge in Saskatchewan Province, and then assure her that she must not worry about the horse, we would look after him. I remember being immensely impressed by the hospital on my arrival. It was almost opulent by comparison to those I knew in England, beautiful polished floors, large windows and the kindest and most attentive staff. Spotlessly clean everywhere, smart chairs and comfortable areas to sit. I returned to Flying Horse horrified that I had lost my best rider and feeling so very sorry for her. That it should happen to the person whom I considered to be Canada's probable best bet, was simply awful. The doctor said that the x-rays showed a fracture, but that did little to lift the feeling of despondency. I had become attached to Cathy and would miss her intelligent conversation and her determined application. Three days later, the Canadian team was due to travel to Bromont and once more all my attention had to return to the team. We would be in French-speaking Canada to compete *hors concours*.

Chapter Nineteen – Pan-American Games

When we got there, I rode Gamble until Jim Henry arrived, then I switched to Sunny. I was becoming more and more aware of the reverence in which the Canadians held Jim Day, and there was no way I could hold the respect which was due to me as team trainer whilst the press were interested only in what this one member of the team was saying, which caused upset and resentment, and Jim Day continued to do as he pleased, sure that none of the committee men would have the guts to take him on. I then named our first team: Jim Day with Mr Superplus; Liz Ashton with Abracadabra; and Jim Henry on Law and Order. Our second team was comprised of: Jim Day with Deep South; Peter Howard with Bright Patrick; and Liz Ashton with Fine and Dandy.

We were competing in what the Canadians were calling the Mini-Olympics, with intermediate rating, meaning that the fences would have a maximum height of 145 cm, a speed and endurance course of approximately ten miles and the competition run over three days. Our first team won the gold medal and in the individual placings Jim Day took second and fourth positions with Superplus and Deep South, whilst Jim Henry with Law and Order was fifth. Liz Ashton took third and seventh places with Abracadabra and Fine and Dandy. Ginny Holgate had won the Bromont Three-Day Event with Jason the IV

Keith, in my absence had been to Spain for a week in between visits to Shenberrow to see how the builders were progressing. His letter told me that I could count on the fact that he would behave himself amongst the brown-eyed beauties. He had this undeniable compulsion to travel and would depart on a sudden whim, perfectly happy with his own company. He said he would fly to Canada and arrive at Bromont to see how my Canadians were progressing with their eventing and then return to Blue Ridge with me. I was looking forward to being distracted from Jim Day and his delight in upsetting everyone, except for the press, who he needed on his side. Meanwhile Keith wandered around at Bromont as the fancy took him, staying away from our hotel at night, and I could feel that there was something different about him.

Finally, we were all back at Blue Ridge and on this night, Keith would be in my bed in the apartment. I would no longer be alone. Our first night was not what I thought it would be. We were hardly in bed and he was on top of me and thrusting inside me with all the force he could muster. This was not like him at all. There had been no teasing foreplay, nor looking at each other with a mixture of lust and love. It did not feel like love to me, it was more like vengeance, but I put it down to pent up feelings of frustration whilst we had been apart. I asked him, "What was the matter?" and he replied, "Nothing." He lay there, looking up at the ceiling, so I decided to play with him, to move my hands all over him, to kiss him deep down and then to withdraw my mouth and sit on top of him. My Dutch cap had been inside me almost as soon as I could get into the bathroom after we entered the apartment. I kept stopping him from reaching the point of ejaculation and he suddenly came to life, throwing me on my back again, waiting over me before entering again and coming with great force as if I were an enemy.

Suddenly, there was a crash and the sound of splintering wood. The legs on the top half of the bed had gone straight through the floorboards and were resting at a precarious angle on the joists below. Keith said he didn't care and fell asleep and I slipped out of bed and went into the bathroom to use my spray and take out the Dutch cap. To my horror I realised it had been knocked sideways, leaving a gap. To modern women it would appear incomprehensible that the only aid to prevent pregnancy was a vulnerable cap, and this night, and indeed this week with Keith, was just the time when what I needed was the morning after pill, not yet invented. It was also going to be very embarrassing to ask for my bed to be mended.

During the next few days Keith and I went off in the afternoons to view the surrounding countryside and take a good look at Toronto. In the morning, he drove off in the jeep or explored the farm. He decided to drive one of the tractors and he took several men to rescue it when it got bogged down. We continued to argue over nothing and it was a miserable time.

At the end of July, I was due to visit Calgary to look at riders competing at the Red Deer Event and to hold a clinic the next day.

203

My instructions were to try to find someone capable of becoming a team member. Keith came too, amusing himself happily in exploring the area, whilst I picked out a girl called Fran McVity from the crowd of eventing hopefuls. I thought she had potential and she was duly asked to turn up at Blue Ridge. Apparently, she had performed way above her best at the clinic and back at Blue Ridge, Bruce and Denny Whittaker said she was nowhere near team material, and that it would be as good as murdering her if we were to put her on our big, strong, class horses. She rode Gamble at Joker's Hill and it was frightening watching her go cross-country on a real horse, I had to send her home quickly. Bruce and Denny had been absolutely right.

Keith and I flew on from Calgary to Mexico where I was due to meet Colonel Sarcedo Caullo to discuss the Canadian needs for the forthcoming Pan-American Games in the middle of October. After our meeting when the men drank tequila together we went back to the Camino Real Hotel, a wonderful nesting place, where Keith, thawed and we returned at last to something approaching our old love, with its longing for each other. We stayed there for a few days and returned to Blue Ridge in August, on the day on which my period was due to start. I tried to calm myself down with the thought that all that dashing around had done something to my insides. I wrote to Keith, telling him that I might be in trouble, and those gremlins within him stoked up. Keith could so easily have counted from the days of my previous period of mid-July and faced the fact that we had had 16 nights of opportunity after Bromont from the 28th July to the 13th of August. I still find it very hard to forgive him for this interpretation and his rejection of the fact that he was the only man who could possibly have made me pregnant.

I went to a gynaecologist and seven days after my period should have appeared I went into hospital for a D and C operation. The next day I was riding again, pretending to myself that nothing had happened.

I wrote a letter to Keith, who had arrived back in England, asking what was the matter with him when he was in Canada. I also told him of what I had had to do to terminate the pregnancy and saying that the least he could do was pay that account. He refused. Still he did not tell me that he had assumed that the show jumper had been a visitor at Blue Ridge. He had convinced himself that this man was the father of the aborted child. I cannot imagine how a man of Keith's intelligence could have been stupid enough not to ask, and then to behave in so strange a manner.

I tried to distract myself by thinking about the Pan-American Games and then I was determined to leave. I was constantly being undermined by Jim Day and it was far too annoying. There was still one more event before the Mexico Games at Joker's Hill and we would use this event as a practice. Again, the team would be riding *hors concours*. All the riders understood this. They were to go steadily round the cross-country, honing their skills at bringing their horses into each fence on a perfect stride so that at the end of the course the horses would have thoroughly enjoyed themselves and should be in just the right state of mind for the Pan-Am Games.

On the 27th August Jim Day and Liz Ashton were due to go to the Fitness Institute in Toronto. The press was waiting for them and Jim Day told them that he would be competing at Joker's Hill, despite Liz saying that they were competing *hors concours*. We all read about this in the newspaper. The eventing ruling committee decreed that unless he withdrew his entry to 'compete' and rode *hors concours* then he would lose his place on the team of the Pan-Am Games. The press picked up this story with delight. Jim decided that the cards were stacked in his favour with the press and the public behind him. When I was asked for my opinion I said that Jim Day had broken an unwritten rule, he had spoken to the press about team business which was not for him to discuss or over-rule.

I could not believe how reluctant the committee was in failing even to summon Jim Day before them. Denny Whittaker said that he would go and talk to him, he was sure that he could change his mind. The next day Jim appeared as determined as ever to ride into the dressage arena as a competitor and the result would be immediate suspension. Just before he was due to ride in he announced that he would be riding *hors concours*. I admired him for his brinkmanship. It was superb. He had managed to upset the team, trainer and the committee, and got clean away with it, except for a reprimand, which must have made him smile in derision.

All the horses went well at Joker's Hill and we returned with all of them sound and well in themselves, having acquired much more valuable experience. Jim Day was not reprimanded. We then went to Mexico. I had quite a few days working intensively with the team

205

before the competition began and Jim Day could not escape some rather exhausting dressage practice.

At the end of the dressage day the Americans were in the lead both for the individual and team event, occupying three of the first four places. The leader was Tad Coffin with Bally-Cor on 34.34 penalties with the Mexican Captain Mariano Bucio riding Cocaleco in second on 38. The Mexicans had small, wiry but blood type horses, eminently suited to dressage with their high paces and lightness in hand. Beth Perkins with Furtive was third on 39.34, Bruce Davidson on Golden Griffin fourth on 41.67, then Jim Henry with Law and Order on 44 penalties. A second Mexican on Canaleto was close to Jim's score on 44.67. Superplus was eighth, Abracadabra was tenth on 50.34 and Peter Howard with Deep South, twelfth on 55.67.

There was a call for me to go to the weighing out tent, where I was told that Jim Day had arrived there with his saddle and had stepped on the scales carrying not only the required saddle, but also his whip, the latter in direct contravention of the rules. He had been promptly eliminated, for carrying his whip on the scales was clearly a violation of the rules. Privately, I thought this served him right, he had been too arrogant to read the rules properly, but as team trainer, I argued on his behalf with all saddlery and equipment carried by the horse, EXCEPT BRIDLE AND WHIP at the start of Phase A, and before the show jumping on the third day. I could not argue against the fact that Jim Day had been carrying his whip when he stood on the scales, but I read out to them from the FEI's rule book which stated only two reasons for eliminating a competitor, namely "Failure to be weighed in front of the official steward, or failure to carry at least the minimum weight. Both involve elimination." My team member had weighed out in front of the official steward and the scales declared him over 75 kgs or 165 lbs, which conformed with the rules. There was no doubt that the rule writer had intended that anyone carrying a whip onto the scales would provide a third reason for elimination along with those who transgressed by not having been weighed in front of the steward, or not carrying enough weight, but the person at the FEI headquarters in Switzerland had failed to make clear that carrying a whip on to the scales was the committee's third reason for immediate elimination from the competition. After protracted arguments, it was decided that Jim Day should be allowed to compete.

He set off on the first phase of the roads and tracks, jumped round the steeplechase course and completed the long phase of the second roads and tracks. Meanwhile, a committee was discussing the matter of the whip appearing on the scales in private, and as Superplus came in for the ten-minute break, he was told that he had been eliminated from the competition. I promptly objected and for forty minutes I battled hard on Jim's behalf. They gave way and with Superplus now very well rested, Jim was thrown up into the saddle and set off round the four and a half miles of cross-country. He promptly rewarded my success in keeping him in the competition by having two falls, one just outside the penalty zone. His elimination was then confirmed, my objection had now been over-ruled. Jim would take no further part in this international three-day event which probably he would prefer rather than finish well down the field having hit the ground twice. This was his first personal blow and it might just make him wonder if he really was an event rider.

Meanwhile, the speed and endurance test proceeded, I managed to drive to the racetrack. I wanted to see how easily Jim Henry, Liz Ashton and Peter Howard coped at a fast speed over the steeplechase course, and how long it had taken them after that to recover their breath on phase C, the second roads and tracks. The Americans, with both riders and horses experienced in all three aspects of eventing under their now long-term trainer, Jack le Goff, should win by the proverbial mile.

I was waiting at the racetrack when I saw one of the members of the Guatemalan team come down the hill and start to cross the racetrack. It was obvious to anyone that this rider was going to miss the red and white flags on top of poles which marked the end of the first roads and tracks. An Army General was strutting about with colourful ribbons all over his chest saw that disaster was about to strike. He decided that he simply could not allow an elimination when there were so few competitors so he shouted at the two army men, standing either side of the flags, to pick the supporting posts out of the ground and carry them at full speed to a spot where they were in front of the rider, and they overtook her just in time for her to pass between the red and white flags. She was then classified as having finished phase A even if the finish position had been moved. If no-one objected, which they did not, she could proceed to the start of the steeplechase and carry on round the rest of the speed and endurance test. I could hardly believe my eyes. I thought the whole episode hilariously funny.

Then I realised that Jim Henry would be aiming for the original position. I hurried over to the General as quickly as I could, telling him in halting Spanish and waving my arms that the men must return the finishing posts to their original place so that my rider saw them where he was expecting to see them. I did not tell Jim what had happened until the evening. Law and Order and Jim galloped round the steeplechase course with aplomb. I watched him slow down his horse in a gentle reducing manner and pass on to the second roads and tracks, and then I jumped into the jeep, driving back as fast as I could to the camp, in the hope of seeing something of his passage over the cross-country course.

As a matter of interest, the Guatemalan woman rider, Silvia Luna, had the worst dressage score of 76.67, but she was the only one of the Guatamalan team to survive the entire three-day event and jumped one of just five clear rounds on the final day's show jumping to finish in eighth place, with Elizabeth Ashton on Abracadabra in ninth and Peter Howard riding Deep South in tenth. Both of them had been in unnecessary trouble on the cross-country.

Law and Order, with his months of dressage work with me at Stanton behind him, was fifth after the first day's competition, with Tad Coffin riding Bally-Cor in the lead on 34.34, the Mexican Captain Mariano Bucio and Cocaleco on 38, Beth Perkins a close third with 39.34. Fourth was Bruce Davidson riding Golden Griffin with 41.67 and then Jim on Law and Order on 44. Of the original 15 on dressage day, 11 survived to jump in the ring on the third day. Our three horses, Deep South, Abracadabra and Law and Order ran up sound in the veterinary examination on the final day's show jumping. Liz with Abracadabra had one foot in the water for 10 penalties, Peter Howard rode a clear round on Deep South. Law and Order, looking as if he could do the entire competition again, was controlled beautifully by Jim Henry, and earned 2 penalty points on time. Jim had succeeded in riding a very careful clear round and finished in fourth place, just missing out on the individual bronze medal.

I was disappointed that Liz and Peter had not done better over the speed and endurance. They had made silly mistakes and paid the penalty and no doubt they would have learnt a valuable lesson to put into practice for the future. Jim Day had managed to get himself eliminated through not having bothered to read the rule book he had been given, and his effect on my riders with his attitude from the moment I arrived at Blue Ridge had been to turn them against me. To my mind, it was fairly miraculous that we had managed to do as well as we had. Despite our failure to produce a better challenge to the Americans, we still emerged as the silver medallists, with Mexico in third place, but I was sad, for I knew we could have performed so much better. Cathy and City Fella had been very much missed. When all the horses and riders and spectators had disappeared from the show jumping ground, Jack le Goff and I were leaning on the rails and discussing the course and our experiences over the last three days. Jack was well aware that I was resigning after my return to Blue Ridge and that it was a result of Jim Day's behaviour and bad influence, and his continuous lack of co-operation. He also knew that I was going to stay with Neil and Helen Ayer at Ledyard before returning to England, and that I had also been invited to visit the home of Bruce Davidson's fiancée, Carol, in Pennsylvania. It had also been suggested to me that I should spend six months of every year in the States working with event horses. This was a very tempting idea and meant that the Americans held my methods in high regard and would not object if I were to train in their country.

Three days later I flew back to Toronto and went to Bruce's office to sort out my resignation and the payment of all the money still owing to me for the purchase of the horses, saddlery and tack from England. Bruce and the Hooves syndicate were delighted with the silver medal from the Pan-Am Games. Bruce honoured the agreement that Sunny, my personal horse, was to be flown back to England. The building extensions at Shenberrow were now completed and awaiting me and I had to put the whole Canadian experience behind me. When I went to actually say good-bye to the team members I felt unexpectedly emotional, and in particular I had to say good-bye to Gamble. I got to New York and the hotel did not serve dinner and I had to venture out into the street to find a restaurant. Usually Keith, and before him Ted, would have arranged such matters and I felt incredibly alone. I felt cared for at the Davidson's place and then at the Ayers but when I flew home to England I felt that I had been cured of gallivanting around the world for a long time to come.

Chapter Twenty – The Bechtolsheimer Years

I let out a sigh of relief when we touched down at Heathrow. Keith was waiting for me and I was uncertain of the state of our relationship. He had not even replied to my letter about the D and C operation. He seemed in a good mood, so I didn't bring up this subject. We drove to Gloucestershire and I looked out at the quintessentially English countryside and the little villages with a new appreciation. I couldn't wait to see Shenberrow with the new extensions.

We came around the corner and I was amazed at the difference in my property. It looked much more important, less of a cottage. Inside the proportions of the extended length of the sitting room were just right. The living room was much lighter and airier. Upstairs, my bedroom was now an elegant oblong instead of a sturdy square and there were two windows to the front instead of one. Glen had gone wild with excitement when he heard the tyres of Keith's car crunching the gravel. He nearly knocked me over with his enthusiastic welcome. He rushed around, then back again to make sure I really had come home. Keith and I enjoyed this time alone and it seemed as if it was back to the way it had been between us. Keith announced that he was going to live with me permanently.

I had to decide what I was going to do now. I dismissed the idea of spending six months a year in the USA training because of the disruption this would cause. In the end I decided that I would buy horses, train them and then sell them on. For this I would need more looseboxes.

Keith and I travelled regularly to the Doncaster sales to purchase horses. I had a number of young women working for me and they all learnt how to judge a horse, my methods of stable management and how to train a horse. I continued to ride Sun and Air, training him for Grand Prix dressage. I had one issue my right leg would fly out of the stirrup causing the stirrup to flap against his side. I tried riding without stirrups and although there was an uproar over this, as if somehow it gave me an advantage, there was nothing in the rules to say that it was not permissible. Eventually, we came up with a solution. The blacksmith produced a curve of iron and soldered it on to one side of the right stirrup. Then my foot could be literally shoved tightly into the iron semi-circle, where it would be wedged. We also used near-invisible laces from the stirrup to the girth to stop my right foot from moving too far away from Sunny's sides.

Then I received a letter from a sixteen-year-old, Mary Thomson who was living at The School House, Salcombe Regis, Sidmouth in Devon. Her father was verger in the local church and none of the family were horsy. She said that she was mad keen on eventing and had decided that she ought to come to Shenberrow to work for me and be properly trained. She enclosed a letter from the head teacher at her school, extolling her many virtues, and her popularity with the other girls. Mary said in her letter that she was prepared to work very hard. I asked her to come for an interview although I did wonder if she were a bit young. She was a tall girl with broad shoulders, whipcord long limbs, the athletic type. She was clearly very keen to learn all about eventing. She was to stay at Shenberrow for three years. She had a very pleasing personality, and everyone loved her. She was the sort of girl who would have no problem were she to be put up for adoption. There should have been a queue.

Mary was an attentive pupil. She quickly learnt how to produce inside and outside positions, shoulder-in, renvers and travers and also how important it was when she was riding round the arena that the horse's hind legs followed in the tracks of his front ones, and that on a circle of going round the corners, it had to be done with length bend. Mary was very strong and had to be taught to create lightness and freedom in the horse's mouth and his pace. She was training the horses to go over the show jumps in the small arena by the house. After that would come preparation for cross-country jumping. I was thrilled to have found a rider who was capable of riding well, with a combination of strength and lightness and a dedication to succeed that none of the other riders possessed. Although it did become clear that she did not have the God-given gift of possessing a natural eye for a stride. So, I taught her how to 'see a stride' by walking backwards from a fence, when walking the course, for as many as ten strides and to find some sort of marker for her to aim at on her approach so that she would have time to adjust the stride and meet the fence for a safe take-off. Some years later she married and is now called Mary King.

In July 1979 a young German doctor, Wilfried Bechtolsheimer, from Monsheim had read my training book, *The Event Horse*, and contacted me. He felt that he must come and meet me. He and his

211

wife, Ursula arrived at Stanton on 8th July and none of us could ever have imagined that this meeting heralded a new epoch in all our lives.

During the war Ursula's father was 18 years old and had several nasty escapes whilst hiding from the Nazis. At the end of the war Ursula's parents, starting from scratch, making clothes in one small room above a shop began a business that was to grow into the Massa empire, a huge hypermarket chain all over Germany.

When Wilfried and Ursula Bechtolsheimer arrived, I had arranged for them to rent a Cotswold stone cottage in Buckland. They spent 26 days at Shenberrow while I trained Wilfried. Keith and I became friends with them. They decided that they needed a better horse and bought a chestnut six-year-old called Après Vous from me. They later renamed him Sir Thomas. During Wilfried's lessons Ursula watched attentively and she would later remind Wilfried of the correct aids to be used.

Wilfried and Ursula decided that they wanted to buy a holiday house in England, so that they could come to me for training. I helped them to find a local cottage and they purchased The Sheppey, which was a new-build in Stanton. We were virtually next door and the horses could be billeted at Shenberrow. The Bechtolsheimers were about to become a central feature of our lives.

It was at about this time that Keith began to wonder if life with me was worthwhile. Yet he could not let go. Nor would I have wanted him to do so, for I still loved him. In early January, 1982, my bank manager at Stow-on-the-Wold rang me and asked me to come and see him. He told me in no uncertain terms that the overdraft was too large, and something must be done about it. Keith had been dealing with all our finances and I had had no premonition of what was to come. I burst into tears. The bank manager was a kind man and he asked me if I wanted a cup of tea. He suggested that I get my own solicitor, and I realised later that he must have known that Keith was going to leave me.

Then Keith and I began to row, and he threatened me with physical violence but stopped short of the act. He told me that I was no good to him ever since I had broken my back. He was drinking a lot and had hidden bottles of whiskey and brandy around the house. He had started a course at Leicester University, which at the age of 54 was a little strange but he would return to Shenberrow every weekend and go straight to the corner where the drinks were kept. He would drink until he got nasty and then would begin to criticise me.

Keith and I were then summoned to the bank and told that the overdraft was to be extended until October that year, and in the meantime the horses had to be sold. A few weeks later Keith arrived and proceeded to remove all his paintings and bronzes. Two days later he returned and brought them back with him.

The Bechtolsheimers had to be told of the disintegration of Keith's and my relationship and completely out of the blue they suggested that I should take my dressage horses to Germany and stay with them at their house in Monsheim where they would convert part of a building into a comfortable apartment for me and I could join them for family lunch in the big house every day. Cherry came over and we talked at length and came to the conclusion that this might be the answer to all my troubles.

In February 1983 I left for Germany with three horses, Olive my employee, and a great deal of luggage. It was planned that I should sell my dressage horses in Germany where the market was better than England. In the meantime, Wilfried was still following his ambition to be an event rider. It was decided that he needed a better horse and we went to the Verden sales in April and bought him Davidoff, who had a terrific jump and a wonderful temperament. He turned out to be multi-talented and a real star. We were training every day now except Sunday, improving his dressage, show jumping and cross-country riding.

Wilfried went to the Waldorf Three-Day Event and at the end of the first day he was in second place - 2.4 points behind the leader. The three of us walked the cross-country course twice and Wilfried knew what he had to do with the exact route he must follow to allow his horse a good clear view of what he had to jump. Ursula and I decided to go and watch them over the water jump with its very narrow, second part in the middle of a man-made pond. Wilfried and his horse came in full of running, jumped the first element off dry land into the water, drove hard to the narrow upright. It was obvious that the pair of them were about to arrive on a totally wrong stride. They took off almost against it and turned straight over in a big arc. Water everywhere, and a very wet Wilfried and horse. Masses of time was

213

wasted before Wilfried was back in a wet saddle which would make the rest of the course a nightmare, and at the end of the second day, he had dropped from second place to 23rd of 26 starters. In the future, Wilfried was going to have to concentrate on working out how to arrive at a fence on the right stride.

Advanced dressage competitions were going on at the same venue of Waldorf and Ursula and I joined the ranks of the dressage supporters who sat, elegantly dressed and coiffed, on low benches, watching the Prix St George and Intermediate 1 tests. It was certainly very different from watching the dressage in England where the dress code for the very few interested enough to sit and watch its progress was mostly of scruff order, except at the biggest competitions. There were a number of dogs there, leashed at the side of their owners, and when the judges called half time, the onlookers stood up and took their dogs off the leash. I copied them and set Gyp free. He went up the field, wagging his tail hard in friendly greeting, and stopped at one of the benches still bearing the delectable scent of another dog. Not appreciating the fact that the dog's owner had placed her designer mackintosh carefully on the bench out of harm's way, Gyp raised his leg against it, giving it a good spray and then he set off in search of new friends.

The very elegant lady owner turned to pick up her mackintosh and one could see her horror as she registered the fact of what had happened. She looked around, but it was impossible to identify the culprit with so many dogs loose, and she was clearly furious. I dreaded to think what her purchase must have cost. I thought it prudent not to call Gyp and draw attention to ourselves until the bell rang to warn the spectators that the dressage judging was about to re-start, and Ursula and I sat there, watching, a picture of innocence.

On Friday, 13th May, I believed that it was an ill-omened day but decided that it would be feeble not to ride and I would school my horse Christian. Olive and Ursula were watching me. We began with our usual working-in and then started to practice the more difficult parts of the test which we would be producing at our imminent début into top competition. We reached the point where I would ask him for changes of leg at the canter every two strides. He could do this perfectly well and had no difficulty in keeping dead straight and maintaining his balance and impulsion in the changes from one leading leg to the other. We came around the corner on the left rein in a balanced, collected canter out of the short side of the arena past where the judges would be sitting in a competition, and smoothly turned left at the immediate quarter marker, to cross the arena over the centre X and arrive at the far quarter marker on the other side. Christian was not feeling co-operative and we were engaged in a battle of wills. Then he quite deliberately threw himself straight over backwards. We crashed to the floor and I smashed into the fence.

I tried to get up, but my back was badly injured again, and I could not move to turn over or go sideways. I realised that this must be serious. Ursula and Olive rushed over to me. I knew that I had wrecked my back again, and that I had no proper feeling. Ursula ran back to the house to telephone for an ambulance. She also had the presence of mind to go to my apartment and collect the 1971 x-rays which showed the previous damage to my thoracic spine when I had been paralysed.

Keith was informed and as before he rose to the occasion in an emergency and said that he would come over to Germany as soon as I was out of hospital. This fall was nowhere near as bad as that which had paralysed me in 1971 and, after a week, I was allowed to get out of bed and try to walk. Ursula and Wilfried came to visit me when they could but I did feel terribly lonely in hospital. Not being able to speak in German was also a distinct disadvantage. No-one wanted to buy my three horses so Wilfried and Ursula very kindly purchased them from me and sent them to Herbert Rehbein. Two weeks after my fall Keith arrived for five days. It was agreed that I should return to Shenberrow as quickly as possible.

I was still going to have to sell Shenberrow so I thought I should start looking for another house. I decided to buy The Old Post House in the village of Stanton. The Bechtolsheimers would sell The Sheppey and buy Shenberrow off me. I would then be very close at hand to continue to give them advice regarding training the horses.

Keith was still coming and going. He would arrive, drink a huge tumbler of whiskey, take down all his paintings and bronzes and leave, then he would bring them back a few days later as if nothing had happened. I never knew where I was with him and it was very traumatic. He slept in the guest bedroom. It seemed that Keith couldn't let go although his primary feelings for me were extremely negative, it was as if it were impossible for him to cut the Gordian knot which tied us together. I had moved into the Post House and he

215

continued to visit me, staying the night in the guest bedroom. However, I was now free of financial stress, I had paid all my debts with the sale of Shenberrow so I was my own mistress.

I had to get used to not having horses and I began to collect paintings, I found them very soothing, and seemed to replace my previous passion for horses. I was amazed that this change of mind had taken place and thought how thrilled Mummy would have been. Now both she and Daddy were gone I missed them more than I ever could have imagined. They had allowed me such a wonderful life. I also began to appreciate the advantages of not having to ride and train and monitor the horses seven days a week, rain or shine. Nor did I need to worry about the girls who were looking after them. I was stepping into a different world.

Late in November, Keith arrived, saying that he had now made an important decision. He had decided that we must part, finally. Like a fool, I believed him and found the prospect very sad and upsetting. He said that he had intended to stay the night, but this was too much for us both, and he decided not to prolong the pain. For a week I was in great distress and just as I was thinking that I would get used to it, he came back, opening the wound again and twisting the knife. He took away pieces of furniture, his paintings and his bronzes. In a bid to reclaim my own life I went out and bought a beautiful bronze of a seated Boxer dog which always made me smile as I passed it, sitting on top of a polished piece of furniture. Then again Keith returned a few days later returning a saucer that he had taken by mistake.

I settled into The Old Post House and a life without horses. I was looking out of the windows one day and saw a young man standing in the Ryland approach to the house. He looked unsure of what he was going to do next. Then I knew immediately who he was, his legs were just the same as John Waddington's, my ex-husband. I went outside and said to him that he must be Charles, my son. He came into the house and there was the start of our relationship. We both took to each other. He was engaged to marry Lucy, who came from a very happy family background with Windermere roots. Their wedding was to be held at her family home in the Lake District.

I bought a very beautiful outfit to show the Waddingtons that I could still look like a pretty woman. But then I began to worry about the logistics of attending the wedding. It was too far for me to drive myself, and with my back and my spasms I was verging on incontinence. I was terrified of an embarrassing incident. I could not bear to disgrace myself and embarrass Charles and I came to the conclusion that the best thing I could do was to stay safe in Gloucestershire.

Later on, Charles brought Lucy to meet me and her features reminded me of portraits of ladies in the Elizabethan era. In fact, one of her ancestors was Lady Jane Grey. I could see that he had chosen to marry someone with a strong and close family background, someone who was keen to have children, and who loved him deeply. After their marriage they spent their first years in London then moved to a large family house not far from Colchester, from where Charles would catch the early London train five days a week. In time, they produced three fine healthy boys.

In January 1985 there was a knock on the main entrance door. It was a woman and her daughter who wanted to buy The Old Post House. I showed them round and they were determined to have it, and immediately agreed to the asking price. I perked up at the idea of having to find a new house.

I very much wanted to remain in the Cotswolds and eventually I found Coppice House in the hamlet of Temple Guiting. It was tucked out of sight on the edge of the village. It certainly had the 'wow' factor and I was very impressed. House hunting had become my new passion. There were three upstairs bedrooms and two bathrooms, overlooking the garden with long views of rolling Cotswold countryside and I knew that this would suit Gyp very well. There was plenty of parking space for several cars at the front of the house, with the lawn starting at its side and turning to a south westerly aspect, with the French windows of the drawing room opening onto a sunny terrace. I walked around the gardens and did not know that the neighbours ran a haulage company and their lorries were kept on the other side of what was my stone wall below the main bedroom window. Early in the morning, the engines of these lorries would be started up, getting ready to deliver stone, sand and gravel all over the country, but when I visited there was no clue that there was anything else but the view of the undulating Cotswold farmland stretching as far as the eye could see.

At the same time Wilfried and Ursula had decided to move to England. They asked me to find them a large family house with land and staff quarters. They wanted a home with an air about it, spacious rooms, ancillary accommodation and obviously land for stables, an indoor and outdoor schools and level paddocks for the horses. I collected up brochures of houses for sale and they came over and we went around viewing them. The last house we looked at was a large estate at Ampney St Peter, a few miles west of Cirencester. It was the home of Lieutenant Colonel Mike Watson, ex-Lord Lieutenant of the County and his wife Sybil and their children.

This was the house for them, it had a lovely family feel to it. I helped with the first stages of getting planning permissions to set it up in the way that they wanted. Talking to Mike Watson as the sale went through he told me that his daughter, who rode as a child, would pretend to be me competing at an event. One day she had hurled her pony at the ha-ha falling straight off into it, breaking two teeth in the process, giving her mother and himself an exceedingly nasty shock. He said it had been very traumatic and was definitely all my fault. I liked the Colonel and the twinkle in his eye.

I continued to be involved in all sorts of arrangements, not only for the building work of the house but the construction of the equestrian facilities. I had noticed a big barn on the property and I told Wilfried and Ursula how such barns were being transformed into character houses in England. They said they couldn't imagine such a thing but after they had moved in and settled they offered to transfer this barn into my name. I was astounded but after thinking about it decided that it was a splendid plan. Although I was happily settled at Coppice House the trucks waking me up each morning was a distinct drawback. When the barn was transferred into my name they included a narrow oblong stretch of land running parallel with the rough track and the low Cotswold stone boundary wall. Part of this became more lawn to the left of my property which I was to call Blithe Barn.

The work on Eastington House was extensive but finally on the 1st of May,1986 the huge German pantechnicons containing the household belongings, the horses, their tack and all other horsy necessities rolled into the farm drive of Eastington House. I was thrilled to see Olive emerging from one of the horseboxes. She reminded me of the good old times we had had at Shenberrow, before we had packed up and gone to Germany, and now she was back.

The Bechtolsheimers had four children, three sons, Felix, Till and Goetz and the only daughter, the baby of the family was just 18 months old. Her name was Laura, and now she is married she is Laura Tomlinson, and very well-known in dressage. She was given an MBE, and as of June 2012, at thirty years of age was ranked third in dressage by the FEI. She won a gold medal in the team dressage, and the bronze in the individual, in the 2012 Olympic Games in London.

The Bechtolsheimers settled in happily and I would go along and watch the training sessions of the horses currently in work. Heinz Schwestriess was employed as a rider. I had been warned that I should never ride again after Christian had reared over backwards and I had gone crashing into the fence. I was feeling frustrated at not being able to ride and in the end, I mounted Chester and had a go. The next morning, I paid the price of riding as I was very stiff.

Wilfried had recently purchased Rubelit von Unkenruf from Christine Stückelberger. He was not a top horse, but his work was very good. Christine was concentrating on the bigger, and far more spectacular Granat. Wilfried and Ursula decided to buy him, and his stable name was Unki. I rode this horse and found him very easy and co-operative. He would make a wonderful teacher for Wilfried when he was ready for Grand Prix competition. He passed an examination with our Gloucestershire vet, Charlie McCartan, and travelled to England and joined the other horses at Eastington House. Unki was very popular in that he was such an easy horse to ride and I could not resist working him with Ursula and Heinz watching me and advising whether or not our work looked good enoug for top competition. Wilfried invited the members of his Lions Club back in Monsheim to visit Eastington, and he especially wanted them to see all the horses shown in hand and Unki was to give a demonstration in advanced dressage with me riding him. I was immensely keen to do the horse justice and pushed myself too far. I pulled a muscle in my left groin and was silly enough to continue. Wilfried and Ursula and I had devised a special show for the visitors. They enjoyed it, but my leg was agony and I had to stop riding and allow it to mend. Still I thought I would be cured in time for Unki and myself to compete at the indoor Grand Prix Dressage competition at Stoneleigh.

Wilfried and Heinz were also competing on the other horses and we had a very long schedule. The Grand Prix was to be judged in the big indoor arena in the evening, with a crowd of dressage aficionados in the grandstand, and by the time I was due to compete, I was already in a lot of pain. The groin injury had come back with a vengeance. Wilfried and Ursula were probably doubtful of my ability, but I was carried away with the idea of riding at Grand Prix level again and with a nervous Wilfried giving me a leg up into the saddle, Unki and I went through our preparation and then answered the call to go into the arena. It was sheer disaster for my groin screamed with pain soon after we began the test and despite all my efforts I was incapable of showing just how well Unki and I could perform together. As I gave my final salute to the judges, I was utterly ashamed of our performance, and desolated that I could have let down the Bechtolsheimers and Unki and myself in this stupid manner.

After this a very hard decision had to be made and I faced the fact that I would not ride again. This really was the end to my life with horses. Gyp and I would sit in solitary splendour in Blithe Barn.

I still enjoyed living at Blithe Barn, but it was an expensive house in terms of upkeep, and I could see the horses and the stables, and this painfully reminded me of that part of my life that was finished. Eventually, after some legal issues, I was to sell the house. At the time that this autobiography was published Laura Tomlinson was living there with her family.

Around this time, Ted Marsh telephoned. He had been in hospital several times over the years and he was back again. He would never say what was the matter with him, in those days such things were private, and one had to observe this. Once I knew he was in Birmingham, being treated, I would send him a card every day, in the hope of cheering him up. I wondered what my life would have been, had I stood up to my parents, and married him when I was just twenty-two years old and so in love with him. I was sure that had we married it would have been very successful, for we liked each other as well as loving. I'm sure that he too must have wondered what might have happened had we been married.

Epilogue

220

Sheila died on 9th June 2017 after suffering from Alzheimers. She is survived by her son Charles. A Requiem Mass was held for her at St Gregory's Church, Cheltenham on June 30th, 2017. Her record of winning three successive Badmintons has never been equalled or bettered.

Printed in Great Britain
by Amazon